T0211132

Lecture Notes in Computer Science　　12870

Founding Editors

Gerhard Goos
Karlsruhe Institute of Technology, Karlsruhe, Germany

Juris Hartmanis
Cornell University, Ithaca, NY, USA

Editorial Board Members

Elisa Bertino
Purdue University, West Lafayette, IN, USA

Wen Gao
Peking University, Beijing, China

Bernhard Steffen
TU Dortmund University, Dortmund, Germany

Gerhard Woeginger
RWTH Aachen, Aachen, Germany

Moti Yung
Columbia University, New York, NY, USA

More information about this subseries at http://www.springer.com/series/7408

Simon McIntosh-Smith ·
Bronis R. de Supinski · Jannis Klinkenberg (Eds.)

OpenMP: Enabling Massive Node-Level Parallelism

17th International Workshop on OpenMP, IWOMP 2021
Bristol, UK, September 14–16, 2021
Proceedings

 Springer

Editors
Simon McIntosh-Smith ⓘ
University of Bristol
Bristol, UK

Bronis R. de Supinski ⓘ
Lawrence Livermore National Laboratory
Livermore, CA, USA

Jannis Klinkenberg ⓘ
RWTH Aachen University
Aachen, Germany

ISSN 0302-9743   ISSN 1611-3349 (electronic)
Lecture Notes in Computer Science
ISBN 978-3-030-85261-0   ISBN 978-3-030-85262-7 (eBook)
https://doi.org/10.1007/978-3-030-85262-7

LNCS Sublibrary: SL2 – Programming and Software Engineering

© Springer Nature Switzerland AG 2021
Chapter "FOTV: A Generic Device Offloading Framework for OpenMP" is licensed under the terms of the
Creative Commons Attribution 4.0 International License (http://creativecommons.org/licenses/by/4.0/). For
further details see license information in the chapter.
This work is subject to copyright. All rights are reserved by the Publisher, whether the whole or part of the
material is concerned, specifically the rights of translation, reprinting, reuse of illustrations, recitation,
broadcasting, reproduction on microfilms or in any other physical way, and transmission or information
storage and retrieval, electronic adaptation, computer software, or by similar or dissimilar methodology now
known or hereafter developed.
The use of general descriptive names, registered names, trademarks, service marks, etc. in this publication
does not imply, even in the absence of a specific statement, that such names are exempt from the relevant
protective laws and regulations and therefore free for general use.
The publisher, the authors and the editors are safe to assume that the advice and information in this book are
believed to be true and accurate at the date of publication. Neither the publisher nor the authors or the editors
give a warranty, expressed or implied, with respect to the material contained herein or for any errors or
omissions that may have been made. The publisher remains neutral with regard to jurisdictional claims in
published maps and institutional affiliations.

This Springer imprint is published by the registered company Springer Nature Switzerland AG
The registered company address is: Gewerbestrasse 11, 6330 Cham, Switzerland

Preface

OpenMP is a widely used application programming interface (API) for high-level parallel programming in Fortran, C, and C++. OpenMP has been supported in most high-performance compilers and by hardware vendors since it was introduced in 1997. Under the guidance of the OpenMP Architecture Review Board (ARB) and the diligent work of the OpenMP Language Committee, the OpenMP specification has evolved up to version 5.1, with version 5.2 soon to be released. OpenMP has become the most widely used HPC language as a result of its continuing evolution.

The latest proposed specification, which is documented in OpenMP Technical Report 10 (TR10), will be the basis of OpenMP 5.2 when the ARB releases it later this year. This version primarily reorganizes and refactors the specification of the directives and clauses that the language provides. These changes necessarily identified inconsistencies in the specification, particularly for the directive and clause syntax and the restrictions that apply to it. Thus, it will replace syntax inconsistencies with the form used more generally throughout the specification in addition to ensuring that common restrictions are consistently and clearly specified.

While these changes are small advancements, work has also begun on the next version of the specification: OpenMP 6.0. Larger changes that we anticipate for that version include the ability for a thread to create a task to be executed by a thread in a different parallel team and to enable free-agent threads to execute tasks in addition to the threads explicitly created for that team. While the details of the latter functionality are still under discussion, this volume includes a paper that explores a proposed mechanism for it. The papers that appear at IWOMP are one avenue through which the OpenMP Language Committee carefully evaluates and incorporates community needs into the OpenMP specification.

OpenMP is important both as a stand-alone parallel programming model and as part of a hybrid programming model for massively parallel, distributed memory systems consisting of homogeneous manycore nodes and heterogeneous node architectures, as found in leading supercomputers. As much of the increased parallelism in the exascale systems will be within a node, OpenMP has become widely used in top-end systems. Importantly, the features in OpenMP 6.0 will further support applications on such systems in addition to facilitating portable exploitation of specific system attributes.

The community of OpenMP researchers and developers is united under the cOMPunity organization. This organization has held workshops on OpenMP around the world since 1999: the European Workshop on OpenMP (EWOMP), the North American Workshop on OpenMP Applications and Tools (WOMPAT), and the Asian Workshop on OpenMP Experiences and Implementation (WOMPEI) attracted annual audiences from academia and industry. The International Workshop on OpenMP (IWOMP) consolidated these three workshop series into a single annual international event that rotates across Europe, Asia-Pacific, and the Americas. The first IWOMP workshop was organized under the auspices of cOMPunity. Since that workshop, the

IWOMP Steering Committee has organized these events and guided development of the series. The first IWOMP meeting was held in 2005, in Eugene, Oregon, USA. Since then, meetings have been held each year, in Reims, France; Beijing, China; West Lafayette, USA; Dresden, Germany; Tsukuba, Japan; Chicago, USA; Rome, Italy; Canberra, Australia; Salvador, Brazil; Aachen, Germany; Nara, Japan; Stony Brook, USA; Barcelona, Spain, and Auckland, New Zealand. Each workshop draws participants from research, program developer groups, and industry throughout the world. In 2020, IWOMP continued the series with technical papers and tutorials presented through a virtual conference, due to the COVID-19 pandemic. We thank the generous support of sponsors that help make these meetings successful, they are cited on the conference pages (present and archived) at the iwomp.org website.

The evolution of the specification would be impossible without active research in OpenMP compilers, runtime systems, tools, and environments. The OpenMP research community is vibrant and dedicated to continuing to improve OpenMP. As we move beyond the present needs, and adapt and evolve OpenMP to the expanding parallelism in new architectures, the OpenMP research community will continue to play a vital role. The papers in this volume demonstrate the adaption of new features found in OpenMP 5.0 and 5.1 and show how the OpenMP feature set can significantly enhance user experiences on a wide range of systems. These papers also demonstrate the forward thinking of the research community, and potential OpenMP directions and further improvements for systems on the horizon.

The IWOMP website (www.iwomp.org) has the latest workshop information, as well as links to archived events. This publication contains proceedings of the 17th International Workshop on OpenMP, IWOMP 2021. The workshop program included 15 technical papers and tutorials on OpenMP. All technical papers were peer reviewed by at least four different members of the Program Committee. The work evidenced by these authors and the committee demonstrates that OpenMP will remain a key technology well into the future.

September 2021

Simon McIntosh-Smith
Bronis R. de Supinski
Jannis Klinkenberg

Organization

General Chair

Simon McIntosh-Smith — University of Bristol, UK

Program Committee Chair

Bronis R. de Supinski — Lawrence Livermore National Laboratory, USA

Publication Chair

Jannis Klinkenberg — RWTH Aachen University, Germany

Tutorial Chairs

Yun (Helen) He — National Energy Research Scientific Computing Center (NERSC), USA
Tom Deakin — University of Bristol, UK

Local Organiser Chair

Tim Lewis — Croftedge Marketing, UK

Program Committee

Patrick Atkinson	NVIDIA, UK
Eduard Ayguade	Universitat Politècnica de Catalunya, Spain
Mark Bull	University of Edinburgh, UK
Sunita Chandrasekaran	University of Delaware, USA
Florina M. Ciorba	University of Basel, Switzerland
Bronis R. de Supinski	Lawrence Livermore National Laboratory, USA
Tom Deakin	University of Bristol, UK
Johannes Doerfert	Argonne National Laboratory, USA
Alex Duran	Intel Iberia, Spain
Deepak Eachempati	HPE, USA
Jini George	AMD, USA
Oscar Hernandez	Oak Ridge National Laboratory, USA
Paul Kelly	Imperial, UK
Jannis Klinkenberg	RWTH Aachen University, Germany
Michael Kruse	Argonne National Laboratory, USA
Kelvin Li	IBM, USA
Chunhua Liao	Lawrence Livermore National Laboratory, USA

Will Lovett	Arm, UK
Larry Meadows	Intel, USA
Kent Milfeld	TACC, USA
Stephen Olivier	Sandia National Laboratories, USA
Joachim Protze	RWTH Aachen University, Germany
Mitsuhisa Sato	RIKEN Center for Computational Science (R-CCS), Japan
Thomas Scogland	Lawrence Livermore National Laboratory, USA
Adrian Tate	NAG, UK
Terry Wilmarth	Intel, USA
Justs Zarins	EPCC, UK

Website

Tim Lewis	Croftedge Marketing, UK

IWOMP Steering Committee

Steering Committee Chair

Matthias S. Müller	RWTH Aachen University, Germany

Steering Committee

Dieter an Mey	RWTH Aachen University, Germany
Eduard Ayguadé	BSC, Universitat Politècnica de Catalunya, Spain
Mark Bull	EPCC, University of Edinburgh, UK
Barbara Chapman	Stony Brook University, USA
Bronis R. de Supinski	Lawrence Livermore National Laboratory, USA
Rudolf Eigenmann	University of Delaware, USA
William Gropp	University of Illinois, USA
Michael Klemm	AMD, Germany
Kalyan Kumaran	Argonne National Laboratory, USA
Lawrence Meadows	Intel, USA
Stephen L. Olivier	Sandia National Laboratories, USA
Ruud van der Pas	University of Delaware, USA
Alistair Rendell	Flinders University, Australia
Mitsuhisa Sato	RIKEN Center for Computational Science (R-CCS), Japan
Sanjiv Shah	Intel, USA
Oliver Sinnen	University of Auckland, New Zealand
Josemar Rodrigues de Souza	SENAI Unidade CIMATEC, Brazil
Christian Terboven	RWTH Aachen University, Germany
Matthijs van Waveren	OpenMP ARB & CS Group, France

Contents

Synchronization and Data

Improving Speculative `taskloop` in Hardware Transactional Memory

Juan Salamanca(✉) and Alexandro Baldassin

IGCE – Sao Paulo State University (Unesp), Rio Claro, SP, Brazil
{juan,alex}@rc.unesp.br

Abstract. Previous work proposed and evaluated Speculative `taskloop` (STL) on Intel Core implementing new clauses and constructs in OpenMP. The results indicated that, despite achieving some speed-ups, there was a phenomenon called the *Lost-Thread Effect* that caused the performance degradation of STL parallelization. This issue is caused by the `nonmonotonic` scheduling implemented in the LLVM OpenMP Runtime Library. This paper presents an improvement in the STL mechanism by modifying the OpenMP runtime to allow `monotonic` scheduling of tasks generated by `taskloop`. We perform an evaluation with two different versions of the OpenMP runtime, both optimized for STL revealing that, for certain loops, infinite slowdowns (deadlocks) using the original OpenMP runtime can be transformed in speed-ups by applying `monotonic` scheduling. The experimental results show the performance improvement of STL using the modified version of the runtime, reaching speed-ups of up to 2.18×.

Keywords: taskloop · Speculative parallelization · OpenMP

1 Introduction

The `taskloop` construct was implemented in OpenMP 4.5 and allows the parallelization of a loop, dividing its iterations into chunks that are executed by a number of tasks [7,18]. The worksharing constructs suffer from certain issues that are overcome by `taskloop`, for example: (a) load imbalance, in the case of `taskloop` the scheduler at runtime will distribute the load in a balanced way using work stealing, whereas in worksharing constructs it is more difficult to achieve this; (b) traditional worksharing can lead to ragged fork/join patterns; and (c) worksharing constructs in inner loops need to create a team of threads (`parallel`) in each call of the outer loop, generating a large overhead in the parallelization. As shown in Fig. 1, it is very difficult to try to create a team of threads just once. However, with `taskloop` this is much simpler and the overhead of opening and closing successive `parallel` regions is avoided, creating the team of threads before the outer loop, as shown in Fig. 2.

This work is supported by FAPESP (grants 18/07446-8 and 18/15519-5).

© Springer Nature Switzerland AG 2021
S. McIntosh-Smith et al. (Eds.): IWOMP 2021, LNCS 12870, pp. 3–17, 2021.
https://doi.org/10.1007/978-3-030-85262-7_1

```
for(iter=0; iter < sc->maxIter; iter++){
  precon(A, r, z);
  ...
  matvec(A, p, q);
  vectorDot(p, q, n, &dot_pq);
  ...
}

void matvec(Mat *A, double *x, double *y){
  ...
  #pragma omp parallel for ...
  for(i = 0; i < A->n; i++) {
  //loop body
  }
  y[i] = y0;
}
```

```
#pragma omp parallel
#pragma omp single
for(iter=0; iter < sc->maxIter; iter++){
  precon(A, r, z);
  ...
  matvec(A, p, q);
  vectorDot(p, q, n, &dot_pq);
  ...
}

void matvec(Mat *A, double *x, double *y){
  ...
  #pragma omp taskloop ...
  for(i = 0; i < A->n; i++) {
  //loop body
  }
  y[i] = y0;
}
```

Fig. 1. Fragment of `Sparse CG`'s code using `parallel for`

Fig. 2. The same code using `taskloop`

A weakness of `taskloop` is that it does not ensure the correct parallelization of a loop when it is non-DOALL, that is, when it is not possible to prove statically that a loop is free of loop-carried dependences. For that case, other parallelization techniques must be used: DOACROSS [2] and Thread-Level Speculation (TLS) [16,17]. DOACROSS parallelization was implemented in OpenMP 4.5 through the `ordered` clause (available in the `for` worksharing construct) and the `ordered` stand-alone directive; on the other hand, TLS has not been officially implemented yet in OpenMP.

The `ordered` construct can be used to mark the `source` and the `sink` of a loop-carried dependence, thus enabling the use of `parallel for` to parallelize DOACROSS loops [7,14]. For instance, Fig. 3 shows the hottest loop of 429.mcf benchmark from SPEC2006. This loop is an example of a *may* DOACROSS loop: it means that is not DOALL and may be DOACROSS depending on the input of the benchmark (if `cond1` and `cond2` are true, a loop-carried dependence in `basket_size` is generated). Previous experiments show that this loop is DOACROSS at runtime for its `reference` input [12], thus it is not correct to parallelize it using `parallel for` or `taskloop`, but one can try to parallelize this loop using the `ordered` construct.

The `ordered` construct is suitable when the loop can be statically considered DOACROSS as also its sequential and parallel components are known—parallel components have to do significant work concerning the loop iteration time to be performant. If the loop is *may* DOACROSS and the presumed sequential component can be known, `ordered` can also be beneficial. However, the most difficult task for the programmer is to recognize these loop components. In the example of Fig. 3, a *may* DOACROSS loop, it is possible to separate components to make use of fine-grained `ordered`. However, a non-trivial loop restructuring is required (Fig. 4) because it is not possible to give a correct value to `sink` in `depend(sink:) basketsize++` due to the indeterminism of the control flow and

```
1   arc=arcs + group_pos
2   for(; arc<stop_arcs; arc+=nr_group){
3     if (arc->ident>BASIC)){ //cond1
4       red_cost = arc->cost - arc->tail->potential + arc->head->potential;
5       if (bea_is_dual_infeasible(arc,red_cost)){ //cond2
6         basket_size++;
7         perm[basket_size]->a=arc;
8         perm[basket_size]->cost=red_cost;
9         perm[basket_size]->abs_cost=ABS(red_cost);
10      }
11    }
12  }
```

Fig. 3. mcf's hottest loop

```
1   #pragma omp parallel for ordered(1)
        shared(basket_size)...
2   for(i=0; i<iterations; i++){
3     arc=...;
4     cond1=arc->ident->BASIC;
5     if (cond1)){
6       red_cost=...;
7       cond2=bea_is_dual_infeasible(...);
8     }
9     #pragma omp ordered depend(sink:i-1)
10    if (cond1 && cond2){
11      basket_size++;
12      basket_sizeL=basket_size;
13    }
14    #pragma omp ordered depend(source)
15    if (cond1 && cond2){
16      perm[basket_sizeL]->a=arc;
17      ...
18    }
19  }
```

```
1   #pragma omp parallel num_threads(N_CORES)
2   #pragma omp single
3   #pragma omp taskloop tls(S_SIZE)
        spec_private(basket_size)...
4   for(arc=init; arc<stop_arcs; arc+=nr_group)
5   {
6     if (arc->ident>BASIC)){
7       red_cost=...;
8       if(bea_is_dual_infeasible(...)){
9         #pragma omp tls if_read(basket_size)
10        basket_size++;
11        #pragma omp tls if_write(basket_size)
12        perm[basket_size]->a=arc;
13        perm[basket_size]->cost=red_cost;
14        perm[basket_size]->abs_cost=...;
15      }
16    }
17  }
```

Fig. 4. Restructured mcf's hottest loop with ordered (speed-up = 0.15×)

Fig. 5. The same loop using tls construct, and taskloop tls (speed-up = 1.16×)

the iterator increment variability. Thus, one has to be conservative and assume that the component is sequential for each iteration (`depend (sink:i-1)`). Unfortunately, the parallelization performance of this loop using `ordered` is poor (a speed-up of 0.15× with respect to serial execution on Intel Core using `libomp12` and Clang 12.0), even worse than the sequential execution, because the work of the parallel components (without `ordered` synchronization) is not significant with respect to the total time of the loop iteration, and the synchronization overhead outweighs the parallelized work.

Thread-Level Speculation is a technique that allows for effectively parallelizing *may* DOACROSS loops that have a low probability of materializing their loop-carried dependencies at runtime. The lower this probability the more likely it is to achieve a performant parallelization. In the case that the loop is effectively DOACROSS at runtime, if the fraction of iterations with loop-carried dependences is low with respect to the total number of iterations, TLS can still be performant; however, it also depends on the pattern of distribution of these loop-carried dependencies throughout loop iterations at runtime [12].

Previous work proposed Speculative `taskloop` (STL) to have the best of two worlds: (a) the advantages of task-based parallelism over worksharing constructs described above; and (b) the effectiveness of TLS to parallelize *may* DOACROSS loops where OpenMP DOALL or DOACROSS techniques fail [13]. Another previous work added clauses (`spec_private` and `spec_reduction`) and directives (`tls if_read`, `tls if_write`, etc.) from Speculative Privatization [11] to Speculative `taskloop`, and evaluated the results of this parallelization technique [10]. For instance, Fig. 5 shows the parallelization of the hottest `mcf` loop using Speculative `taskloop` and Speculative Privatization, which offers the advantage of not needing to recognize the components and complex loop restructuring, resulting in better performance (speed-up of 1.16× with respect to serial execution on Intel Core using `libomp12` and Clang 12.0).

However, in both of the previous papers, the performance was hurt by an issue called the *Lost-Thread Effect* [13] caused by the OpenMP runtime. This paper fixes this problem and presents new results using Speculative `taskloop`. In particular, we make the following contributions:

- We modify the LLVM OpenMP Runtime Library to support `monotonic` scheduling of tasks in Speculative `taskloop`, thus improving the results obtained previously;
- We perform an evaluation with two different versions of the OpenMP runtime, both optimized for STL. The experimental results show the improvement of using the modified version of the runtime (Sect. 5). We further compare against the `ordered` construct, which was implemented previously by Shirako *et al.* [14].

This paper is organized as follows. Section 2 describes the background material and discusses related works. Section 3 details the design and implementation of the `monotonic` scheduling in two versions of the OpenMP Runtime Library. Benchmarks, methodology and settings are described in Sect. 4. Section 5 evaluates the performance of STL. Finally, Sect. 6 concludes the work.

2 Background and Related Work

This section presents related works and the main concepts used in this paper: Task-based Parallelism, TLS, Speculative Taskloop, Lost-Thread Effect, and OpenMP Runtime Library.

2.1 Task-Based Parallelism

In this model, the execution can be modeled as a directed acyclic graph, where nodes are tasks and edges define data dependences between tasks. A runtime system schedules tasks whose dependences are resolved over available worker threads, thus enabling load balancing and work stealing [4]. At runtime, the task creation code packs the kernel code pointer and the task operands, and then adds them in the task pipeline; in this way, the generating thread can continue creating additional tasks.

Tasks in OpenMP are blocks of code that the compiler envelops and arranges to be executed in parallel. Tasks were added to OpenMP in version 3.0 [1]. In OpenMP 4.0 [6], the `depend` clause and the `taskgroup` construct were incorporated and, in OpenMP 4.5, the `taskloop` construct was proposed and added to the specification [7]. Like worksharing constructs, tasks are generally created inside of a `parallel` region. To spawn each task once, the `single` construct is used. The ordering of tasks is not defined, but there are ways to express it: (a) with directives such as `taskgroup` or `taskwait`; or (b) with task dependences (`depend` clause).

Variables that are used in tasks can be specified with data-sharing attribute clauses (`private, firstprivate, shared`, etc.) or, by default, data accessed by a task is `shared`. The `depend` clause takes a type (`in, out`, or `inout`) followed by a variable or a list of variables. These types establish an order between sibling tasks. The `taskwait` clause waits for the child tasks of the current task. `taskgroup` is similar to `taskwait` but it waits for all descendant tasks created in the block. Moreover, task `reduction` was introduced in OpenMP 5.0 [8].

The `taskloop` construct was proposed by Teruel *et al.* [18] and allows parallelizing a loop by dividing its iterations into a number of created tasks, with each task being assigned to one or more iterations of the loop. The `grainsize` clause specifies how many iterations are assigned for each task and the number of tasks can be calculated automatically. OpenMP brings another clause called `priority` to specify the level of priority of each task used by the runtime scheduler [7]. `taskloop` is compatible with the `parallel for` construct, the main difference is the lack of the `schedule` clause in the `taskloop` [9].

2.2 TLS on Hardware Transactional Memories

Thread-Level Speculation (TLS) is an environment where threads operate speculatively, performing potentially unsafe operations, and temporarily buffering the state that they generate [20]. Then, the operations of a thread are declared to be correct or incorrect. If they are correct, the thread commits; if they are incorrect, the thread is rolled back and typically restarted from its beginning. The term TLS is most often associated with a scenario where the goal is to parallelize a sequential application. However, in general, TLS can be applied to any environment where speculative threads are executed and can be squashed and restarted [20]. Thread-Level Speculation or Speculative DOACROSS has been widely studied in the past [15–17].

For performance, TLS requires hardware mechanisms that support four primary features: conflict detection, speculative storage, in-order (`monotonic`) commit of transactions, and transaction roll-back. However, to this day, there is no off-the-shelf processor that provides direct support for TLS. Speculative execution is supported, however, in the form of Hardware Transactional Memory

(HTM) available in processors such as the Intel Core and the IBM POWER. HTM implements three out of the four key features required by TLS: conflict detection, speculative storage, and transaction roll-back. Thus, these architectures have the potential to be used to implement TLS [12]. Speculative `taskloop` is based on this approach.

2.3 Speculative `taskloop` (STL)

TLS is a technique to enable the parallel execution of loop iterations in the presence of potential dependences. We proposed adding Hardware-Transactional-Memory-based TLS (TLS-HTM) to `taskloop`—Speculative `taskloop` (STL)—through the addition of the clause `tls` to `taskloop` in a previous work [13]. This clause can be used to speculate about data dependences between tasks generated by a `taskloop` construct in non-DOALL loops, thus STL manipulates multiple tasks of loop iterations in order to exploit task parallelism (load balancing, work stealing, efficient creation of `parallel`, etc.) and to accelerate the loop execution. The addition of Speculative Privatizations [11] to `taskloop tls` was proposed by Salamanca et al. [10], through the clauses `spec_private` and `spec_reduction`, in order to integrate speculative execution into OpenMP task-based parallelization. A sketch of the Fig. 5's code (STL) converted to the OpenMP standard is shown in Fig. 6.

```
1   next_strip_to_commit=init;
2   #pragma omp parallel num_threads(N_CORES)
3   #pragma omp single // or master
4   #pragma omp taskloop grainsize(1) default(none) firstprivate(stop_arcs,init,nr_group)
        shared(basket_size,perm,next_strip_to_commit) private(red_cost,arc)
5   for(arc_s=init; arc_s<stop_arcs; arc+=nr_group*S_SIZE){
6     char flag_r_basket=0, flag_w_basket=0;
7     long basket_sizeL;
8     char speculative = BEGIN(&next_strip_to_commit,arc_s);
9     for(arc=arc_s; arc<stop_arcs && arc-arc_s<S_SIZE*nr_group; arc+=nr_group){
10      if (arc->ident>BASIC)){
11        red_cost = arc->cost - arc->tail->potential + arc->head->potential;
12        if(bea_is_dual_infeasible(arc, red_cost)){
13          if (!flag_r_basket){
14            flag_r_basket = 1;
15            basket_sizeL = basket_size;
16          }
17          basket_sizeL++;
18          flag_w_basket=1;
19          perm[basket_sizeL]->a = arc;
20          perm[basket_sizeL]->cost = red_cost;
21          perm[basket_sizeL]->abs_cost = ...;
22        }
23      }
24    }
25    END(speculative,&next_strip_to_commit,arc_s);
26    if (flag_w_basket) basket_size = basket_sizeL;
27    next_strip_to_commit += nr_group*S_SIZE;
28  }
```

Fig. 6. STL parallelization of the `mcf`'s loop converted to standard OpenMP

2.4   Lost-Thread Effect

In a previous work [13], we were able to verify that, at one point during the STL execution, a thread (the lost thread) begins to execute high iteration counts and therefore suffers from order-inversion aborts[1] almost all the time, in this way it executes almost no effective work and degrades the parallelization performance. We called this issue the Lost-Thread Effect, and it is generated because `taskloop` assigns chunks of iterations to tasks in an order that is usually not the increasing logical iteration order (`nonmonotonic`), thus tasks that execute high iteration counts have to abort due to order inversion and have to wait for tasks executing lower iteration counts.

2.5   LLVM OpenMP Runtime Library

The task-based model relies on the OpenMP runtime to distribute tasks onto worker threads, thus enabling load balancing and work stealing. We study two versions: (a) the version `libomp20160808` of the runtime used in the previous papers [10,13]; and (b) the latest stable version in LLVM 12.0, `libomp12`.

`libomp20160808` [5] – The mechanism for `taskloop` in this runtime is implemented in the `kmpc_taskloop` function in the `kmp_tasking.c` file. When `taskloop` is executed by the thread that encounters the construct (the generating thread that also encounters `single`), the `kmp_tasklooop_linear` function is invoked. Then, it generates tasks following the increasing order of the loop iterations. These tasks are pushed into the thread's deque (double-ended queue) and thus scheduled to be executed (`kmp_push_task`); however, if the deque is full, the task is immediately executed by the thread. If this task corresponds to a high iteration count, the Lost-Thread Effect is generated in STL. The size of each deque has been defined as 256 tasks. On the other hand, each thread that is part of the team created in the `parallel` region executes the `kmp_execute_tasks_template` function, where it first executes the tasks of its own deque, and then it tries to steal tasks from deques of other threads. When a thread looks for its own tasks, it invokes the `kmp_remove_my_tasks` function which removes tasks from the tail of its deque; in this way the thread executes a high iteration count of loop causing the Lost-Thread Effect in STL.

`libomp12` [19] – The mechanism for `taskloop` in this runtime is also implemented in the `kmpc_taskloop` and the `kmp_taskloop` functions. The main difference between `libomp20160808` and `libomp12` is that `libomp12` is implemented in C++ (`kmp_tasking.cpp`). Another important difference is that `kmp_taskloop` not only invokes the `kmp_taskloop_linear` function to split the iteration space, but also the `kmp_taskloop_recur` function which recursively partitions the loop

---

[1] An abort caused by order-inversion rolls back a transaction that completes execution out of order using an explicit abort instruction (`xabort`).

iterations into chunks to generate tasks until reaching a threshold. This kind of partition is nonmonotonic because it does not follow the increasing order of the loop iterations and could cause a complete Lost-Thread Effect (all thread lost or deadlock) in STL. Tasks are also pushed into the thread deque or executed immediately if the deque is full (libomp12 has the same deque size of 256 tasks). As in libomp20160808, each thread that is part of the team executes the function kmp_execute_tasks_template.

3   Implementation

This section presents a description of the changes made to each OpenMP runtime to enable the monotonic scheduling in Speculative taskloop.

3.1   First Attempt: Use priority Clause

To avoid modifying the runtime, as a first idea to implement monotonic scheduling, we tried to use the priority clause, giving higher priorities to tasks executing low iteration counts and lower priorities to tasks executing high iteration counts. However, in taskloop, all the tasks created have the same priority assigned through the priority clause, thus we transform the loop with strip mining and use the task construct: the outer loop generates tasks and the inner loop (with S_SIZE iterations) is marked with the task construct and the respective priority clause, as shown in the Fig. 7.

```
1  next=init;
2  prty=omp_get_max_task_priority();
3  #pragma omp parallel num_threads(N_CORES)
4  #pragma omp single
5  for (arc_s=init; arc_s<stop_arcs; arc+=nr_group*S_SIZE){ //outer loop
6    prty--;
7    #pragma omp task priority(prty) shared(basket_size,perm,next)...
8    { ...
9      int spec=BEGIN(&next,arc_s);
10     for(arc=arc_s; arc<stop_arcs && arc-arc_s<S_SIZE*nr_group; arc+=nr_group){ //inner loop
11       ...//loop body
12     }
13     END(spec,&next,arc_s);
14     next+=S_SIZE;
15   }
16 }
```

Fig. 7. First attempt: using tasks and priority clause in mcf's hottest loop

In libomp20160808, it was observed in our experiments that the priority clause for tasks is not implemented. Anyway, the partitioning of the iterations in libomp20160808 is linear and in the increasing order of the iterations, so using priority would have had the same result. The causes of the Lost-Thread Effect in this runtime are, as explained above: (a) the immediate execution of tasks by the generating thread when its deque is full; and (b) the thread that encounters **single**, after finishing generating the tasks, begins to remove tasks from its own deque to be executed starting from the deque's tail (higher iteration count).

On the other hand, **libomp12** implements a recursive partition of iterations. Using the **task** construct, as in Fig. 7, it is possible to avoid the deadlock generated by the **taskloop** construct that are due to the recursive partition of the iterations (which introduce a **nonmonotonic** scheduling), and to obtain a linear partition generated by the outer loop after the loop transformation. However, the same two issues found in **libomp20160808** persist and generate the Lost-Thread Effect despite using strip mining and **task priority**.

3.2   Recursive Partition of Iterations

The first problem causing the Lost-Thread Effect is the recursive partitioning of iterations by **taskloop** in the OpenMP runtime (only in **libomp12**). **kmp_taskloop_recur** function uses a binary splitting approach in which the iteration space is recursively split into chunks. Each chunk is assigned to a new task that continues binary splitting until a minimal chunk size is reached. This function in invoked when the number of tasks is greater than the minimum number of tasks (threshold). In this way, when Speculative **taskloop** is executed (**kmp_taskloop** function), we set **num_task_min** to the total number of tasks so that **kmp_taskloop_linear** can always be executed and to avoid the Lost-Thread Effect, as shown in Fig. 8.

```
1  if (speculative_taskloop) num_tasks_min = num_tasks;
2  if (num_tasks>num_tasks_min) __kmp_taskloop_recur(..); else __kmp_taskloop_linear(..);
```

Fig. 8. Modification in **kmp_taskloop** function

```
1  if(thread_data->td.td_deque_ntasks >=
        TASK_DEQUE_SIZE(thread_data->td)){
2    if ((!speculative_taskloop) &&
        __kmp_enable_task_throttling &&
        ...)
3      return TASK_NOT_PUSHED;//immediate exec
4    } else {
5      if(thread_data->td.td_deque_ntasks >=
          TASK_DEQUE_SIZE(thread_data->td))
6        __kmp_realloc_task_deque(thread,
            thread_data);
7    }
8  }
```

Fig. 9. kmp_push_task

```
1  if (speculative_taskloop){
2    taskdata= thread_data->
          td.td_deque[thread_data->
          td.td_deque_head];
3    thread_data->td.td_deque_head=
          (thread_data-> td.td_deque_head+1)
          & TASK_DEQUE_MASK(thread_data->td);
4  }else{
5    tail= (thread_data->td.td_deque_tail-1)
          & TASK_DEQUE_MASK(thread_data->td);
6    taskdata=thread_data->td.td_deque[tail];
7  }
8  ...
9  if (!speculative_taskloop)
10   thread_data->td.td_deque_tail = tail;
```

Fig. 10. kmp_remove_my_task

3.3 Immediate Execution When Deque is Full

The second problem that results in the Lost-Thread Effect is the immediate execution of tasks by the generating thread in `taskloop` when its deque is full. The deque size of the threads, especially the one of the generating thread, which is the deque that stores all the tasks generated by `taskloop`, is critical. Both versions of the OpenMP runtime have an initial deque size of 256 tasks (`TASK_DEQUE_BITS = 8`).

`libomp12` – To implement `monotonic` scheduling in this runtime, it is necessary to prevent a task that cannot be pushed onto a full queue from being executed immediately. This can be accomplished by reallocating the deque to an increased size. In the `libomp12` runtime, reallocation is already implemented but it depends on a variable called `kmp_enable_task_throttling`, which is `true` and prevents reallocation. The condition can be modified in `kmp_push_task` so that when the deque is full and the task being pushed was generated by Speculative `taskloop`, it is not allowed to start immediately (as shown in Fig. 9). Another way to achieve the non-execution of the task is to increase the initial size of the deque. A reasonable value is 1024, which does not allow the deque to be full in the evaluated loops. In terms of performance, the second option is faster because it avoids copying the deque to another portion of memory, and this was confirmed in the experiments carried out; however, it is not a complete solution. We use a combination of both.

`libomp20160808` – The main difference with the other version studied is that here `kmp_push_task` did not invoke `kmp_realloc_task_deque` in any case, so a mechanism, similar to `libomp12`, had to be implemented from scratch. The deque size was also increased to 1024.

3.4 Removal from Tail of Thread's Deque

When the generating thread finishes sweeping all the iterations, it runs `kmp_execute_tasks_template` to start executing tasks and, firstly, it checks its own deque. As the deque of the generating thread has all the tasks generated by `taskloop`, there are already team threads stealing tasks from it (from the head), so it starts removing from the deque's tail (high iteration counts in a linear partition). To implement a `monotonic` scheduling it is necessary to ensure that the generating thread also removes its own tasks from the head. To accomplish this, the `kmp_remove_my_task` function was modified as shown in the Fig. 10. This is similar in the two versions of the runtime.

4 Benchmarks, Methodology and Experimental Setup

The performance assessment in this work reports speed-ups and abort/commit ratios (transaction outcome) for the STL (Speculative `taskloop`) [10,13]

and `ordered` parallelizations of *may* DOACROSS loops from the Collective
Benchmark[3] (`cBench`) and SPEC benchmark suites running on Intel Core. For
all experiments, the default input is used for the `cBench` benchmarks and the
reference input for `mcf`. The baseline for speed-up comparisons is the serial execution of the same benchmark program compiled at the same optimization level.
Loop times are used to calculate speed-ups. Each software thread is bounded to
a unique core. Each benchmark was run twenty times and the average time is
used. Runtime variations were negligible and are not presented.

We compiled the programs with Clang 4.0 and used `libomp20160808` [5] as
the OpenMP Runtime Library in two flavors: (a) the original version; and (b)
the one modified to allow `monotonic` scheduling, explained in Sect. 3. However,
to validate that these changes work not only for an older version of the OpenMP
runtime but also for the latest version, we also used `libomp12` [19] in the experiments. For compatibility reasons, in the experiments that use `libomp12`, the
programs were compiled with Clang 12.0 [19] to generate a more updated code
for the runtime. However, the `tls` clause for `taskloop`, and the clauses and
directives for Speculative Privatization are not yet implemented in Clang 12.0,
therefore we made manual code transformations to the evaluated loops following the algorithms described in previous works [10,13] thus obtaining the STL
parallelization of the benchmarks. They were then executed using an Intel Core
i7-6700HQ machine, and their speed-ups measured with respect to sequential
execution. Table 1 lists the loops used in the study.

The benchmarks were compiled with Clang 4.0 when `libomp20160808` was
used (`stl-12016`), and with Clang 12.0 when `libomp12` (`stl-112`) was used,
both at optimization level -O3 and with the set of flags specified in each benchmark program. Code compiled by `clang -fopenmp` was linked against the respective version of the OpenMP runtime in two flavors: `monotonic` (`stl-1x-mon`)
and `nonmonotonic` (`stl-1x-nm`). `ordered` parallelization of the benchmarks
was compiled with Clang 12.0 and linked against `libomp12`. To guarantee
that each software thread is bound to a unique core, the environment variable `KMP_AFFINITY` was set to `granularity = fine,scatter`. This experimental evaluation was carried out on an Intel Core i7-6700HQ processor with 4
cores with 2-way SMT, running at 2.6 GHz, with 16 GB of memory on Ubuntu
18.04.5 LTS (GNU/Linux 4.15.0-139-generic x86_64). The cache-line prefetcher
is enabled by default. Each core has a 32 KB L1 data cache and a 256 KB L2
unified cache. The four cores share an 6144KB L3 cache.

5   Experimental Results and Analysis

This section presents results and analysis. The first part of Table 1 shows the
information of loops: (1) the ID of the loop in this study; (2) the benchmark of
the loop; (3) the file/line of the target loop in the source code; (4) %Cov, the
fraction of the total execution time spent in the loop; and (5) the number of
invocations of the loop in the whole program. The features used to characterize
the loops are shown in the second part of Table 1: (1) N, the average number of

Table 1. Characterization and STL Execution of Loops.

Loop ID	Loop Information				Loop Characterization				STL Execution				ordered
	Benchmark	Location	%Cov	Invocations	N	%lc	Average Iteration Size	S_SIZE	libomp2016 Speed-ups nonmonotonic	monotonic	libomp12 Speed-ups nonmonotonic	monotonic	Execution Speed-up
A	automotive_bitcount	bitcnts.c,65	100%	560	1125000	100%	12 B	5020	1.61	1.69	-	1.55	0.21
E	automotive_susan_s	susan.c,725	100%	22050	600	0%	14 B	25	1.71	1.98	1.79	2.0	0.75
H	automotive_susan_e	susan.c,1117	18%	374	442	0%	3 KB	1	1.91	2.18	-	1.24	1.00
I	automotive_susan_e	susan.c,1056	56%	374	444	0%	4 KB	1	1.13	1.17	-	1.04	0.93
V	automotive_susan_c	susan.c,1614	7%	782	440	34%	1 KB	8	1.06	1.12	-	1.16	0.81
mcf	429.mcf	pbeampp.c,165	40%	21854886	300	3.1%	300 B	75	1.17	1.13	1.16	1.11	0.15

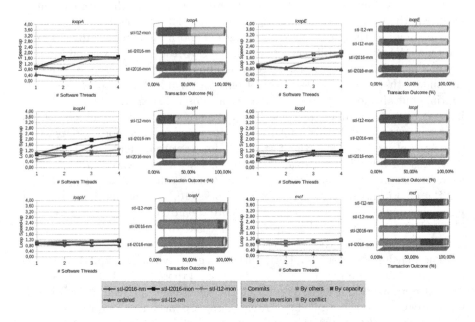

Fig. 11. Speed-ups and abort ratios (4 threads) for STL (with two different OpenMP runtime versions) and **ordered** parallelizations on Intel Core

loop iterations; (2) %lc, the percentage of iterations that have actual RAW loop-carried dependences for the default input of cBench loops and the reference input of mcf; and (3) the average size in bytes read/written by an iteration. The parameters in the third part of Table 1 describe: (1) **S_SIZE**, the *strip size* used for the experimental evaluation of STL parallelization; (2) the average speed-ups with four threads for stl using the original version of libomp2016 (**nonmonotonic**) and the modified version (Sect. 3) to support **monotonic** scheduling; (3) the average speed-ups with four threads for STL using the original (**nonmonotonic**) and the modified (**monotonic**) version of libomp12; (4) the average speed-ups with four threads for ordered using schedule(auto). Symbol '-' in speed-ups means that the loop did not finish due to a deadlock.

Firstly, the performance of the STL parallelization of the benchmarks improves with the implementation of **monotonic** scheduling in the two OpenMP runtime libraries. This is more noticeable with two threads—where STL-parallelization slowdowns using **nonmonotonic** scheduling are transformed to substantial performance improvements—since the Lost-Thread Effect causes a large number of aborts due to order inversion (almost 100% of the transactions started with 2 threads[2]) and removing it by applying a `monotonic` scheduling decreases the ratio of order-inversion aborts.

On the other hand, it is important to note that it is possible to achieve speed-ups using STL and the modified `libomp12` (`stl-l12-mon`) in loops that did not even finish (deadlock) with `nonmonotonic` scheduling (`stl-l12-nm`). This and the reduction of order-inversion aborts in all evaluated loops, with respect to `nonmonotonic` scheduling (as shown in Fig. 11), confirms the effectiveness of `monotonic` scheduling of tasks in STL parallelization.

The performance improvements of STL using both runtimes with `monotonic`-scheduling support is similar, except for `loopH`. This is because, in `loopH`, the execution time of the serial version using Clang 12.0 is much shorter (even compiling with -O1) than that generated by Clang 4.0. Even so, it is possible to get a speed-up of 1.24× with 4 threads in `stl-l12-mon`. However, with 2 threads there are slowdowns (0.86×) because the overhead of creating tasks outweighs the parallelized work.

As mentioned before, in `stl-l12-nm` parallelization, a complete Lost-Thread Effect is generated causing no thread to progress due to the recursive partition of the iteration space, which is completely `nonmonotonic`; however, the results in Fig. 11 show that `loopE` completed its execution for three and four threads. After investigating the `libomp12` code, it was observed that the value of the variable `num_tasks_min` is equal to the minimum between the initial value of the thread deque (256) and the result of multiplying the number of threads by 10 (40 and 30 for four and three threads respectively). Since the number of iterations of this loop is 600 and its S_SZE value is 25, the number of tasks generated by `taskloop` is 24. Thus, when the condition `num_tasks > num_tasks_min` is reached in the `kmp_taskloop` function, it will be false and it will invoke `taskloop_linear` function rather than the `taskloop_recur`. As shown in Fig. 11, the performance of `stl-l12-nm` for `loopE` is worse than the `monotonic` version, and very similar to `stl-l16-nm`.

`loopA` has the same or better speed-ups with three threads than with four threads when `monotonic` scheduling is used in both versions of the runtime because the abort ratio due to order inversion drops dramatically using three threads compared to four threads. The abort overhead, in this case, outweighs the work parallelized by one more thread. In `loopV`, the ratio of aborts due to conflict increases using `monotonic` scheduling. This is because the thread that was lost and repeatedly aborting participates in the parallelization, decreasing the ratio of aborts due to order inversion but conflicting with the other threads for the variable n (loop-carried). The number of commits also increases using

---

[2] In `nonmonotonic` scheduling, there are 100% aborts due to order inversion using two threads because one thread generates tasks and the another consumes them slowly and not speculatively (only one consuming thread). When the generating thread finishes generating all the tasks, it executes iteration $n - 1$ and aborts due to order inversion repeatedly until the another thread arrives.

this type of scheduling, which generates a performance improvement; however, the percentage of transactions committed remains almost the same due to the increase in transaction aborts due to conflict.

The `mcf` hottest loop is a particular case because, with the S_SIZE used, only four tasks are generated. Two of three exposed issues that generate the Lost-Thread Effect do not affect the STL-parallelization of this loop: a) when using four threads or less, the partition will be linear (and no recursive) due to the same reasons explained above for `loopE`; and b) the deque of the generating thread will never be packed because only four tasks are generated (the deque has a capacity of 256 tasks).

Moreover, if the generating thread removes tasks from the tail (`nonmonotonic` scheduling), since there are only four tasks, the Lost-Thread Effect does not occur because the other three threads will execute the three first tasks (strips) and will arrive quickly when the generating thread is executing the fourth strip. On the other hand, using `monotonic` scheduling, the generating thread tries to remove tasks from the head of its deque, which causes more competition for this resource and a performance detriment. Only for this particular reason, the `nonmonotonic` version of this loop offers better speed-ups with four threads than the `monotonic` version.

For the parallelization with `ordered`, `schedule (auto)` clause is used, otherwise the performance is even worse (`loopA` had slowdowns up to $0.01\times$ for 4 cores). In general, `ordered` should be used in (*may*) DOACROSS loops where: (a) their (possible) dependences and components (parallel and serial) can be statically known; and (b) their parallel components do significant work with respect to the iteration time. In the evaluated loops, the performance is poor because either it is not possible to distinguish parallel/serial components or the work of the parallel components is not significant.

6   Conclusions

This paper confirms our claim in previous work about the performance detriment of the Lost-Thread Effect and shows that the implementation of `monotonic` scheduling improves the performance of Speculative `taskloop`. We present an evaluation with two different versions of the OpenMP runtime, both optimized for STL, that reveals that, for certain loops, slowdowns or infinite slowdowns (deadlocks), using the original OpenMP runtime, can be transformed in speed-ups by applying `monotonic` scheduling.

Acknowledgments. The authors would like to thank the anonymous reviewers for the insightful comments.

References

1. Ayguade, E., et al.: The design of OpenMP tasks. IEEE Trans. Parallel Distrib. Syst. (TPDS) **20**(3), 404–418 (2009)

2. Cytron, R.: Doacross: beyond vectorization for multiprocessors. In: International Conference on Parallel Processing (ICPP), pp. 836–844 (1986)
3. cTuning Foundation: cBench: Collective benchmarks (2016). http://ctuning.org/cbench
4. Gayatri, R., Badia, R.M., Ayguade, E.: Loop level speculation in a task based programming model. In: 20th Annual International Conference on High Performance Computing, pp. 39–48 (2013)
5. Intel: Intel OpenMP runtime library, version 20160808 (2016). http://clang-omp.github.io/
6. OpenMP-ARB: OpenMP application program interface version 4.0 (2013)
7. OpenMP-ARB: OpenMP application program interface version 4.5 (2015)
8. OpenMP-ARB: OpenMP application program interface version 5.0 (2018)
9. Podobas, A., Karlsson, S.: Towards unifying OpenMP under the task-parallel paradigm. In: Maruyama, N., de Supinski, B.R., Wahib, M. (eds.) IWOMP 2016. LNCS, vol. 9903, pp. 116–129. Springer, Cham (2016). https://doi.org/10.1007/978-3-319-45550-1_9
10. Salamanca, J., Baldassin, A.: Evaluating the performance of speculative doacross loop parallelization with taskloop. In: IEEE International Conference on High Performance Computing and Simulation (HPCS), Barcelona, Spain (2020)
11. Salamanca, J., Baldassin, A.: Using hardware transactional memory to implement speculative privatization in OpenMP. In: International Workshop on Languages and Compilers for Parallel Computing (LCPC), New York, USA (2020)
12. Salamanca, J., Amaral, J.N., Araujo, G.: Performance evaluation of thread-level speculation in off-the-shelf hardware transactional memories. In: Rivera, F.F., Pena, T.F., Cabaleiro, J.C. (eds.) Euro-Par 2017. LNCS, vol. 10417, pp. 607–621. Springer, Cham (2017). https://doi.org/10.1007/978-3-319-64203-1_44
13. Salamanca, J., Baldassin, A.: A proposal for supporting speculation in the OpenMP taskloop construct. In: Fan, X., de Supinski, B.R., Sinnen, O., Giacaman, N. (eds.) IWOMP 2019. LNCS, vol. 11718, pp. 246–261. Springer, Cham (2019). https://doi.org/10.1007/978-3-030-28596-8_17
14. Shirako, J., Unnikrishnan, P., Chatterjee, S., Li, K., Sarkar, V.: Expressing DOACROSS loop dependences in OpenMP. In: Rendell, A.P., Chapman, B.M., Müller, M.S. (eds.) IWOMP 2013. LNCS, vol. 8122, pp. 30–44. Springer, Heidelberg (2013). https://doi.org/10.1007/978-3-642-40698-0_3
15. Sohi, G.S., Breach, S.E., Vijaykumar, T.N.: Multiscalar processors. In: International Symposium on Computer Architecture (ISCA), S. Margherita Ligure, Italy, pp. 414–425 (1995)
16. Steffan, J., Mowry, T.: The potential for using thread-level data speculation to facilitate automatic parallelization. In: High-Performance Computer Architecture (HPCA), Washington, USA, pp. 2–13 (1998)
17. Steffan, J.G., Colohan, C.B., Zhai, A., Mowry, T.C.: A scalable approach to thread-level speculation. In: International Conference on Computer Architecture (ISCA), Vancouver, British Columbia, Canada, pp. 1–12 (2000)
18. Teruel, X., Klemm, M., Li, K., Martorell, X., Olivier, S.L., Terboven, C.: A proposal for task-generating loops in OpenMP*. In: Rendell, A.P., Chapman, B.M., Müller, M.S. (eds.) IWOMP 2013. LNCS, vol. 8122, pp. 1–14. Springer, Heidelberg (2013). https://doi.org/10.1007/978-3-642-40698-0_1
19. The LLVM Project: LLVM 12.0.0 (2021). https://github.com/llvm/llvm-project
20. Torrellas, J.: Speculation, Thread-Level, pp. 1894–1900. Springer, Boston (2011)

Vectorized Barrier and Reduction
in LLVM OpenMP Runtime

Muhammad Nufail Farooqi[✉] and Miquel Pericàs

Chalmers University of Technology, Gothenburg, Sweden
{nufail,miquelp}@chalmers.se

Abstract. Barrier synchronization is a well known operation in parallel processing that can be an obstacle for getting performance in parallel programs, particularly for high thread counts. Similarly, reduction is a collective communication pattern frequently used in parallel applications and needs to be optimized for applications to achieve their best performance. With the introduction of multi-core and many-core processors several new barrier and reduction implementations have been proposed. As the number of cores per node continues to grow, implementation of these primitives need to be revisited and adapted for upcoming architectures. We see an opportunity to improve synchronization by exploiting vector units present in modern and future CPU designs based on vector ISAs such as ARM's Scalable Vector Extension and the RISC-V Vector extension. In this work we propose vectorized barriers and reductions using the vector length agnostic paradigm and implement them in the LLVM OpenMP runtime. Our barrier implementation achieves up to 2.2× and 1.4× speedup over the default LLVM OpenMP implementation on Intel KNL and Fujitsu A64FX, respectively.

Keywords: OpenMP · Vectorization · Barrier · Reduction

1 Introduction

In a fork/join parallel pattern, a group of threads running in parallel to perform a task or computation often requires to coordinate their execution flow by waiting for a specific task to be completed or a data item to be updated before proceeding further execution for correctness. This is achieved by a *barrier*, that is, a point in a program where all participating threads or processes wait to reach before continuing its execution. Similarly, algorithms often combine a number of values into a single value by applying an arithmetic operation. This pattern is known as *reduction*. Barriers and reductions are two commonly used operations in parallel programs.

A major concern about synchronization is that it causes threads to idle as a result of load imbalance, leading to performance degradation and resource underutilization. However, the barrier itself is a costly task and can be subject to scaling issue with increasing number of threads [6]. This is shown in Fig. 1

© Springer Nature Switzerland AG 2021
S. McIntosh-Smith et al. (Eds.): IWOMP 2021, LNCS 12870, pp. 18–32, 2021.
https://doi.org/10.1007/978-3-030-85262-7_2

where the time spent in EPCC's barrier and reduction benchmarks [3] is observed to increase as one increases the number of threads from 2 to 256 on Intel Knights Landing (KNL) machine. The barrier overhead has been identified as an obstacle for getting performance in parallel programs [22,25]. Similarly, reductions have been observed to scale badly with increasing number of threads [6].

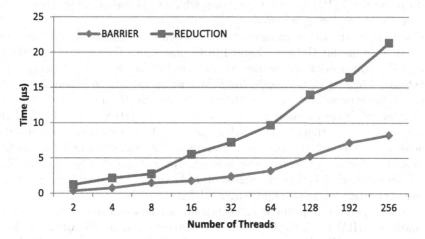

Fig. 1. OpenMP barrier and reduction construct overheads using the EPCC benchmark on Intel Knights Landing (KNL). One threads per core is used until 64 threads and 2, 3, 4 threads per core for 128, 192, 256 threads, respectively.

OpenMP is the most widely used shared memory parallel programming model. Two types of barriers occur frequently in OpenMP: explicit or implicit barriers. Explicit barriers are inserted via the barrier pragma (#pragma omp barrier) and implicit barriers are employed automatically at the end of many OpenMP constructs, e.g. OpenMP *parallel, for* and *single*. Reductions are explicitly specified via a *reduction* clause that includes reduction variable/s and the corresponding reduction operation. Each participating OpenMP thread performs the reduction operation on a subset of the values and then the local results from all threads are further reduced to a single value that is shared among all threads.

On chip parallelism is increasing and is expected to raise even more at exascale, thus posing a challenge to keep the cost of barriers low as the number of cores on chip rise. At the same time, vector units are being added to microprocessor chips in order to perform certain operations more efficiently. For example, Fujitsu's A64FX processor includes a 512-bit vector unit based on ARM-SVE [21]. Vector units are designed to process multiple data items in parallel. Barriers and reductions involve operations that are applied to multiple data items, and can be applied simultaneously to all items. This raises the following question: Can modern vector units be used to accelerate synchronization and reduction operations?

Many algorithms for barrier synchronization have been developed over the past four decades. A discussion of the most relevant proposals is given in Sect. 2. The performance of barriers depends on many factors, like the number of threads to synchronize, the underlying hardware architecture, the application type and the system load at the time of synchronization [15,17]. Barriers implemented with a tree synchronization pattern are well suited for high number of threads [1]. We focus on the LLVM OpenMP runtime, which implements a few state of the art tree based barrier algorithms.

Caballero et al. [4,5] implemented a tree based barrier algorithm in the Intel OpenMP runtime for the Intel Xeon Phi Coprocessor. They utilize the SIMD unit in the coprocessor for barrier synchronization as well as for performing reductions. Their work is specific for SIMD while we aim to generalize it for vector architectures. Furthermore, they implement SIMD specific reduction in the runtime while we use *clang*'s code generator to generate vectorized LLVM-IR reduction code. The runtime approach requires an ISA or even machine specific implementation for all standard reduction operations and can't be implemented for custom reductions. However, the code generator approach has the capability to generate code that is portable across all ISAs as the LLVM-IR for the Vector Length Agnostic (VLA) programming model standardises.

In this paper, we implement low overhead barriers and reduction in LLVM OpenMP for ARM-SVE, RISC-V Vector Extensions and Intel's Advanced Vector Extensions (AVX) by vectorizing the threads arrival flag check and release operation in barriers. We also vectorize reduction operation to reduce partially reduced values from all threads. Our contributions are as follows:

- We implement vectorized barrier and reduction support in LLVM OpenMP runtime for ARM-SVE, RISC-V Vector Extensions and AVX.
- We implement LLVM-IR generator in clang to generate vectorized reduction function.
- We provide performance measurement and comparison of Fujitsu A64FX and Intel KNL, and validate the correctness for RISC-V Vector Extensions. Our evaluation shows that the vectorized barrier achieves 2.2× speedup on an Intel KNL and 1.52× speedup on a Fujitsu A64FX.

The rest of the paper is organised as follows: Sect. 2 gives background about different types of barriers that are found in the literature and of the implementation of barriers and reduction in the LLVM OpenMP runtime. Section 3 presents the vectorized barrier algorithm and the LLVM-IR generation for vectorized reduction in clang. Performance results are then discussed in Sect. 4, while Sect. 5 concludes the paper.

2 Background and Related Work

In this section, first we discuss different types of barriers found in the literature. We classify barriers mainly on the underlying data structure used for implementation. Here, we also explain how barriers and reduction are implemented in LLVM OpenMP.

2.1 Types of Barriers in Literature

Two types of data structures are usually used for barrier implementation. One is centralised data structure where a single variable that is shared among all threads is used for synchronization. The other data structure is to use a dedicated flag for each thread. The actual pattern of how the synchronization is performed also depends on the data structure used.

The types of barriers with centralised data structure implementation uses a single shared variable as counter. Each thread, upon reaching at synchronization point, increment the counter variable to mark its arrival. Access to the shared counter is controlled via locks or is incremented through atomic operations. These type of barriers do not scale with increasing number of threads due to the lock contention that is required by threads before modifying the counter [18]. There exist a number variants for centralised barrier algorithms [10,13,23,24] that are based on this type of data structures. A major variant is software combining tree barrier [26] that uses multiple shared counters organised as a tree where each counter is dedicated for a subgroup of threads to reduce contention.

Barriers implemented using dedicated flags has a fixed variable for each thread that is used to mark its arrival at the synchronization point. The flag variable can be either a variable in thread's own data structure or a dedicated location in a shared array. This type of implementation can scale well with increasing number of threads because each thread only modifies its dedicated location and do not require any lock. The drawback is that all flags are required to be checked to ensure the arrival of all threads at the synchronization point.

Dissemination Barrier [9,10], Tournament Barrier [10,14], Static Tree Barrier [15], Multi-Degree SIMD Combining Tree Barrier Algorithm [5] and barrier implementations in the LLVM OpenMP runtime uses dedicated flags to mark threads arrival. The Dissemination Barrier takes places in multiple stages where at a stage x each thread synchronizes with its 2^xth adjacent thread. Tournament and Static Tree synchronizes in a tree manner with dedicated array for each tree level. The difference between the two is that Static Tree Barrier uses a static thread to synchronize sibling threads in a subgroup at a level and mark arrival of subgroup at higher level while the in Tournament Barrier a winner thread performs this task. The winner thread is selected dynamically depending on its time of arrival. Diego's [5] algorithm is similar to Static Tree Barrier except that tree levels can have variable number of nodes.

Besides software barriers, there are also efforts at the hardware level to implement low cost synchronization. These are either fully in hardware [11,16,19] or a hybrid of software and hardware [20].

2.2 Barriers and Reductions in OpenMP

Barriers: The clang code generator replaces every #pragma omp barrier with a call to the OpenMP runtime's barrier subroutine. The LLVM OpenMP runtime implementation of a barrier is composed of two phases: A *Gather* and a *Release* phase. In *Gather* phase, all threads marks their arrival at synchronization point by incrementing their flags and then wait to be released. Any task e.g. reduction that is needed to be performed is carried out. Then followed by the *Release* phase where parent threads releases child threads by resetting the flags.

The LLVM's OpenMP runtime, based on use of a barrier in a program, implement two barrier models. One is *Fork-join* model that is used implicitly with OpenMP parallel construct and the other is *Plain* model that is used everywhere else both for implicit and explicit barriers. The *Fork-join* model as compared to the *Plain* model is implemented with an additional assumption that a threads' data may not exist because either it is not created yet or it deleted its data after leaving the barrier at the end of a parallel region. That is why it is used for parallel construct because threads are created at the beginning of a parallel construct and destroyed at the end.

The runtime, for synchronization of threads in a team implements four types of patterns: Linear, Tree, Hyper and Hierarchical.

- Linear: A single master thread is responsible for ensuring arrival of all team member threads at a barrier and performs any required task before releasing them.
- Tree: This pattern uses a balanced tree approach with a branching factor in powers of 2 where threads at a level l work as master thread for child threads at level $l+1$.
- Hyper: This is hypercube-embedded tree like pattern with a branching factor in powers of 2. Hypercube is explained at [7].

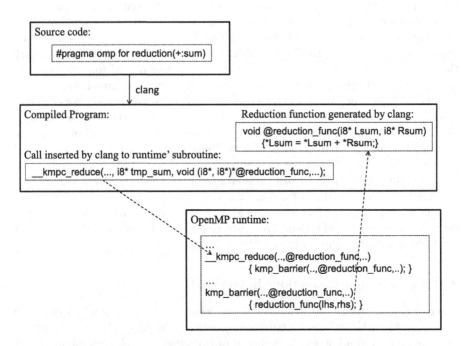

Fig. 2. An example of how reduction is handled in LLVM OpenMP.

– Hierarchical: Similar to a tree pattern but the tree structure is based on machine hierarchy.

Reductions: There are two components involved in implementation of a reduction. One is the clang code generator that automatically generate a reduction function @*reduction_func* that performs the reduction operations specified in the reduction clause. The other involve inserting a call to the runtime's subroutine _*kmpc_reduce* for the reduction. A function pointer to the reduction function @*reduction_func* and pointer to reduction variables are passed as parameter to the subroutine. During program execution all threads encounter a call to the runtime subroutine _*kmpc_reduce*. This subroutine in turn calls the reduction function @*reduction_func* using the function pointer between the *Gather* and *Release* phases of an embedded barrier. Figure 2 shows an example of what a compiler generates when it encounters a reduction clause and then how the compiled program interacts with the OpenMP runtime.

3   Low Overhead Barrier and Reduction in OpenMP

We present low overhead barrier and reductions implementation in LLVM's OpenMP runtime by utilizing the vector unit in the modern processors. We added this as an optional feature in the LLVM OpenMP that can be enabled by −fopenmp_use_vbr compiler command line option.

3.1   Vectorized Barrier

We changed both the data structure and the synchronization pattern in the runtime for vectorized barrier implementation. The existing OpenMP runtime uses dedicated flags, embedded in each thread's own data structure, to mark the arrival of threads at synchronization point. However, vector units are designed to processes a contiguous chunk of data. Therefore we added an array per team that is shared among all threads in a team and is used to mark the arrival of threads at barrier. The same array is also used to signal the release of threads after processing any required task. All the flags are initialized to 1 when the shared flags array for a team is allocated.

The *Gather* and *Release* phases of the synchronization pattern for a *Plain* barrier model implementation are shown in Fig. 3. In the *Gather* phase, each thread marks its arrival by setting the dedicated location to 0 in the shared flags array and start waiting on the same flag at the *Release* phase except the master thread. Threads in a team need to wait at a synchronization point until all the threads arrive. Thus master thread continuously loads a part of the shared array (depends on the vector length) and perform bitwise or operation between the loaded part and a temporary vector register until the entire array is processed in the inner loop. The master thread then in an outer loop checks if any of the threads did not reach yet by looking for any bit that is still set in the temporary vector register. After arrival of all threads the master thread completes any task that need to be performed and then release all child threads in the *Release* phase by setting their flags equal to 1.

We use tree pattern for barrier synchronization where branching factor can be set using an environment variable and allocate a dedicated shared array for each tree level.

Gather phase:

```
vec_array[thread_id]=0;
if(master_thread){
do {
    tmp_vec[1:VLEN]=0;
    for (i=0; i<nThreads; i+=VLEN) {
        tmp_vec |= vector_load(&vec_array[i], VLEN);}
} while (tmp_vec);
```

Release phase:

```
if(master_thread){
    vec_array[1:nThreads]=1;
} else {
    while(!vec_array[thread_id]);
}
```

Fig. 3. Pseudocode for barrier (Gather and Release phases). VLEN is length of the vector unit and nThreads are number of threads participating in the barrier.

3.2 Vectorized Reduction

The OpenMP runtime and the clang code generator for OpenMP are both modified to implement vectorized reduction.

In the OpenMP runtime, a shared array per team for each reduction variable in a reduction clause is created. The same arrays are reused for subsequent reduction clauses, if any. The partial reduction result from each thread is copied to the shared reduction array during the *Gather* phase of a barrier that is embedded inside the runtime's reduction subroutine. The master thread then computes the reduction result by calling the vectorized *@reduction_func* function. We modify signature of the reduction subroutine __kmp_reduce for vectorized reduction. A parameter is added to pass the reduction variables sizes to the runtime that is later used to copy the partial reduction results for each thread into the shared reduction array. The signature of pointer to the reduction function that is passed to __kmp_reduce is also changed because of an additional parameter in the vectorized reduction function.

The code generator is adapted to generate vectorized LLVM-IR code for the reduction operation in the *@reduction_func* function. Pseudocode for the vectorized reduction function is shown in Fig. 4. The function signature is changed by passing the number of threads as additional parameter that indicates the number of elements to be reduced. The default reduction function perform the reduction operation on two variables while the vectorized reduction function

```
void @reduction_func(i8* Lsum, i8* RedArr, nThreads) {
    vec_gather[1:VLEN] = 0; // initial value suitable for reduction
    for(i=0; i<nThreads; i+=VLEN) {
        vec_gather += Gather_Load(&RedArr[i], VLEN, PaddingLength); }
    *Lsum = Vector.Reduce.Add(vec_gather);}
```

Fig. 4. Pseudocode for vectorized reduction function

reduces an array with elements equal to the number of threads in a team. We use the reduction method described in [12]. The code generator also inserts a call to __kmp_reduce with the modified signature.

Our implementation of LLVM-IR code generator for vectorized reduction function in clang supports AVX, ARM-SVE and RISC-V Vector Extensions. Currently, there is no standardised LLVM-IR for scalable vectors so the LLVM-IR generated is different for each instruction set.

4 Performance Results

We carried out performance measurements using EPCC's parallel, barrier and reduction benchmarks on Intel KNL for AVX and Fujitsu A64FX for Arm SVE. EPCC's parallel, barrier, for and reduction benchmarks measures the performance of (#pragma omp parallel), (#pragma omp barrier), (#pragma omp for) and (#pragma omp parallel reduction(+:sum)) pragmas, respectively. The EPCC's reduction benchmark measures the overhead of reduction by appending the reduction clause to OpenMP *parallel* pragma. Measuring the pure overhead of a reduction clause is not possible. Therefore, we also write another benchmark to measure the overhead of reduction where we append the reduction clause to OpenMP *for* pragma as (#pragma omp for reduction(+:sum)). Table 1 shows machine specifications for Intel KNL and Fujitsu A64FX. In all experiments, LLVM OpenMP's default barrier and reduction are used as baseline for comparison with vectorized barrier and reduction. The runtime uses hypercube-embedded tree barrier pattern as default.

Table 1. Machine specifications.

	Intel KNL	Fujitsu A64FX
Cores	68	48
L1	32 KB	64 KB
L2	34 MB (private)	32 MB (shared)
Memory	192 GB	32 GB
Bandwidth	90 GB/s	1 TB/s

For RISC-V Vector Extension, we validated the functional correctness of implementation using qemu [2] and vehave emulator [8]. We could not perform any performance studies because, currently, there is no machine or simulator available that can be used to carry out performance studies for multithreaded RISC-V Vector Extension.

We ran experiments with different branching factors for the tree pattern that we use for barrier synchronization. For both Intel KNL and A64FX, the best performance is achieved when branching factor is maximum and all the threads are at same level that is equivalent to a linear pattern.

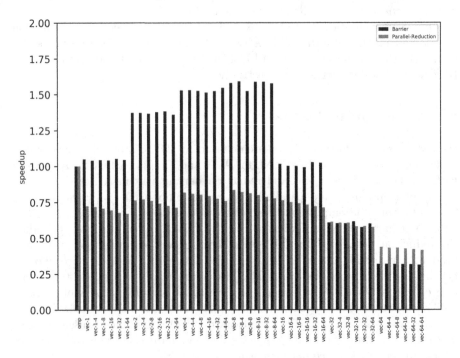

Fig. 5. Performance of vectorized barrier and reduction with varying padding for barrier flags and reduction array (256 Threads on Intel KNL with snc4 cluster mode).

4.1   Intel KNL

We analysed the effect of padding the shared flags array for vectorized barriers and the reduction array on Intel KNL. Figure 5 shows speedup for parallel, barrier and reduction benchmarks running on Intel KNL for 256 threads. On the x-axes, *omp* is the default OpenMP and *vec-x-y* is for OpenMP with vectorized barrier and reduction where x is the number of bytes used for a barrier flag (including the padding) and y is the number of bytes used for an element of reduction array (including the padding). In *vec-x*, no padding is used for reduction array and vector loads to are used to load the reduction array instead of a gather instruction. The performance of vectorized barrier increases as we increase the padding until 8 bytes (i.e. 8 threads sharing a cache line) and then starts degrading with further increase in the padding. The performance initially increases due to the reduction in false sharing that is caused by threads sharing a cache line but starts degrading with further increase in the padding because of an increase in the on-chip memory traffic. The maximum performance is achieved when the balance between false sharing and on-chip memory traffic is optimal. For reduction, the maximum performance is without padding and performance declines when the padding is increased.

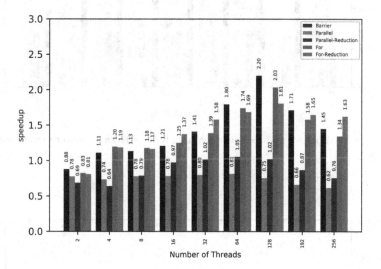

Fig. 6. Vectorized barrier and reduction on Intel KNL with snc4 cluster mode (padding: 8 bytes).

Figure 6, 7 and 8 shows scaling results in terms of speedup for the barrier, parallel, parallel-reduction, for and for-reduction benchmarks when using 8, 16 and 32 bytes padding for each thread's barrier flag on Intel KNL with snc4 clustering mode. The vectorized barrier was able to achieve a maximum of 2.2× speedup for 128 threads when a padding of 8 bytes is used. In all the three cases, the performance increase as we increase the number of threads until the optimal balance between false sharing and on-chip memory traffic is achieved and then deteriorates with further increase in the number of threads. For lower number of threads when we increase the padding the performance also increase because it reduces the false sharing while the on-chip network is still not saturated due to memory traffic.

The performance penalty in the parallel benchmark is due to the extra overhead caused by the initialization of barrier and reduction arrays that are created at entry to the parallel region and destroyed at the exit. The performance gain

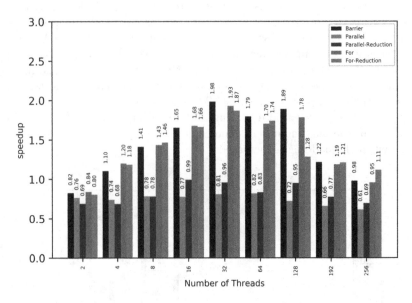

Fig. 7. Vectorized barrier and reduction on Intel KNL with snc4 cluster mode (padding: 16 bytes).

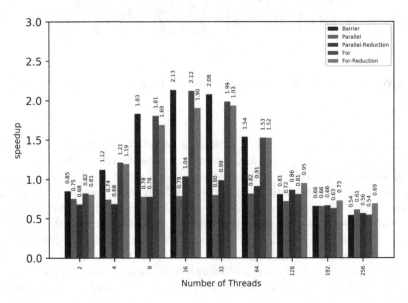

Fig. 8. Vectorized barrier and reduction on Intel KNL with snc4 cluster mode (padding: 32 bytes).

in the for benchmark is due to the implicit barrier that is used to synchronize all threads threads at the exit.

The parallel-reduction and for-reduction benchmarks are implemented by adding the reduction clause to the OpenMP parallel and for pragmas, respectively. Thus the performance measured using these benchmarks is the combined performance of the pragma used and the reduction. The vectorized parallel-reduction do not achieve a clear performance improvement over the default parallel-reduction. However, the benefit of vectorized reduction is visible from the additional speedup achieved by the parallel-reduction compared to the parallel benchmark and the for-reduction compared to the for benchmark when the number of threads are high.

4.2 Fujitsu A64FX

Padding the shared flags array for vectorized barriers and the reduction array was also analysed on Fujitsu A64FX. Maximum performance was observed when using a padding of 64 bytes for barrier and no padding for reduction array. Figure 9 shows scaling results in terms of speedup for barrier, parallel, parallel-reduction, for and for-reduction benchmarks on A64FX using a padding of 64 bytes for barrier i.e. a single cache line per thread. On A64FX, the vectorized barrier achieved a maximum speedup of 1.4x for 8, 16 and 32 cores i.e. when number of cores are in multiple of 8. Vectorized reduction couldn't outperform the default implementation on A64FX as the number of threads are low as compared to Intel KNL.

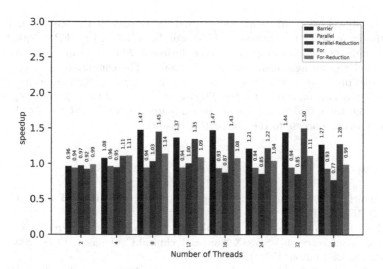

Fig. 9. Vectorized barrier and reductions on A64FX (64 byte padded array for barrier flags and no padding for reduction array).

5   Conclusions

In this paper, we implemented low overhead barriers and reduction in LLVM OpenMP by vectorizing the threads arrival flag check and release operation in barriers and reduction operation to reduce partially reduced values from all threads. The goal was to utilise vector/SIMD units available in modern architectures to prepare the OpenMP runtime for the massive cores counts that is expected in exascale era. Our implementation supports ARM-SVE, RISC-V Vector Extension and Intel's Advanced Vector Extensions. We carried out performance studies on Fujitsu A64FX for ARM-SVE and on Intel KNL for AVX. The vectorized barriers achieved 2.2x speedup on Intel KNL for 128 threads and 1.4x speedup on A64FX for 32 threads over the default OpenMP barrier implementation. Measuring the pure overhead of a reduction clause is not possible as it used as an additional clause to OpenMP pragma like *parallel* and *for*. The vectorized reduction show performance improvements on Intel KNL when performance of parallel is compared with parallel-reduction and for with for-reduction benchmark. However, the reduction benchmark on A64FX do not show performance improvements.

In experimentation with different padding sizes for barrier flags, we found that the cache coherency protocol plays an important role in the performance of vectorized barriers. Reducing the overhead of barriers and reduction further by doing optimization only in the software is not a trivial task and would benefit from hardware support. In the future, we are planning to work on the cache coherency mechanism to provide support for synchronizations and reductions in the cache hierarchy.

Acknowledgements. This work has been done as part of the European Processor Initiative project. The European Processor Initiative (EPI) (FPA: 800928) has received funding from the European Union's Horizon 2020 research and innovation programme under grant agreement EPI-SGA1: 826647. The computations were enabled by resources provided by the Swedish National Infrastructure for Computing (SNIC) at HPC2N, partially funded by the Swedish Research Council through grant agreement no. 2018–05973. We thank Barcelona Supercomputer Center (BSC-CNS) for their support and providing access to the CTE-ARM cluster.

References

1. Arenstorf, N.S., Jordan, H.F.: Comparing barrier algorithms. Parallel Comput. **12**(2), 157–170 (1989)
2. Bellard, F.: Qemu, a fast and portable dynamic translator. In: Proceedings of the Annual Conference on USENIX Annual Technical Conference, ATEC 2005, p. 41, USENIX Association, USA (2005)
3. Bull, J.M., Reid, F., McDonnell, N.: A microbenchmark suite for OpenMP tasks. In: Chapman, B.M., Massaioli, F., Müller, M.S., Rorro, M. (eds.) IWOMP 2012. LNCS, vol. 7312, pp. 271–274. Springer, Heidelberg (2012). https://doi.org/10. 1007/978-3-642-30961-8_24

4. Caballero, D.: SIMD@OpenMP: a programming model approach to leverage SIMD features. Ph.D. Thesis, Universitat Politecnica de Catalunya (2015)
5. Caballero, D., Duran, A., Martorell, X.: An OpenMP* Barrier Using SIMD instructions for intel® Xeon PhiTM coprocessor. In: Rendell, A.P., Chapman, B.M., Müller, M.S. (eds.) IWOMP 2013. LNCS, vol. 8122, pp. 99–113. Springer, Heidelberg (2013). https://doi.org/10.1007/978-3-642-40698-0_8
6. Doodi, T., et al.: OpenMP runtime instrumentation for optimization. In: de Supinski, B.R., Olivier, S.L., Terboven, C., Chapman, B.M., Müller, M.S. (eds.) Scaling OpenMP for Exascale Performance and Portability. Lecture Notes in Computer Science, pp. 281–295. Springer International Publishing, Cham (2017)
7. https://people.eecs.berkeley.edu/~demmel/cs267-1995/lecture10/lecture10.html
8. https://repo.hca.bsc.es/gitlab/epi-public/risc-v-vector-simulation-environment
9. Han, Y., Finkel, R.A.: An optimal scheme for disseminating information. In: Proceedings of the International Conference on Parallel Processing, ICPP '88, The Pennsylvania State University, University Park, PA, USA, August 1988. Volume 2: Software, pages 198–203. Pennsylvania State University Press (1988)
10. Hensgen, D., Finkel, R., Manber, U.: Two algorithms for barrier synchronization. Int. J. Parallel Program. **17**, 1–17 (1988). https://doi.org/10.1007/BF01379320
11. Hetland, C., et al.: Paths to fast barrier synchronization on the node. In: Proceedings of the 28th International Symposium on High-Performance Parallel and Distributed Computing, HPDC 2019, pp. 109–120. Association for Computing Machinery, New York, NY, USA, (2019)
12. Lin, H., Sips, H.: Parallel vector reduction algorithms and architectures. J. Parallel Distrib. Comput. **5**(2), 103–130 (1988)
13. Lubachevsky, B.D.: An approach to automating the verification of compact parallel coordination programs. I. Acta Inf. **21**(2), 125–169 (1984)
14. Lubachevsky, B.D.: Synchronization barrier and related tools for shared memory parallel programming. Int. J. Parallel Prog. **19**(3), 225–250 (1991)
15. Mellor-Crummey, J.M., Scott, M.L.: Algorithms for scalable synchronization on shared-memory multiprocessors. ACM Trans. Comput. Syst. **9**(1), 21–65 (1991)
16. Mondal, H.K., Cataldo, R.C., Marcon, C.A.M., Martin, K., Deb, S., Diguet, J.-P.: Broadcast-and power-aware wireless NoC for barrier synchronization in parallel computing. In: 2018 31st IEEE International System-on-Chip Conference (SOCC), pp. 1–6 (2018)
17. Nanjegowda, R., Hernandez, O., Chapman, B., Jin, H.H.: Scalability evaluation of barrier algorithms for OpenMP. In: Müller, M.S., de Supinski, B.R., Chapman, B.M. (eds.) IWOMP 2009. LNCS, vol. 5568, pp. 42–52. Springer, Heidelberg (2009). https://doi.org/10.1007/978-3-642-02303-3_4
18. Pfister, G.F., Norton, V.A.: "hot spot" contention and combining in multistage interconnection networks. IEEE Trans. Comput. C **34**(10), 943–948 (1985)
19. Sampson, J., Gonzalez, R., Collard, J.-F., Jouppi, N.P., Schlansker, M., Calder, B.: Exploiting fine-grained data parallelism with chip multiprocessors and fast barriers. In: 2006 39th Annual IEEE/ACM International Symposium on Microarchitecture (MICRO 2006), pp. 235–246 (2006)
20. Sartori, J., Kumar, R.: Low-overhead, high-speed multi-core barrier synchronization. In: Patt, Y.N., Foglia, P., Duesterwald, E., Faraboschi, P., Martorell, X. (eds.) HiPEAC 2010. LNCS, vol. 5952, pp. 18–34. Springer, Heidelberg (2010). https://doi.org/10.1007/978-3-642-11515-8_4
21. Sato, M., et al.: Co-Design for A64FX Manycore Processor and "Fugaku". In: SC20: International Conference for High Performance Computing, Networking, Storage and Analysis, pp. 1–15, November 2020

22. Satoh, S., Kusano, K., Sato, M.: Compiler optimization techniques for OpenMP programs. Sci. Program. **9**(2–3), 131–142 (2001)
23. Tang, P., Yew, P.: Processor self-scheduling for multiple-nested parallel loops. In: Hwang, K., Jacobs, S., Swartzlander, E. (eds) Proceedings of the International Conference on Parallel Processing, Proceedings of the International Conference on Parallel Processing, pp. 528–535. IEEE, December 1986
24. Tang, P., Yew, P.-C.: Software combining algorithms for distributing hot-spot addressing. J. Parallel Distrib. Comput. **10**(2), 130–139 (1990)
25. Tatebe, O., Sato, M., Sekiguchi, S.: Impact of OpenMP optimizations for the MGCG method. In: Valero, M., Joe, K., Kitsuregawa, M., Tanaka, H. (eds.) High Performance Computing. Lecture Notes in Computer Science, pp. 471–481. Springer, Berlin, Heidelberg (2000). https://doi.org/10.1007/3-540-39999-2_44
26. Yew, P.-C., Tzeng, N.-F.: Lawrie: distributing hot-spot addressing in large-scale multiprocessors. IEEE Trans. Comput. C **36**(4), 388–395 (1987)

Tasking Extensions I

Enhancing OpenMP Tasking Model: Performance and Portability

Chenle Yu[1,2]([⊠]), Sara Royuela[1]([⊠]), and Eduardo Quiñones[1]([⊠])

[1] Barcelona Supercomputing Center, Barcelona, Spain
{chenle.yu,sara.royuela,eduardo.quinones}@bsc.es
[2] Universitat Politècnica de Catalunya, Barcelona, Spain
chenle.yu@upc.edu

Abstract. OpenMP, as the *de-facto* standard programming model in symmetric multiprocessing for HPC, has seen its performance boosted continuously by the community, either through implementation enhancements or specification augmentations. Furthermore, the language has evolved from a prescriptive nature, as defined by the thread-centric model, to a descriptive behavior, as defined by the task-centric model. However, the overhead related to the orchestration of tasks is still relatively high. Applications exploiting very fine-grained parallelism and systems with a large number of cores available might fail on scaling.

In this work, we propose to include the concept of Task Dependency Graph (TDG) in the specification by introducing a new clause, named *taskgraph*, attached to *task* or *target* directives. By design, the TDG allows alleviating the overhead associated with the OpenMP tasking model, and it also facilitates linking OpenMP with other programming models that support task parallelism. According to our experiments, a GCC implementation of the `taskgraph` is able to significantly reduce the execution time of fine-grained task applications and increase their scalability with regard to the number of threads.

Keywords: OpenMP specification · Tasking model · Runtime overhead

1 Introduction

OpenMP is a parallel programming model widely used on shared memory systems by virtue of its programmability, portability, and competitive performance. OpenMP 3.0 introduced support for fine-grained irregular parallelism with the so-called task-centric model. Later, OpenMP 4.0 introduced fine-grained data-driven synchronization mechanisms in the form of task dependencies. Since this preliminary support for task parallelism, the OpenMP specification has evolved from a *prescriptive* to a *descriptive* paradigm, enabling users to define what has to be parallelized rather than how to parallelize it. Interestingly, the tasking model can be now used not only for *task parallelism*, by using the `task` construct, but also for *data parallelism*, by using the `taskloop` construct.

© Springer Nature Switzerland AG 2021
S. McIntosh-Smith et al. (Eds.): IWOMP 2021, LNCS 12870, pp. 35–49, 2021.
https://doi.org/10.1007/978-3-030-85262-7_3

Despite the clear benefits of the tasking model (including flexibility, dynamism, and independence from the underlying resources), the implementations of this model typically introduce a considerable overhead related to the management of the parallel execution of tasks. As a result, these overheads have been extensively studied [8,13,15], concluding that a sufficiently coarse granularity of tasks (i.e., workload assigned to a task) is the keystone to obtain the expected performance gains. However, the smaller the granularity is, the greater the overhead will represent the end-to-end execution time. Although the runtime overhead is substantially dependent on each particular implementation, the observations made on the studies are independent of the compiler and the runtime used in the experiments.

To overcome the limitations derived from classic OpenMP implementations, different works propose alternative solutions. Castelló et al. presented an implementation using lightweight threads (LWT) instead of POSIX threads [2] and G.Tagliavini et al. designed and implemented an OpenMP runtime environment specifically for the Kalray MPPA 256 [5], a many-core processor for embedded systems. Despite the effectiveness of these solutions, they are either difficult to apply on mainstream OpenMP runtime implementations, or they are not portable to diverse shared memory systems.

This paper takes into account the limitations of the previous solutions, and proposes a new feature in the OpenMP specification to allow users to define *taskgraph* regions, i.e., regions of an OpenMP task-based program that can be implemented more efficiently. This enhancement in the implementation is substantiated on the Task Dependency Graph (TDG) used to represent the execution of a task-based program (or region), and is only possible if either (a) the TDG of the selected region can be completely expanded at compile-time (i.e., all tasks instances and their dependencies can be decided statically), or (b) the region is going to be executed multiple times and the same TDG can be exploited several times.

The approach proposed can reduce, by design, the runtime overhead related to task management, and it has a higher abstraction level than previously presented methods. Hence, existing OpenMP implementations, including aforementioned work, can easily integrate taskgraph, thus benefiting from several layers of optimization. Our main contributions are the following:

- A new approach for accelerating the OpenMP tasking model by reducing task runtime overhead, together with the analysis of the use cases that can benefit from this new approach.
- A new clause, namely `taskgraph`, providing the syntax and the semantics thereof, and the characterization of the implications on the execution and memory models of OpenMP.
- Preliminary results on the benefits that can be extracted from this new feature considering (a) performance gain by virtue of a lighter implementation of the OpenMP runtime, and (b) interoperability provided by the TDG, which allows using OpenMP as a high-level API that can be lowered to different programming models.

2 Motivation

The main sources of overhead in the OpenMP runtime for handling tasks include: (a) the contention caused by different threads accessing simultaneously to shared resources, for instance, acquiring the lock that protects a shared data element; and (b) the cost of handling tasks, including task creations, dependency resolutions and task deletions. While the former is proportional to the number of threads running concurrently and the amount of parallelism exposed in the application, the latter scales with the number of tasks, which tends to be large in modern HPC applications. This can be explained by the increased workloads and the growing number of logical threads incorporated in high-end modern processors.

On the whole, to achieve the levels of performance provided by modern multi-core and many-core accelerated architectures, the number of tasks exposed in an application must be, at least, as large as the number of threads during most part of the execution. However, using more threads does not systematically mean higher performance, according to the sources of overhead stated above. Therefore, reducing task-related overhead is of paramount importance for the success of OpenMP task-based frameworks.

In a perfect world, where the compiler can statically determine the data associated to all task instances and all dependencies among tasks, the allocation of tasks and the resolution of the dependencies can be done at compile time. We use an in-house implementation in the GCC 7.3.0 framework that uses a pre-computed Task Dependency Graph to allocate tasks and decide dependencies beforehand in order to illustrate the benefits of this approach. Figure 1 shows the execution time[1] of an optimized heat transfer simulation where the problem size is fixed (2048×2048 matrix), and the block size is changed throughout the experiment, generating from 640 tasks (with 256×256 block size) to 16000 tasks (with 52×52 block size). The line annotated as $GCC+taskgraph$ corresponds to the optimal case where the TDG is fully pre-calculated at compile-time, whereas the line annotated as $GCC + original\ GOMP$ runs the vanilla implementation of GCC GOMP runtime. Essentially, the figure shows when the number of tasks increases (and so the granularity of the tasks decreases because of the fixed total workload) the modified version does not lose performance, while the original version does once the number of tasks exceeds 4000.

Applications in the HPC domain are however commonly dynamic, in the sense that their data is only known at runtime. As a consequence, compilers are not able to automatically apply the optimizations explained above. However, some HPC applications show other patterns that can also benefit from a similar approach to reduce overhead. This is the case of applications that expose multiple levels of parallelism, where the outer levels are dynamic and the inner levels are static, e.g., the sLASs linear algebra solver [19], the Specfem3D simulator [6]

---

[1] The execution has run in a node of the Marenostrum IV [1] supercomputer, equipped with an Intel Xeon Platinum 8160 CPU, having 2 sockets of 24 physical cores each, at 2.1 GHz and 33 MB L3 cache.

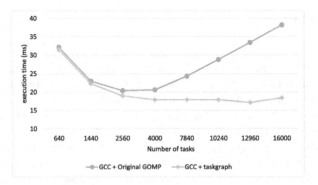

Fig. 1. Execution time of Heat transfer simulation using Gauss-Seidel method while changing the number of tasks and reducing the task granularity.

and the Quantum ESPRESSO material modeling tool [4]. In these cases, where inner TDG can become static after their first execution, benefits similar or even better than the ones shown in Fig. 1 can be expected.

Nonetheless, it is unattainable for a compiler to detect these cases and lower the code accordingly so the runtime does not create and destroy the inner (and stable) TDGs each time they have to run. As a consequence, this paper proposes to enable programmers to explicitly define the regions of their applications that are static (i.e., decidable at compile-time) or stable (i.e., these will run several times without changing the TDG and consumed data). In order to fit in the OpenMP specification without introducing unnecessary changes, we propose a new clause called `taskgraph` which, together with the `task` and `target` directives, acts as a hint to the compiler and the runtime system to recognize the task region to optimize.

Furthermore, the possibility of pre-building a TDG opens the door for programs to be lowered, not only to the common OpenMP runtime (e.g., GCC, LLVM), but also to other APIs in order to exploit the heterogeneity. This is of particular interest in modern supercomputers as, for instance, 6 of the 10 most powerful supoercomputers in the world now incorporate Nvidia GPUs to scale their computation power [18], and various applications are legacy code, or are highly tuned for a specific accelerator device. Thus, increasing the portability of OpenMP to these models, as well as enhancing the programmability of low-level APIs is crucial. Previous works [20] have already tackled this issue, and a detailed analysis on these aspects is further provided in Sect. 4.2.

3   The Taskgraph Model

Despite the fact that application developers often use TDGs to express and study their programs, the OpenMP specification does not include the concept of TDG per se. We propose to introduce this concept, named *taskgraph*, in the OpenMP specification to tackle the challenges mentioned in Sect. 2. To do so, this section presents the *taskgraph* mechanism and discusses how to integrate this feature into the current OpenMP specification. Concretely, it defines first the syntax of a new `taskgraph` clause and its semantic, considering its impact on the execution and memory models of OpenMP; and then exhibits the conditions required by the OpenMP program to use the *taskgraph* feature correctly.

3.1 The `taskgraph` Mechanism

Implementations supporting `taskgraph` shall be able to generate a TDG, either at compile-time or at run-time, from a region annotated with the `taskgraph` clause. By leveraging the information contained in the TDG, the compiler or the runtime is capable of replacing the entire taskgraph region (meaning the user code) with the execution of the TDG. Therefore, not only the overhead related to task creation, dependency resolution and task deletion is alleviated, but also loop and conditional statements can be skipped.

Figure 2 illustrates the *taskgraph* mechanism. Particularly, Fig. 2a shows a snippet of a Heat transfer simulation implemented with OpenMP tasks and using the `taskgraph` clause, and Fig. 2b shows an overview of the TDG extracted from that application.

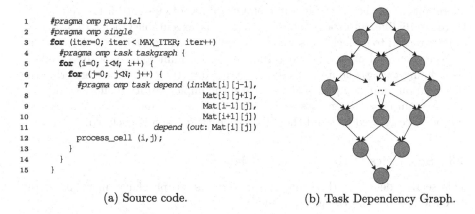

```
1    #pragma omp parallel
2    #pragma omp single
3    for (iter=0; iter < MAX_ITER; iter++)
4      #pragma omp task taskgraph {
5      for (i=0; i<M; i++) {
6        for (j=0; j<N; j++) {
7          #pragma omp task depend (in:Mat[i][j-1],
8                                   Mat[i][j+1],
9                                   Mat[i-1][j],
10                                  Mat[i+1][j])
11                       depend (out: Mat[i][j])
12         process_cell (i,j);
13        }
14      }
15    }
```

(a) Source code.   (b) Task Dependency Graph.

Fig. 2. Heat transfer simulation implemented with the Gauss-Seidel iterative method, using the proposed *taskgraph* clause

The main limitation of the *taskgraph* appears when the TDG has to be computed at run-time and, although the shape is stable for some time, there are conditions in the application that can make this TDG change. For those cases, the `taskgraph` clause can be declared with a list of variables, i.e., `taskgraph(list)`, which can be monitored at runtime, and so when a variable changes, the TDG is destroyed and rebuilt again. This mechanism is further described in Sect. 3.3.

3.2 Syntax of the `taskgraph` Clause

The proposed syntax for exposing a *taskgraph* region in OpenMP is as a new clause attached to the `task` or the `target` directives, as described next:

    #pragma omp target|task [clause...] taskgraph [(list)]

With `clause` being the clauses currently allowed to be used with the corresponding directive, and *list* being the list of variables that shape the TDG, e.g., the loop boundaries if tasks are instantiated within a loop statement.

Although *taskgraph* allows a new execution model for OpenMP (named *define-once-run-repeatedly*, and described in the next subsection), there are some reasons leading us to define it as a clause instead of a new directive: (a) taskgraphs can be applied to both host and accelerator models, and so defining it as a directive would force to introduce additional clauses to describe where the taskgraph is to be executed; and (b) the *taskgraph* region can be seen as an implicit task with nested parallelism and, as such, it can benefit from clauses already defined for `task` directive like dependencies, priorities, and data-sharing clauses, or those defined specifically for `target` directive, like mapping clauses. Another option would be to add the new `taskgraph` clause to the `taskgroup` directive. However, this will remove the possibility of defining dependencies between the tasks in a taskgraph and previous/next tasks, and also reduce interoperability with the accelerator model. Overall, as of OpenMP 5.1 specification, there are 16 different types of constructs (that is, executable OpenMP directives, often attached to a block of user code), and 28 various constructs without counting the combined ones, each construct may have numerous associated clauses. By defining `taskgraph` as a clause to existing directives, we avoid rendering the specification more complex and we reduce the implementation effort it induces, because clauses as `depend` associated with tasks are currently implemented and can be directly used to build the TDG when `taskgraph` is declared.

3.3 Semantics of the `taskgraph` Clause

This section describes the semantics of the `taskgraph` clause in terms of the execution model and the memory model.

Execution Model. When a thread encounters a `task` or `target` directive declared with `taskgraph` clause, it will be exposed to one of the following situations: (a) there is missing information in the TDG of the taskgraph region, or (b) the TDG contains all task-related information in its structured-block, and its execution is equivalent (in terms of functionality) to the execution of the source code in the associated region. The procedure varies depending on the case:

- In the first case, the thread encountering the `taskgraph` clause executes the corresponding *taskgraph* region, and is also in charge of saving the missing information in the TDG runtime structures by, for instance, recording and saving the data captured during the execution of the inner tasks.

– In the second case, when the TDG is already complete, the encountering thread needs to launch its execution so that other idle threads can execute the TDG jointly. The user code in the `taskgraph` region will not drive the execution of the tasks, but the TDG instead.

Additionally, if `taskgraph` *(list)* is declared, the variables included in *list* shall be copied and saved when the region is executed for the first time. In other words, these are considered as *firstprivate* variables to the taskgraph region. While the program is running, the original copies of these variables in *list* can change. In this case, the update will be propagated to the TDG the next time we enter the `taskgraph` region, at which time the rebuild process of the TDG will start. The *list* is user-defined and shall include only variables defining the shape of the TDG, i.e., the variables defining the boundaries of loops or the branches taken in conditional statements enclosing the inner tasks, or the variables in the dependencies, if these change the memory object being dependent.

The TDG-driven execution can obtain its maximum efficiency when the *taskgraph* is defined once and replayed multiple times. This is the so-called *defined-once-run-repeatedly* execution model (as for CUDA graphs). Hence, implementations of `taskgraph` are recommended to build the TDG either at compile-time (if conditions allow, i.e., data size is known, loop boundaries are static, etc.) or after running the `taskgraph` region for the first time, at run-time, in order to maximize the performance gain of the subsequent executions.

The execution of the taskgraph region is synchronized by an implicit *taskgroup*. In other words, tasks created in the `taskgraph` structured-block belong to the same taskgroup set. The taskgroup is implicit and is declared as if it was surrounding the task defined by the directive combining with `taskgraph`.

Memory Model. The new `taskgraph` clause does not affect the existing OpenMP memory model regarding both the current global memory model, i.e. relaxed-consistency shared-memory model, and the interpretation of the data-sharing clauses that are attached to the task directives. However, the context generated by the `taskgraph` clause manages its data environment differently from how it is managed in a task.

More specifically, upon encountering a task directive (meaning `task` or `target`), all the clauses declared with the directive are immediately evaluated, including `taskgraph`. If `taskgraph` is executed, the declared data-sharing clauses also apply for the Task Dependency Graph. Inner-tasks may have different data-sharing clauses over the same data, e.g., a variable being global to the taskgraph can be set as private to tasks within it, using `firstprivate` or `private` clauses. Unlike `task` and `target`, where data environments are destroyed at completion, when a task accompanied by a `taskgraph` clause finishes its execution, all its data is recommended to be preserved, so the subsequent iterations can start without initialization. Programs that rely on saving the context of a `taskgraph` region after its completion to execute correctly are non-conforming and result in unspecified behavior.

3.4   Requirements of the `taskgraph` Region

A *taskgraph* region can be represented as a TDG, and so, it only stores information related to the execution of the inner tasks. As a result, the `taskgraph` clause is only applicable to those regions of code that are *completly taskified*, i.e., all the computation is done within the inner tasks, and the code in between only decides the control flow, so there cannot be sequential code in-between tasks.

While analyzing the `taskgraph` region, it can happen that the inner tasks contain nested tasks, as allowed in the current OpenMP specification. While syntactically correct, defining nested *taskgraphs* is however prohibited. In other words, *a `taskgraph` region can contain nested tasks, but none of them can be declared with `taskgraph` clause.* The reason is that taskgraph contains all information related to the execution of the tasks declared in its associated region, meaning that an inner taskgraph is entirely included in its outer taskgraph. Therefore, it is pointless to have nested taskgraphs, and it would break the semantics of the outer taskgraph if an inner taskgraph changes its shape in a different point in time than the outer one.

4   Projected Results

This section presents the expected results from integrating the `taskgraph` clause into the OpenMP specification. Two aspects are covered: (a) the potential performance gain from alleviating task management overhead and (b) the portability facilitated by the TDG to map OpenMP into other programming models.

4.1   Potential Performance Gain

The `taskgraph` clause targets the reduction of the overhead due to the orchestration of the parallel execution of tasks, comprising task creation, task enqueue and dependency resolution. According to Gautier et al. [3], who consider the LLVM libOMP runtime library, resolving task dependencies represents the major overhead source (up to 90%) when executing dependent tasks, and it further scales with the number of threads. In other words, using `taskgraph` can optimally relieve the greatest task overhead source and enhance the program scalability by alleviating the overhead related to multi-threading.

The results of our experiments support this statement, as shown in Fig. 3. In this example, we consider the heat transfer simulator and the HOG (Histogram of Oriented Gradients) object detection application, run on a Marenostrum cluster node, described in note 1. While the problem size and the task granularity are kept invariant, we modify the number of threads across the experiment. Both applications run for 128 iterations. Finally, the charts compare the execution using the original libgomp runtime library, labelled named *GOMP*, with the enhanced libgomp supporting the recording of the TDG at runtime, named *Taskgraph*. Particularly, *Taskgraph* version records the TDG in the first iteration and reuses it for the next 127 iterations. The figure shows that using the proposed *taskgraph* feature not only provides equivalent or better speedup than the original libgomp in all considered scenarios, but it also allows the application to further benefit from the thread scaling.

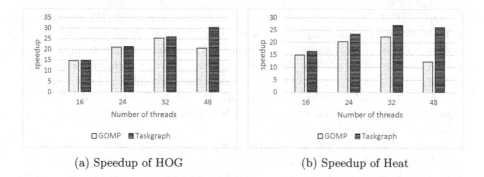

(a) Speedup of HOG   (b) Speedup of Heat

Fig. 3. Speedup of Heat Transfer Simulation (using Gauss-Seidel method) and HOG object detection application, running 128 iterations, using original GOMP runtime library and a modified version with support for `taskgraph`

While the results seem promising, we must underline that it is preferable to use `taskgraph` for repeated task region (e.g., the computation loop inside simulators as N-body simulation or iterative problem solvers as the Gauss-Seidel method), because the first iteration will be charged by the generation of the TDG, incurring greater runtime overhead than the original runtime system. This is illustrated by Table 1, where we execute the kernels only once, with fixed number of threads (24 threads in this case, assigned to a single socket). The execution times are in milliseconds. GOMP execution corresponds to the time needed to execute the applications with the native GOMP runtime library. Similarly, Recorded execution is obtained with the modified library. The Record overhead is simply Record execution time minus the GOMP execution time. As the table depicts, the overhead incurred by the record mechanism increases when the task number increases. Another factor that may impact the cost of recording is the number of dependent variables, that is, the number of variables defining the dependency relationship among tasks. More specifically, the more dependent variables there are, the longer the dependency resolution will last, resulting in a longer record process.

Table 1. Time needed (millisecond) to execute the kernels once, with 24 threads

Application name	# tasks	GOMP execution	Recorded execution	**Record overhead**
Heat transfer	2560	20.3	23	**2.7**
	4000	19.8	23.9	**4.1**
HOG application	3600	48.5	52.1	**3.6**
	8040	46.9	54.4	**7.5**

4.2   The TDG: A Door for Expanding Portability

Task-based parallelism is very effective in uncovering the parallelism available in HPC applications. There are several programming models supporting tasking, e.g., OpenMP, Cilk++ [9], Intel TBB [7] and CUDA graphs [11] are among the more extended. The major success of OpenMP in front of its competitors substantiates in many factors: (a) it relies on relatively simple compile-time directives to expose parallelism (hence avoiding the need of refactoring sequential applications); (b) it is supported by a vast majority of compiler and chip vendors (including Intel, GCC and LLVM in the former, and Intel, ARM and PowerPC in the latter); and (c) it offers a great trade-off between programmability and performance, among others.

The Task Dependency Graph representing an OpenMP task-based application is however equivalent to that extracted when using other APIs to expose the parallelism. Figure 4 illustrates the portability enabled by means of the TDG. More specicifically, Fig. 4a shows a simple sequential code snippet, Fig. 4b shows the TDG representing the concurrency available in the sequential code, and Figs. 4c, 4d, 4e and 4f show the Cilk++, OpenMP, TBB and CUDA graph implementations of the TDG, respectively.

As the Figure depicts, OpenMP effectively offers better programmability by only introducing compile-time directives in an exact same version of the sequential code. Conversely, all Cilk++, TBB and CUDA graphs require some refactoring from the code for different reasons: (a) Cilk++ does not provide data-flow dependencies, but full synchronizations instead; (b) TBB decouples the description of the graph from its execution, and requires specific functions for starting the graph and joining results; and (c) CUDA graphs provide a low-level API that forces programmers to manage data copies and point-to-point synchronizations. The performance comparison between these models is out of the scope of this paper, but several works have already tackled this topic showing performance results for OpenMP competitive to the other parallel models [12, 17].

Previous works already studied the portability provided by the TDG to transform OpenMP task-based applications into CUDA graphs [20]. This approach uses the static computation of the TDG to lower the code into calls to the CUDA graph API instead of calls to a regular OpenMP implementation (e.g., GOMP or LLVM).

OmpSs is another example of interoperability based on the TDG. This programming model, developed by Barcelona Supercomputing Center, has been a forerunner of OpenMP with respect to the tasking model. Therefore, it supports tasked-based parallelism, and also heterogeneous computing with devices like GPUs and FPGAs [14]. The TDG extracted, at runtime, from the compile-time directives defined with OmpSs is used to manage tasks across heterogeneous architectures supporting different programming models like CUDA and OpenCL. Results show how OmpSs can fully replace the host API of both CUDA and OpenCL in a portable way.

```
1   int fn1(int v) {...}
2   int fn2(int v) {...}
3   int fn3(int v) {...}
4   int tmp1, tmp2, res=0;
5   for(int i=1; i<=2; ++i) {
6       tmp1 = fn1(i);
7       tmp2 = fn2(i);
8       res += fn3(tmp1, tmp2);
9   }
```

(a) Serial version

(b) TDG

```
1   tmp1 = cilk_spawn fn1(1);
2   tmp2 = cilk_spawn fn2(1);
3   tmp3 = cilk_spawn fn1(2);
4   tmp4 = cilk_spawn fn2(2);
5   cilk_sync;
6   res += fn3(tmp1, tmp2);
7   res += fn3(tmp3, tmp4);
```

(c) Cilk++

```
1   #pragma omp parallel shared(res)
2   #pragma omp single
3   for(int i=1; i<=2; ++i) {
4       #pragma omp task \
5           depend(inoutset:tmp1) \
6           shared(tmp1)
7       tmp1 = fn1(i);
8       #pragma omp task \
9           depend(inoutset:tmp2) \
10          shared(tmp1)
11      tmp2 = fn2(i);
12      #pragma omp task \
13          depend(in:tmp1,tmp2) \
14          depend(inout:res) \
15          firstprivate(tmp1,tmp2) \
16          shared(res)
17      res += fn3(tmp1, tmp2);
```

(d) OpenMP

```
1   graph g;
2
3   broadcast_node<int> start(g);
4   function_node<int,int> n1(
5       g, unlimited, fn1());
6   function_node<int,int> n2(
7       g, unlimited, fn2());
8   join_node<tuple<int, int>,
9       queueing> jn(g);
10  function_node<tuple<int,int>, int>
11      n3(g, serial, fn3(res));
12
13  make_edge(start, n1);
14  make_edge(start, n2);
15  make_edge(n1, input_port<0>(jn));
16  make_edge(n2, input_port<1>(jn));
17  make_edge(jn, n3);
18
19  for(int i=1; i<=2; ++i)
20      start.try_put(i);
21  g.wait_for_all();
```

(e) TBB

```
1   cudaGraph_t g;
2   cudaGraphCreate(&g, 0)
3
4   cudaGraphNode_t n1, n2, n3, n4, n5, n6;
5   cudaKernelNodeParams n1_args, n2_args, n3_args,
6                        n4_args, n5_args, n6_args;
7   n1_args.func = (void*) fn1;
8   void *kernelArgs_n1[2] = {&i_1, &tmp1};
9   n1_args.kernelParams = (void**) kernelArgs_n1;
10  cudaGraphAddKernelNode(&n1, g, NULL, 0, &n1_args);
11
12  // similar to n1, but n2 uses fn2 and tmp2 instead
13  ...
14  n3_args.func = (void*) fn1;
15  void *kernelArgs_n3[2] = {&i_2, &tmp3};
16  n3_args.kernelParams = (void**) kernelArgs_n3;
17  cudaGraphAddKernelNode(&n3, g, NULL, 0, &n3_args);
18  // similar to n3, but n4 uses fn2 and tmp4 instead
19  ...
20  n5_args.func = (void*) fn3;
21  void *kernelArgs_n5[3] = {&tmp1, &tmp2, &res};
22  n5_args.kernelParams = (void**) kernelArgs_n5;
23  std::vector<cudaGraphNode_t> n5_deps;
24  n5_deps.push_back(n1); n5_deps.push_back(n2);
25  cudaGraphAddKernelNode(&n5, g, n5_deps.data(),
26                         n5_deps.size(), &n5_args);
27  n6_args.func = (void*) fn3;
28  void *kernelArgs_n6[3] = {&tmp3, &tmp4, &res};
29  n6_args.kernelParams = (void**) kernelArgs_n6;
30  std::vector<cudaGraphNode_t> n6_deps;
31  n6_deps.push_back(n3); n6_deps.push_back(n4);
32  n6_deps.push_back(n5);
33  cudaGraphAddKernelNode(&n6, g, n6_deps.data(),
34                         n6_deps.size(), &n6_args);
35
36  cudaGraphExec_t gExec;
37  cudaGraphInstantiate(&gExec, g, NULL, NULL, 0);
38  cudaStream_t gStream;
39  cudaStreamCreate(&gStream);
40  cudaGraphLaunch(gExec, gStream);
41  cudaStreamSynchronize(gStream);
42  cudaGraphExecDestroy(gExec);
43  cudaGraphDestroy(g);
44  cudaStreamDestroy(gStream);
```

(f) CUDA

Fig. 4. TDG representation and high-level description of a simple code parallelized with different task-based parallel programming models.

5   Related Work

The imminent advent of exascale computing raises new challenges in on-node parallelism, such as the efficient exploitation of modern many-core processors and the increasing heterogeneity of HPC systems. OpenMP is the current *de facto* standard parallel programming model, and it needs to address these challenges. Although the OpenMP tasking model is a convenient method to parallelize applications, many authors have investigated to tackle the overhead this model incurs [8,13,15]. That work is considered Sect. 1. This section focuses on work related to the Task Dependency Graph representation and its benefits.

M. Serrano et al. [16] provided a timing analysis over OpenMP tasks, where tasks with timing properties are represented in a TDG. This work strengthened the possibility of using OpenMP untied tasks (i.e., once such task is suspended by the initial thread, it can be correctly resumed by any idle thread within the same OpenMP team) on safety-critical embedded systems. A. Munera et al. [10] showed how statically generated TDGs can reduce the dynamic memory usage of OpenMP tasks, so that the tasking model can be used on embedded systems conveniently, where the amount of dynamic memory is often limited by safety constraints. Taskgraph makes OpenMP more suitable for safety-critical embedded systems by reinforcing their work:

- The `taskgraph` clause can be used with both `tied` and `untied` tasks, making the analysis of [16] still valid for taskgraph. As a result, taskgraph can perform the associated region in shorter time by reducing the runtime overhead, which eases the scheduling of the region within a larger real-time application.
- Techniques used in [10] rely on the static generation of the TDG, the information from which can be leveraged by the *taskgraph* clause to enhance the performance. Therefore, by including the new clause in their method, the resulting framework should deliver better performance than the current OpenMP tasking model, and also use less dynamic memory throughout the execution.

C. Yu et al. [20] proposed a framework to generate a CUDA graph [11] from OpenMP task directives. The new execution model proposed by Nvidia, where each node represents a CUDA kernel and edges express the dependencies among them, is interestingly similar to the taskgraph structure. This work shows, on the one hand, how OpenMP could benefit from a *define-once-run-repeatedly* execution model, as that enabled by CUDA graphs, in terms of performance. On the other hand, it shows how the programmability of CUDA graphs could be enhanced by reducing the number of lines required from the programmer, going from 15500 to 4 in a Cholesky implementation used for illustration purposes.

6 Conclusion

This work describes a new method to tackle the OpenMP task overhead at a higher abstraction level, that is, by introducing the concept of Task Dependency Graph in the OpenMP specification through `taskgraph` clause.

Our preliminary results, based on GCC GOMP runtime library, validate the effectiveness of the TDG, as a representation of a region of code that can be boosted by the OpenMP framework. When the TDG holds the complete execution of a part of the user's code, this code can be replaced by the execution of the TDG. This results in the reduction of the overhead introduced by the access to shared resources, like task queues, and the management of tasks, including creation, orchestration and destruction.

The concept of TDG also allows a new execution model in OpenMP, the *define-once-run-repeatedly* model, equivalent to that described by CUDA graphs. This mechanism, which is a hint for the implementation and shall not change the functional behavior of the program, allows further alleviating the overhead in applications running several times the same TDGs. Interestingly, this proposed mechanism can promote the use of the OpenMP API as a door for effectively exploiting CUDA graphs.

Future investigations include implementing the `taskgraph` clause in major compilers and runtime systems, such as LLVM, to further validate our results. As a prediction, we expect `taskgraph` to deliver significant performance gain in LLVM, as in GOMP library. This assumption is supported by Fig. 5, where we run different applications with the OpenMP runtime libraries from LLVM and GCC. Although the LLVM is better optimized in these cases (shorter execution time), its runtime overhead increases when the task granularity shrinks, similar to the GOMP library. Other research lines comprise (a) thoroughly testing the performance impact of the new clause in larger applications and different processor architectures; (b) using the taskgraph in applications with tasks inside a taskgraph region and tasks outside the region; and (c) exploring usages and improvements of other programming models through the use of the TDG generated by OpenMP `taskgraph`.

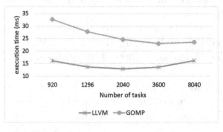

(a) HOG object detection application

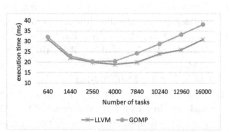

(b) Heat transfer simulator

Fig. 5. Execution time (in ms) analysis of different applications with original GCC GOMP library and LLVM OMP runtime library, fixing the number of threads to 24

Acknowledgements. This work has been supported by the EU H2020 project AMPERE under the grant agreement no. 871669.

References

1. BSC: Marenostrum IV User's Guide (2017). https://www.bsc.es/support/MareNostrum4-ug.pdf
2. Castello, A., Seo, S., Mayo, R., Balaji, P., Quintana-Orti, E.S., Pena, A.J.: GLTO: on the adequacy of lightweight thread approaches for openmp implementations. In: Proceedings of the International Conference on Parallel Processing, pp. 60–69 (2017)
3. Gautier, T., Perez, C., Richard, J.: On the impact of OpenMP task granularity. In: de Supinski, B.R., Valero-Lara, P., Martorell, X., Mateo Bellido, S., Labarta, J. (eds.) IWOMP 2018. LNCS, vol. 11128, pp. 205–221. Springer, Cham (2018). https://doi.org/10.1007/978-3-319-98521-3_14
4. Giannozzi, P., et al.: Quantum espresso: a modular and open-source software project for quantum simulations of materials. J. Phys. Condens. Matter **21**(39), 395502 (2009)
5. Kalray MPPA products (2021). https://www.kalrayinc.com/
6. Komatitsch, D., Tromp, J.: SPECFEM3D Cartesian (2021). https://github.com/geodynamics/specfem3d
7. Kukanov, A., Voss, M.J.: The foundations for scalable multi-core software in intel threading building blocks. Intel Technol. J. **11**(4), 309–322 (2007). http://citeseerx.ist.psu.edu/viewdoc/download;jsessionid=79B311F4CEB9A4B6 10520177C7144D57?doi=10.1.1.71.8289&rep=rep1&type=pdf
8. Lagrone, J., Aribuki, A., Chapman, B.: A set of microbenchmarks for measuring OpenMP task overheads. In: Proceedingis of International Conference on Parallel and Distributed Processing Techniques and Applications II, pp. 594–600 (2011). http://citeseerx.ist.psu.edu/viewdoc/download?doi=10.1.1.217.9615&rep=rep1&type=pdf
9. Leiserson, C.E.: The Cilk++ concurrency platform. J. Supercomput. **51**(3), 244–257 (2010)
10. Munera, A., Royuela, S., Quinones, E.: Towards a qualifiable OpenMP framework for embedded systems. In: Proceedings of the 2020 Design, Automation and Test in Europe Conference and Exhibition, DATE 2020, no. 2, pp. 903–908 (2020)
11. Nvidia: CUDA Graph programming guide (2021). https://docs.nvidia.com/cuda/cuda-c-programming-guide/#cuda-graphs
12. Olivier, S.L., Prins, J.F.: Evaluating OpenMP 3.0 run time systems on unbalanced task graphs. In: Müller, M.S., de Supinski, B.R., Chapman, B.M. (eds.) IWOMP 2009. LNCS, vol. 5568, pp. 63–78. Springer, Heidelberg (2009). https://doi.org/10.1007/978-3-642-02303-3_6
13. Perez, J.M., Beltran, V., Labarta, J., Ayguade, E.: Improving the integration of task nesting and dependencies in OpenMP. In: Proceedings - 2017 IEEE 31st International Parallel and Distributed Processing Symposium, IPDPS 2017, pp. 809–818 (2017)
14. Sainz, F., Mateo, S., Beltran, V., Bosque, J.L., Martorell, X., Ayguadé, E.: Leveraging OmpSs to exploit hardware accelerators. In: 2014 IEEE 26th International Symposium on Computer Architecture and High Performance Computing, pp. 112–119. IEEE (2014)

15. Schuchart, J., Nachtmann, M., Gracia, J.: Patterns for OpenMP task data dependency overhead measurements. In: de Supinski, B.R., Olivier, S.L., Terboven, C., Chapman, B.M., Müller, M.S. (eds.) Scaling OpenMP for Exascale Performance and Portability, pp. 156–168. Springer International Publishing, Cham (2017)
16. Serrano, M.A., Melani, A., Vargas, R., Marongiu, A., Bertogna, M., Quiñones, E.: Timing characterization of OpenMP4 tasking model. In: 2015 International Conference on Compilers, Architecture and Synthesis for Embedded Systems, CASES 2015, pp. 157–166 (2015)
17. Stpiczyński, P.: Language-based vectorization and parallelization using intrinsics, openmp, tbb and cilk plus. J. Supercomput. **74**(4), 1461–1472 (2018)
18. TOP500 (2020). https://www.top500.org/lists/top500/2020/11/
19. Valero-Lara, P., Catalán, S., Martorell, X., Usui, T., Labarta, J.: sLASs: a fully automatic auto-tuned linear algebra library based on openmp extensions implemented in ompss (lass library). J. Parallel Distrib. Comput. **138**, 153–171 (2020)
20. Yu, C., Royuela, S., Quiñones, E.: OpenMP to CUDA graphs: a compiler-based transformation to enhance the programmability of NVIDIA devices. In: Proceedings of the 23rd International Workshop on Software and Compilers for Embedded Systems, SCOPES 2020, pp. 42–47 (2020)

OpenMP Taskloop Dependences

Marcos Maroñas[1,2]([⊠]), Xavier Teruel[1], and Vicenç Beltran[1]

[1] Barcelona Supercomputing Center (BSC), Barcelona, Spain
{mmaronas,xteruel,vbeltran}@bsc.es
[2] Huawei Research, Edinburgh, Scotland
marcos.maronas.bravo@huawei.com
http://www.bsc.es

Abstract. Exascale systems will contain multicore/manycore processors with high core count in each node. Therefore, using a model that relaxes the synchronization, such as data-flow, is crucial to adequately exploit the potential of the hardware. The flexibility of the data-flow execution model relies on the dynamic management of data-dependences among tasks.

The OpenMP standard already provides a construct, known as `taskloop`, that distributes the loop iteration space into several tasks, but this construct does not support the use of the `depend` clause yet. In this paper we propose the use of the induction variable to define data dependences in tasks created by the `taskloop` construct. By using the induction variable, each task will contain its own dependences based on the partition of work they received.

We also aim to demonstrate that using taskloop with dependences provides an enhancement in terms of programmability with respect to using stand-alone tasks to parallelize a loop. Our implementation does not introduce any significant overhead on the taskloop implementation and, in certain cases, it outperforms the stand-alone task version.

Keywords: OpenMP · Tasking · Loops · Synchronization · Taskloop construct · Depend clause

1 Introduction

The introduction of the first multiprocessor architectures led to the development of shared memory programming models. One of those is OpenMP, which became a *de facto* standard for parallelization on shared memory environments.

OpenMP [12], with its highly optimized fork-join execution model, is a good choice to exploit structured parallelism, especially when the number of cores is small. Worksharing constructs, like the well-known `omp for` construct, are good examples of how OpenMP can efficiently exploit structured parallelism. However, when the number of cores increase and the work distribution is not perfectly balanced, the rigid fork-join execution model can hinder performance.

© Springer Nature Switzerland AG 2021
S. McIntosh-Smith et al. (Eds.): IWOMP 2021, LNCS 12870, pp. 50–64, 2021.
https://doi.org/10.1007/978-3-030-85262-7_4

The `omp for` construct accepts different scheduling policies that can mitigate load-balancing issues; and the `nowait` clause avoids the implicit barrier at the end of an `omp for`. Still, both techniques are only effective in a few specific situations. Moreover, the fork-join execution model is not well-suited for exploiting irregular, dynamic, or nested parallelism.

Task-based programming models were developed to overcome some of the above-mentioned limitations. The first tasking models were based solely on the tasks and taskwaits primitives, which naturally support irregular, dynamic, and nested parallelism. However, these tasking models are still based on the fork-join execution model. The big step forward came with the introduction of data dependences. Thus, replacing the rigid fork-join execution model by a more flexible data-flow execution model that relies on fine-grained synchronizations among tasks. Modern task-based programming models such as Cilk, OmpSs or OpenMP tasking model have evolved with advanced features to exploit nested parallelism [13], hardware accelerators [1,2,6], and seamless integration with message passing APIs such as MPI [14,15].

Exascale systems will contain multicore/manycore processors with high core count in each node. Therefore, using a model that relaxes the synchronization, such as data-flow, is crucial to adequately exploit the potential of the hardware.

Additionally, worksharing techniques are easier to apply compared to tasking. A single worksharing construct is enough to parallelize a loop. In contrast, using tasks, it requires more effort from the user. There must be at least a task per core, to feed all the cores and prevent lack of parallelism. A frequent technique applied to create enough tasks is blocking. This technique partitions a loop in several blocks, and each block is processed by an independent task. Although this is not a complex technique, it requires more effort than the worksharing alternative.

The OpenMP standard contains a directive able to distribute the iteration space of a loop into tasks, which, theoretically, enables users to parallelize a whole loop with a single construct using tasks. This is the `taskloop` construct. However, in practice, it is not useful for a single reason: it does not support data dependences. Thus, a `taskloop` creates a set of tasks that cannot have data dependences, and so, the synchronization must be done using coarse-grained synchronization points (i.e., the implicit taskgroup, or explicit taskwaits). So, basically, we end up in a fork-join model but with increased overhead compared to worksharing constructs.

We propose adding support for data dependences to the `taskloop` construct. Our proposal enables programmers to use the induction variable of the loop to specify data dependences. Thus, each task created by the taskloop will register the data dependences specified by the user. If the induction variable is used to specify any dependence, each task will register the dependence using its own value of the induction variable. As a result, apply blocking is possible using a single construct, enhancing programmability.

2   Tasking Programmability Challenges

Compared to using worksharing techniques, tasks are more complicated to use. If we simply replace worksharing constructs by task constructs, there is very few parallelism, and most of the cores are idle. This is because a worksharing construct distributes the work among all the available cores, that run concurrently. In contrast, an instantiated task is a piece of code that runs only in a single core at a given instant of time. Figure 1 shows such a problem. The figure also shows one possible solution, which is the use of blocking.

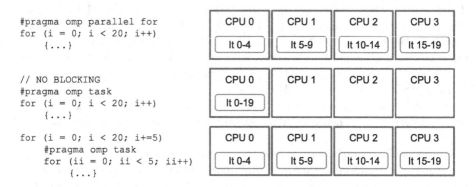

Fig. 1. Illustration of CPU occupation using different parallelism techniques.

Listings 1.1 and 1.2 shows a real code using worksharing constructs and task with blocking respectively. It is possible to see that applying blocking techniques is simple, but also that it requires more effort than using worksharing constructs. For a single loop, worksharing constructs require only three lines of code, while tasks with blockings require five lines of code.

The OpenMP standard already provides a construct known as `taskloop` that distributes work into several tasks. This construct is the natural replacement of worksharing constructs to use tasks. Listing 1.3 shows the very same example using the `taskloop` construct. Notwithstanding, the tasks created using the `taskloop` construct cannot have data dependences, so they can only be synchronized using synchronization points (i.e., keeping the implicit taskgroup region or using explicit taskwaits). As a result, we have a fork-join pattern with its rigid synchronization. So, we moved from worksharing constructs to tasks to benefit from a more lightweight data-flow synchronization, but the impossibility of using data dependences when using the `taskloop` construct prevents us from obtaining all its benefits.

In summary, tasks require more effort from users than worksharing constructs. However, tasks provide key benefits that fit the requirements of Exascale systems better than worksharing constructs. For instance, programmers may parallelize different stages of the program by means of tasks, as long as they guarantee a proper task depend annotation. Then, they can rely on the

Listing 1.1. Simple code using the work-sharing construct

```
#pragma omp for
for(size_t j = 0; j < N; j++)
    b[j] = scalar*c[j];
```

Listing 1.2. Simple code using the task construct (and blocking)

```
for(size_t j = 0; j < N; j+=BS) {
    size_t size = j+BSIZE > N ? N-j : BSIZE;
    #pragma omp task depend(in:c[j:size]) depend(out:b[j:size])
    for(size_t j2=j; j2 < j+size; j2++)
        b[j2] = scalar*c[j2];
}
```

Listing 1.3. Simple code using the taskloop construct

```
#pragma omp taskloop chunksize(BSIZE)
for(size_t j = 0; j < N; j++) {
    b[j] = scalar*c[j];
} // implicit taskgroup region
```

OpenMP run-time library to compute the correct synchronization order among these tasks. In other words, task parallelization improves composability.

In the other hand, the `taskloop` construct enables programmers to use tasks with a similar effort than the effort required by worksharing constructs. Nevertheless, it does not support data dependences, and this prevent users from getting the key benefits of tasking.

3   Related Work

We already mentioned in the previous section that OpenMP supports both loop-based parallelism and task-based parallelism. The most common way of using loop-based parallelism in OpenMP is by means of the worksharing constructs. In terms of programmability, worksharing constructs enable users to parallelize loops using a single construct. Thus, they are very simple to use. In terms of performance, worksharing constructs deliver good performance in the general case. Nevertheless, they contain an implicit barrier at the end of the worksharing region, introducing very rigid synchronization.

The task-based approach is a bit more complex in terms of programmability. It usually requires blocking techniques to uncover parallelism, which require some more code than a single construct. Regarding performance, tasks have a natural ability to deal with load imbalance, but they have associated costs that may introduce some overhead depending on task's granularity. OpenMP provides also the `taskloop` construct, that distributes the iteration space of a loop into several tasks. There is the possibility of specifying a *grainsize* guaranteeing that each of the tasks created executes no less than *grainsize* iterations. Thus, the taskloop construct simplifies the use of task-based parallelism, enabling users to parallelize loops with a single construct. Nevertheless, OpenMP does not support dependences in the taskloop construct. As a result, users must rely on fork-join-like synchronization with explicit synchronization points. Consequently, dropping the data-flow execution model of task-based parallelism, and its benefits. By enabling the use of data dependences in the taskloop construct, we offer users the possibility of parallelizing loops in a single construct while keeping the benefits of the data-flow execution model. Additionally, the use of the taskloop construct, may reduce the tasking overhead because allocations could be optimized to be done as a whole, instead of one by one. However, the number of tasks that will be created and scheduled is still proportional to the problem size.

On the other hand, OpenMP 4.5 [11] already included the `doacross` dependences for work-sharing loops based on the *source* and *sink* dependence types and the extension of the `ordered` construct to support the `depend` clause. This feature allows to express general cross-iteration loop dependences and thereby support doacross parallelization [16]. The loop dependencies that cross the iteration space are enforced via point-to-point synchronization injected where the compiler finds the `ordered` construct. The main advantage of this extension is that only applying to a unique iteration space, it could be easily implemented by a single 2D matrix of *per chunk* relationships, imposing a very low overhead to the runtime. This advantage is also its main drawback, as it does not allow to dynamically connect to other loop iteration spaces (neither combine it with any other work-sharing or task generating constructs).

Intel Cilk presents the `cilk_for` [7], which is used to parallelize loops. The body of the loop is converted into a function that is called recursively using a divide and conquer strategy for achieving better performance. However, there is a `cilk_sync` at the end of each iteration. Therefore, synchronization is quite rigid, similarly to OpenMP worksharings. Moreover, Cilk tasks do not support data dependencies between tasks.

The CUDA programming model [8,10] allows expressing kernel dependencies using proper streams and events. This approach will be similar to the stand-alone task model implemented by the OpenMP standard and requires manually transform the loop to its blocked version, to decompose the iteration space. Furthermore, the use of multiple streams and their synchronization via events could be non-trivial in some cases. On the other hand, CUDA offers the option to capture and reuse such task instantiation using the CUDA graph set of routines, offering an extra optimization by reducing the overhead. The CUDA graph functionality is out of the scope of this paper and should be considered as an extension that can be widely used, not only in taskloop constructs but in any portion of code parallelized with tasks.

4   Taskloop with Dependences

In this section, we detail the syntax of our proposal to support data dependences in the `taskloop` construct. In short, we propose the use of the induction variable

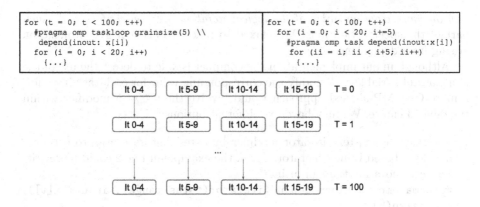

```
for (t = 0; t < 100; t++)          for (t = 0; t < 100; t++)
  #pragma omp taskloop grainsize(5) \\     for (i = 0; i < 20; i+=5)
  depend(inout: x[i])                #pragma omp task depend(inout:x[i])
  for (i = 0; i < 20; i++)             for (ii = i; ii < i+5; ii++)
    {...}                                 {...}
```

Fig. 2. Partition of work and dependences between tasks created using taskloop

to define data dependences in tasks created by the `taskloop` construct. By using the induction variable, each task will contain its own dependences based on the partition of work they received. Figure 2 shows an example. There is an outer loop and an inner loop parallelized using the enhanced `taskloop` construct with data dependences. As we can see, the data dependences contain the induction variable. In this case, it means that each of the tasks register a dependence over the i-th element of x. As each of the tasks receive a part of the iteration space, each of the tasks will have different values for i, thereby allowing them to run concurrently, but defining a dependence with tasks of the next and previous t iteration that work over the same data. Figure 2 also includes the code to get equivalent behavior using regular tasks.

With this mechanism, expressivity is enhanced and the `taskloop` construct becomes usable in many real-world examples while keeping the key benefits of tasking.

We would like to point out that the mechanism to define the granularity of a task created by the `taskloop` construct is the `grainsize` clause, as shown in Fig. 2. As the loop iteration distribution should be deterministic and visible to the programmer (in order to allow him/her to combine tasks generated by the taskloop with stand-alone generated tasks), the use of taskloop dependences will assume the strict modifier within the `grainsize` clause. If no `grainsize` is provided, default applies.

A second observation relates the task instantiation order and the dependence computation. Currently, taskloop does not guarantee any task creation order, while the proper dependence computation relies on it. Although the implementation does not need to actually create tasks in such order, it must compute dependencies AS IF they were created in the logical iteration order. The OpenMP runtime can easily follow this behavior due to it can compute the number of tasks and the corresponding task boundaries when encountering the taskloop construct. In addition, the current specification says *"Programs that rely on any execution order of the logical iteration are non-conforming"*; such part of the specification must be relaxed to take into account synchronization arising from dependences.

Although in our implementation the compiler is able to detect the use of the loop control variable and modify the corresponding value for each task instance, a more OpenMP-aligned approach would involve the use of a modifier within the depend clause. We may have two different options:

- Leverage the existent iterator modifier by extending its syntax to accept a new loop-based value generator. Then, the example in Fig. 2 could be rewritten by annotating the loop using:
  ```
  #pragma omp taskloop depend(iterator(t=taskrange), inout: x[t])
  grainsize(5).
  ```
- Define a new modifier based on the task loop boundaries. Again, the example in Fig. 2 could be rewritten using:
  ```
  #pragma omp taskloop depend(taskrange(b=begin), inout: x[b:5])
  grainsize(5).
  ```

While the first option relies in the multiple values generated by the iterator modifer (by means of a new iterator range specifier: *taskrange*); the second one uses the chunk-associated lower bound (by means of the new OpenMP keyword begin and a new depend modifier: *taskrange*) combined with the grainsize parameter in order to define an array section.

Finally, adding taskloop dependences on the OpenMP specification should relax the implicit taskgroup region defined as part of the taskloop construct. It will be recommended to implicitly consider the nogroup clause when the programmer uses any dependence clause on the taskloop construct.

5   Implementation

Our proposal is done in the OmpSs-2 programming model, built on top of the Mercurium compiler and the Nanos6 runtime library. Following, we detail the extensions done in both components to support dependences in the taskloop construct. We also conceptually explain our implementation.

Semantics. The taskloop construct is a convenient "syntactic sugar" to ease the use of tasks. It can be implemented just by applying an automatic blocking technique in the compiler side, similar to a manual blocking done by the end-user. But it also allows smarter implementations that can improve performance by reducing the associated overhead.

Mercurium Compiler. The Mercurium compiler has been extended to support the use of data dependences in the taskloop construct. Mercurium is a source to source compiler, meaning that it receives code as an input, and generates code as an output. Mercurium creates a function to register dependences per each task construct found in the user code. To support the use of the induction variable in the `taskloop` dependences, Mercurium has to accept a new parameter in the functions used to register dependences. Given that in our implementation it is the runtime who partitions the work and assigns iterations to the tasks, Mercurium must receive the information of the assigned iterations to replace the induction variable by its real value.

Additionally, in the same line, Mercurium creates a function per task type including the user code that the task has to run. In this case, it also has to receive an additional parameter: the iterations that each task has to run.

Finally, when creating a `taskloop` entity, Mercurium has to enable some flags to let the runtime system know that this is not a regular task, but a `taskloop`.

Nanos6 Runtime Library. In the runtime system, the first step is to extend the work descriptor of a task to include the iteration space of the loop, and the grainsize specified by the user, if any. This single task will represent the whole taskloop and it will register the whole set of dependencies, which are generated based on the iteration space and the grainsize value. When the task instance that represents the taskloop is executed it will instantiate one sub-task for each partition of the iteration space with its corresponding dependencies. This approach works because we are leveraging the *weak dependencies* and *early release* features of OmpSs-2 [13] that enables the parent task to become ready even if the dependencies are still not fulfilled. In this way, the sub-tasks created behave as if they were created on the dependency domain of the parent taskloop. A side effect of this implementation is that the creation and execution of the taskloop is not blocking, so many of them can be executed in parallel. Each sub-task created inside a task-loop will behave as a regular task, waiting for its data-dependencies before it can become ready.

We would like to point out that our current implementation focuses on programmability. Therefore, we are trying to provide a simpler way of using tasks that introduces no significant overhead compared to using other techniques such as manual blocking. Nevertheless, the `taskloop` construct provides the opportunity to apply further optimizations that cannot be applied in the case of manual blocking. Such optimizations could include a single allocation for all the loop tasks, instead of allocating space for each of them individually; or the application of smarter throttle policies to mitigate memory overuse when there are too many tasks in flight. In this way, throttle policies may take into account the total number of tasks needed to instantiate the whole loop iteration space, rather than consider each of the tasks as an independent entity (i.e., making decisions based on each individual item).

6 Experiment Results

In this section, we wish to demonstrate that the taskloop with dependences provides an enhancement in programmability when using tasks, while introducing no significant overhead compared to a manual equivalent implementation. For that purpose, our evaluation will focus in both programmability and performance.

Regarding programmability, we used several different metrics to compare the different implementations: Source Lines of Code (SLOC) [9], Development Estimate Effort (DEE) [5], and Cyclomatic Complexity (CC) [17]. It is important to highlight that for the SLOC metric we only consider the code related to the parallelization. And it is also important to notice that this metric is an approximation to measure code complexity based only on the number of lines but it ignores that some individual lines can be more complex than others.

In terms of performance, we compare the different implementations to demonstrate that using the `taskloop` construct do not add any significant overhead.

Environment. The experiments were carried out on the Marenostrum 4 supercomputer. It is composed of nodes with 2 sockets Intel Xeon Platinum 8160 2.1 GHz 24-core and 96 GB of main memory.

Regarding the software, we used the Mercurium [3] compiler (v2.3.0) and the Nanos6 runtime library [4] as the baseline components to implement our proposal (described in Sect. 5); the gcc and gfortran compilers (v7.2.0), in order to compile Mercurium and Nanos6 (included here for reproducibility purposes); and the Intel compilers (v17.0.4), as the native compiler used by Mercurium to generate binary code.

Methodology. As previously introduced, we focus our evaluation in two different aspects: performance and programmability. Our experiments will use two different versions of each application/benchmark:

- **T**. Version using regular tasks. It requires manual blocking.
- **TL**. Version using the `taskloop` construct with dependences.

Regarding performance, for each of the benchmarks/applications, we select two different problem sizes, one small-medium size, and one big size. For each of the problem sizes, we try several block sizes to show that the differences between the T and the TL are small or even non-existent in several different scenarios.

All the experiments ran using the interleaving policy offered by the numactl command, spreading the data evenly across all the available NUMA nodes, in order to minimize the NUMA effect.

The results shown in the figures are averages of five different executions. We decided to use only five executions because the variability across different executions was very small.

Related to programmability, we count the SLOC required to parallelize the baseline code for each of the versions, and use the SLOCCount [18] tool and the Lizard [19] tool to retrieve the DEE and CC respectively.

Performance Evaluation. In this section, we evaluate several applications/benchmarks to demonstrate that the use of the `taskloop` construct does not

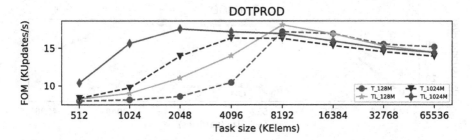

Fig. 3. Evaluation of taskloop using DOTPROD benchmark

introduce overhead compared to a manual alternative. All the figures show the Figure of Merit (FOM) of the application on the y-axis, and different task granularities in the x-axis. All of them have four series: one using the T version with a small-medium problem size, one using the TL version with a small-medium problem size, one using the T version with a big problem size, and one using the TL version with a big problem size. We would like to highlight that the T versions use the usual approach where a single core creates all the tasks.

Figure 3 shows the results of the dot product benchmark. In this case, we repeat the *dotprod* kernel a given number of iterations to make the execution longer. For both problem sizes, the TL version performs better than the T version in the small task sizes. The T version has only a single core creating tasks. When the granularity is small, a single creator cannot create rapidly enough to feed all the cores. As explained in Sect. 5, the TL version may have several cores creating tasks, speeding up the creation, and increasing the overall performance. The TL version may have several cores producing tasks because each iteration of the kernel is a taskloop instance, that can be running in different cores concurrently, while the T version has a single core creating all the iterations sequentially. Finally, from TS = 8192, all the versions perform very similarly.

Figure 4 shows the results of the N-body benchmark. For this benchmark, we see again a difference in the smallest granularity, where the TL version outperform the T version for both problem sizes. Like previously, this is because there are several taskloops that can be creating tasks concurrently in the TL version, while there is a single core creating tasks sequentially in the T version, and it is not quick enough to feed all the cores.

Finally, Fig. 5 shows the results of the Stream benchmark. The results presented are an average of the four different kernels of the Stream benchmark. In this benchmark, there are some differences between the T and TL versions. Firstly, in the smallest granularity, the TL version outperforms the T version in both problem sizes. Like in some previous benchmarks, this is because the TL version has multiple taskloops that can create concurrently rather than a single one, and speeding up the creation improves the overall performance. Then, when TS = 64, for the small problem size the T version outperforms the TL version, and

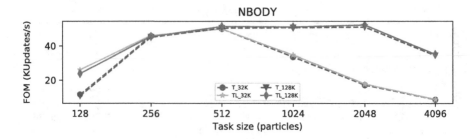

Fig. 4. Evaluation of taskloop using NBODY benchmark

the other way around for the big problem size. Our runtime system has an immediate successor mechanism to exploit data locality between successor tasks. In this case, this mechanism is making the difference. We repeated the experiment with no immediate successor, and the results for both versions were very similar. For the big problem size, the TL version is able to find more immediate successor tasks than the T version, and the other way around for the small problem size.

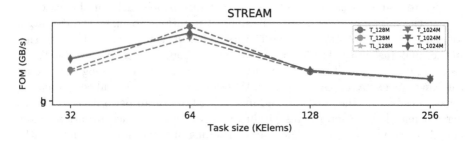

Fig. 5. Evaluation of taskloop using STREAM benchmark

Overall, we see that there are few differences between the T and TL versions, with the TL versions generally outperforming the T versions in fine granularities, thanks to the use of multiple creators. Thus, we can conclude that the TL is not only introducing very few overhead, but it is able to enhance performance in some specific scenarios.

Programmability Evaluation. Table 1 shows the different programmability metrics evaluated in this analysis for different benchmarks. The DEE is a metric that tries to estimate the effort that a developer must spend to write a given code. In this case, it is measured in *person-months*. The size of the code affects the DEE. The CC metric is higher when a code can take more different paths. For instance, adding an `if` increases the CC.

In Table 1, some benchmarks show no difference between the T version and the TL version. As previously explained, a frequent way of parallelize an application

Listing 1.4. Stream code using tasks with blocking

```
for (int k=0; k<nTimes; k++) {
    for(size_t block = 0; block < NUM_BLOCKS; block++) {
        size_t aux = block*BSIZE;
        size_t size = aux+BSIZE > N ? N-aux : BSIZE;
        #pragma oss task in(a[aux;size]) out(c[aux;size])
        for(size_t j2=aux; j2 < aux+size; j2++)
            c[j2] = a[j2];
    }
    for(size_t block = 0; block < NUM_BLOCKS; block++) {
        size_t aux = block*BSIZE;
        size_t size = aux+BSIZE > N ? N-aux : BSIZE;
        #pragma oss task in(c[aux;size]) out(b[aux;size])
        for(size_t j2=aux; j2 < aux+size; j2++)
            b[j2] = scalar*c[j2];
    }
    for(size_t block = 0; block < NUM_BLOCKS; block++) {
        size_t aux = block*BSIZE;
        size_t size = aux+BSIZE > N ? N-aux : BSIZE;
        #pragma oss task in(a[aux;size], b[aux;size]) out(c[aux;size])
        for(size_t j2=aux; j2 < aux+size; j2++)
            c[j2] = a[j2]+b[j2];
    }
    for(size_t block = 0; block < NUM_BLOCKS; block++) {
        size_t aux = block*BSIZE;
        size_t size = aux+BSIZE > N ? N-aux : BSIZE;
        #pragma oss task in(b[aux;size], c[aux;size]) out(a[aux;size])
        for(size_t j2=aux; j2 < aux+size; j2++)
            a[j2] = b[j2]+scalar*c[j2];
    }
}
#pragma oss taskwait
```

with tasks is using blocking, thereby converting a single loop into two loops, one to iterate over blocks, and one to iterate over the elements of each block. The `taskloop` construct prevents users from requiring this twofold loop structure in some cases, saving some lines of code. In the case of the Nbody benchmark, the data layout in our implementation is blocked, so we cannot eliminate the twofold loop. Thus, there is no real improvement in programmability for this benchmarks. In contrast, the Stream benchmark shows improvements in all the different metrics, reaching up to a 3.57x reduction of SLOC. Regarding the CC,

Table 1. Programmability metrics to compare the use of the `taskloop` construct with the manual use of tasks

	T			TL		
	SLOC	DEE	CC	SLOC	DEE	CC
DOTPROD	7	0.07	4	3	0.05	2.5
NBODY	10	0.29	2.6	10	0.29	2.6
STREAM	25	0.37	13.5	7	0.3	9.5

Listing 1.5. Stream code using taskloop

```
for (int k=0; k<nTimes; k++) {
    #pragma oss taskloop grainsize(BSIZE) in(a[j]) out(c[j])
    for(j = 0; j < N; j++) {
        c[j] = a[j];
    }

    #pragma oss taskloop grainsize(BSIZE) in(c[j]) out(b[j])
    for(j = 0; j < N; j++) {
        b[j] = scalar*c[j];
    }

    #pragma oss taskloop grainsize(BSIZE) in(a[j], b[j]) out(c[j])
    for(j = 0; j < N; j++) {
        c[j] = a[j]+b[j];
    }

    #pragma oss taskloop grainsize(BSIZE) in(b[j], c[j]) out(a[j])
    for(j = 0; j < N; j++) {
        a[j] = b[j]+scalar*c[j];
    }
}
#pragma oss taskwait
```

using taskloop reduces it from 13.5 to 9.5 because we are able to remove four different **for** loops, as you can see comparing the code snippets in Listings 1.4 and 1.5. Similarly, in the dotprod benchmark we can remove two **for** loops, reducing the CC.

7   Conclusions and Future Work

The **taskloop** construct is a directive that distributes the iteration space of a loop into several tasks. This gives a boost to productivity when using the tasking model. However, the current implementation of this construct does not cover the vast majority of cases, because it is missing data dependences support. Therefore, users are forced to use explicit synchronization points, like in the fork-join model. As a result, users get a fork-join like structure, with increased overhead compared to worksharing constructs.

By providing support for data dependences to the **taskloop** construct, we enable users to utilize this directive in the majority of cases. Thus, they are able to fully convert their loops into tasks with a single directive, maximizing productivity, while keeping the main benefit of tasks, a lightweight synchronization based on data dependences.

Our evaluation shows that **taskloop** with dependences delivers as much performance as its manual counterpart, but with a reduced number of lines of code. The number of lines of source code required to parallelize a code using **taskloop** with dependences is up to 3.57x times smaller than its manual counterpart.

As future work, we plan to further investigate the interactions of `taskloop` dependences with other OpenMP features. The big challenge will imply combining dependences with the `collapse` clause. As this clause specifies the number of loops that are collapsed into a logical iteration space that then is divided according to the `grainsize` and `num_tasks` clauses; the implementation should take into account partial innermost level loop partition that will hinder the array section definition.

Another opportunity for future research include the study of the interaction with the loop transformation constructs (i.e., the `tile` and the `unroll` constructs). Although it seems the programmer should apply the semantics of the `taskloop` dependences on top of the already transformed loops, such use cases should be considered to discard potential corner cases.

Acknowledgements. This research has received funding from the European Union's Horizon 2020/EuroHPC research and innovation programme under grant agreement No 955606 (DEEP-SEA); and the support of the Spanish Ministry of Science and Innovation (Computacion de Altas Prestaciones VIII: PID2019-107255GB).

References

1. Augonnet, C., Thibault, S., Namyst, R., Wacrenier, P.A.: StarPU: a unified platform for task scheduling on heterogeneous multicore architectures. Concur. Comput. Pract. Exp. **23**(2), 187–198 (2011)
2. Ayguade, E., et al.: A proposal to extend the OpenMP tasking model for heterogeneous architectures. In: Müller, M.S., de Supinski, B.R., Chapman, B.M. (eds.) IWOMP 2009. LNCS, vol. 5568, pp. 154–167. Springer, Heidelberg (2009). https://doi.org/10.1007/978-3-642-02303-3_13
3. Barcelona Supercomputing Center: Mercurium Compiler. https://github.com/bsc-pm/mcxx. Accessed 24 March 2019
4. Barcelona Supercomputing Center: Nanos6 Runtime. https://github.com/bsc-pm/nanos6. Accessed 24 March 2019
5. Wheeler, D.A.: SLOCCount: More about COCOMO. https://dwheeler.com/sloccount/sloccount.html#cocomo. Accessed 05 July 2021
6. Duran, A., Duran, A., et al.: OmpSs: a proposal for programming heterogeneous multi-core architectures. Parallel Process. Lett. **21**(2), 173–193 (2011)
7. Intel: Intel C++ Compiler 19.0 Developer Guide and Reference. https://software.intel.com/en-us/cpp-compiler-developer-guide-and-reference-cilk-for. Accessed 24 March 2019
8. Luebke, D.: Cuda: scalable parallel programming for high-performance scientific computing. In: 2008 5th IEEE international symposium on biomedical imaging: from nano to macro, pp. 836–838. IEEE (2008)
9. Nguyen, V., Deeds-rubin, S., Tan, T., Boehm, B.: A SLOC counting standard. In: COCOMO II Forum 2007 (2007)
10. Nvidia: CUDA C++ Programming Guide 11.4 (June 2021). https://docs.nvidia.com/cuda/archive. Accessed 05 July 2021
11. OpenMP Architecture Review Board: OpenMP Application Programming Interface 4.5 (Nov 2015). Accessed 18 Feb 2021

12. OpenMP Architecture Review Board: OpenMP Application Programming Interface (Nov 2018). https://www.openmp.org/wp-content/uploads/OpenMP-API-Specification-5.0.pdf. Accessed 24 Mar 2019

13. Perez, J.M., Beltran, V., Labarta, J., Ayguadé, E.: Improving the integration of task nesting and dependencies in OpenMP. In: 2017 IEEE International Parallel and Distributed Processing Symposium (IPDPS), pp. 809–818. IEEE (2017)

14. Sala, K., et al.: Improving the interoperability between MPI and task-based programming models. In: Proceedings of the 25th European MPI Users' Group Meeting, pp. 1–11 (2018)

15. Sala, K., Teruel, X., Perez, J.M., Peña, A.J., Beltran, V., Labarta, J.: Integrating blocking and non-blocking MPI primitives with task-based programming models. Parallel Comput. **85**, 153–166 (2019)

16. Shirako, J., Unnikrishnan, P., Chatterjee, S., Li, K., Sarkar, V.: Expressing doacross loop dependences in OpenMp. In: 9th International Workshop on OpenMP, IWOMP 2013, vol. 8122, pp. 30–44 (Sep 2013). https://doi.org/10.1007/978-3-642-40698-0

17. Watson, A.H., McCabe, T.J.: Structured testing: A testing methodology using the cyclomatic complexity metric, vol. 500, no. 235. Technical report., NIST Special Publication (1996)

18. Wheeler, David A.: SLOCCount. https://dwheeler.com/sloccount. Accessed 24 March 2019

19. Yin, T.: Lizard. https://github.com/terryyin/lizard. Accessed 24 March 2019

Applications

Outcomes of OpenMP Hackathon: OpenMP Application Experiences with the Offloading Model (Part I)

Barbara Chapman[5], Buu Pham[1], Charlene Yang[2], Christopher Daley[3],
Colleen Bertoni[4], Dhruva Kulkarni[3], Dossay Oryspayev[5], Ed D'Azevedo[6],
Johannes Doerfert[4], Keren Zhou[7], Kiran Ravikumar[8], Mark Gordon[1],
Mauro Del Ben[3], Meifeng Lin[5], Melisa Alkan[1], Michael Kruse[4],
Oscar Hernandez[6], P. K. Yeung[8], Paul Lin[3], Peng Xu[1(✉)], Swaroop Pophale[6],
Tosaporn Sattasathuchana[1], Vivek Kale[5], William Huhn[4],
and Yun (Helen) He[3]

[1] Iowa State University, Ames, IA, USA
{buupq,mgordon,alkan,pxu,tsatta}@iastate.edu
[2] NVIDIA Corporation, Santa Clara, CA, USA
charleney@nvidia.com
[3] Lawrence Berkeley National Laboratory, Berkeley, CA, USA
{csdaley,dkulkarni,mdelben,paullin,yhe}@lbl.gov
[4] Argonne National Laboratory, Lemont, IL, USA
{bertoni,jdoerfert,mkruse,whuhn}@anl.gov
[5] Brookhaven National Laboratory, Upton, NY, USA
{doryspaye,mlin,vkale}@bnl.gov
[6] Oak Ridge National Laboratory, Oak Ridge, TN, USA
{dazevedoef,oscar,pophaless}@ornl.gov
[7] Rice University, Houston, TX, USA
keren.zhou@rice.edu
[8] Georgia Institute of Technology, Atlanta, TX, USA
kiran.r@gatech.edu,pk.yeung@ae.gatech.edu

Abstract. This paper reports on experiences gained and practices adopted when using the latest features of OpenMP to port a variety of HPC applications and mini-apps based on different computational motifs (BerkeleyGW, WDMApp/XGC, GAMESS, GESTS, and Grid-Mini) to accelerator-based, leadership-class, high-performance supercomputer systems at the Department of Energy. As recent enhancements to OpenMP become available in implementations, there is a need to share the results of experimentation with them in order to better understand their behavior in practice, to identify pitfalls, and to learn how they can be effectively deployed in scientific codes. Additionally, we identify best practices from these experiences that we can share with the rest of the OpenMP community.

Supported by Exascale Computing Project (ECP) OpenMP Hackathon hosted by SOL-LVE and NERSC [25].

© Springer Nature Switzerland AG 2021
S. McIntosh-Smith et al. (Eds.): IWOMP 2021, LNCS 12870, pp. 67–80, 2021.
https://doi.org/10.1007/978-3-030-85262-7_5

Keywords: OpenMP · Device offload · Application experiences

1 Introduction

As the HPC landscape moves to more heterogeneous architectures, we are seeing more efforts from applications to adapt to GPU programming. Programming on GPUs is an attractive solution as GPUs provide tremendous computing capability from their thousands of tiny processing cores while consuming less energy per floating-point operation as compared to traditional CPUs. A GPU's ability to run thousands of threads in parallel make it ideal for single-instruction multiple-data (SIMD) or data parallel workloads. Recently, the focus has moved from more architecture-specific programming to performance portability. OpenMP is one such programming model that can give performance closer to architecture-specific programming interfaces like CUDA while maintaining portability across architectures [22].

In this paper, we explore the use of the capability in OpenMP to offload computational work to a GPU for a variety of HPC applications and mini-apps - BerkeleyGW, WDMApp/XGC (in Part I), GAMESS, GESTS, and GridMini (in Part II) based on different computational motifs. As recent enhancements to OpenMP become available in its implementations, there is a need to share the results of application experiences with the larger OpenMP user-base in order to impart specific lessons learnt, share critical issues that were overcome to achieve better performance, and identify pitfalls and how to overcome them in scientific codes.

2 Platforms Used

The primary platforms used for this study are:

- Cori GPU system at NERSC has 18 nodes total. Each node contains two sockets of twenty-core Intel Xeon Skylake 2.4 GHz CPUs, 384 GB DDR4 memory; and eight NVIDIA Tesla V100 GPUs, each with 16 GB HBM2 memory and connected with NVLink interconnect.
- Summit at OLCF [6] uses IBM Power System AC922 nodes. Each of the approximately 4,600 compute nodes contain two IBM POWER9 processors and six NVIDIA Tesla V100 accelerators with 512 GB of DDR4 memory (for POWER9), 96 GB of HBM2 (for accelerators), and 1.6TB of non-volatile memory that can be used as a burst buffer.

3 Application Experiences

3.1 BerkeleyGW

BerkeleyGW [13] is a massively parallel software package employed to study the excited state properties of electrons in materials by using *GW*, Bethe-Salpeter Equation (BSE) methods and beyond. The first-principle *GW* [18,19] and BSE [23] approaches are among the most accurate and effective electronic excited-stated methods broadly employed to study materials with applications such as energy storage and conversion, photovoltaics, quantum information technologies, and nano-electronics, to cite a few.

3.1.1 Application Overview

The software package[1] is primarily written in Fortran 2003, with auxiliary and post-processing utilities written in C, C++, Python, Perl and Bash. BerkeleyGW supports interfacing with many popular DFT codes, with efficient built-in wrappers for them. These DFT codes include Abinit [16], Octopus [26], Quantum ESPRESSO [15] and SIESTA [24].

BerkeleyGW is comprised of four major modules: epsilon (computes the dielectric function and its frequency dependence), sigma (computes *GW* self-energy matrix elements and quasiparticle eigenvalues), kernel (constructs the electron-hole interaction kernels) and absorption (solves the Bethe-Salpeter equation and outputs exciton eigenvalues and eigenfunctions). The four stand-alone executables allow for flexible configurations for different steps in the *GW* and BSE workflow, and reuse of intermediate products between steps.

BerkeleyGW employs a multi-level parallelization strategy, using MPI for inter-node communication and OpenMP for the many-core implementation at the CPU level. Experimental GPU support has been implemented for all four major modules employing a hybrid CUDA+OpenACC programming model and associated libraries [2]. The version of the code optimized on NVIDIA hardware shows near linear strong and weak scaling up to the full scale of Summit [6] at OLCF, with 27,648 NVIDIA V100 GPUs. At full scale on Summit, the sigma executable achieves 105.9 PFLOP/s double-precision performance (52.7% of the peak) and time to solutions of the order of 10 min for a 2,742-atom structure with over 10,000 electrons in the simulation cell [12]. BerkeleyGW exploits optimized HPC libraries whenever possible for its basic computational kernels:

- **Required:** BLAS, LAPACK, FFTW
- **Recommended:** MPI, ScalaPACK, HDF5
- **Optional:** ELPA, PRIMME, cuBLAS, cuFFT

3.1.2 Application Motif

The work presented in this paper is focused on the porting of the sigma module to GPUs using OpenMP target offload, henceforth referred to as OpenMP-target. Starting from the dielectric function computed by epsilon, sigma evaluates a set of self-energy matrix elements (between 10–1000 depending on the calculation type) employed to solve the Dyson's equations and obtain the electrons' quasiparticle eigenvalues (quasiparticle energies E_{QP}) [13]. This computation, together with the evaluation of the dielectric function by epsilon, represent the

---

[1] The BerkeleyGW software package [1] is distributed under an open-source 4-clause BSD license, with mainline development branch maintained on GitHub [3].

two major bottlenecks of the overall GW workflow, each displaying an $O(N^4)$ growth of the computational complexity with system size.

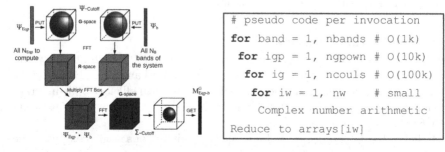

Fig. 1. Left, schematic representation of the MTXEL kernel, and right, pseudocode for the GPP kernel in sigma. Shown on the right of the GPP pseudocode is the relative size of the loops for each kernel invocation for a large scale application.

In sigma, within the Generalized Plasmon-Pole (GPP) model [19], two major computational kernels can be isolated (see Fig. 1):

- MTXEL matrix elements kernel: Calculate intermediate matrix elements between the original system's wave functions and an auxiliary plane-wave (PW) basis. From a computational standpoint this kernel is implemented as a large number of serial FFTs (approximately 100,000 grid points per FFT). For large scale applications, this kernel takes less than 5% of the total computational workload.
- GPP kernel: Represents by far the most intensive computational kernel for large scale applications (>95%). Starting from the matrix elements computed by MTXEL and the dielectric function computed by epsilon, GPP computes self-energy matrix elements, each obtained as tensor-like reduction across different matrices with a complex matrix-vector interdependence.

3.1.3 OpenMP Parallelization Strategy

The approach employed in our porting strategy is summarized as follow:

1. Devise a porting strategy for the major computational bottlenecks based on preliminary analysis of mini-apps[2] simulating the full application running at scale.
2. Add a portability layer to the main applications to switch between various programming models. For the current case we include three layers: (i) multi-threaded OpenMP (CPU) (ii) offload with OpenACC (iii) offload with OpenMP-target.

---

[2] The mini-apps are design to quickly and systematically assess the features of various programming models and associated libraries.

3. Isolate the computational kernels, simulated by the mini-apps, in the main application, organizing each of them within the portability layer framework.
4. Translate from OpenMP (CPU) or OpenACC to OpenMP-target, assessing compiler support, correctness of results and performance compared to other programming models.
5. Improve performance systematically of OpenMP-target implementation, following a similar approach to our original OpenACC porting [27].
6. Test intermediate ports using BerkelyGW's full continuous integration suite.
7. Merge successful ports back into the mainline branch.
8. Report compiler bugs and issues to vendors.

For the case of `sigma` these steps resulted in interfacing to vendor-accelerated FFT and GEMM libraries and translating from OpenMP to OpenMP-target in the `GPP` kernel.

3.1.4 Results

Unless otherwise stated, the benchmark calculations have been obtained on a shared node (interactive queue) on Cori GPU employing 4 GPUs and 16 cores, with a parallel setup of 4 MPI tasks total each comprised of one GPU and 4 OpenMP (CPU) threads. The benchmark system employed for the performance measurements is a small/medium calculation, evaluating $N_{\mathrm{Eqp}} = 2$ quasiparticle energies of a divacancy defect in silicon with 214 atoms in the simulation cell (referred as Si-214) [11]. The NVIDIA HPC SDK 20.11 compiler was used with the compiler flags `-acc -mp=gpu -Mcuda` to enable mixed use of multiple programming models.

```
 1    select case( mtxel_algo )
 2       case (OPENACC_ALGO)
 3 #ifdef OPENACC
 4       if ( fsign > 0 ) then
 5          !$acc host_data use_device(box)
 6          iErr = cufftExecZ2Z(plan, box, box, CUFFT_INVERSE)
 7          !$acc end host_data
 8       else
 9          !$acc host_data use_device(box)
10          iErr = cufftExecZ2Z(plan, box, box, CUFFT_FORWARD)
11          !$acc end host_data
12       end if
13 #else
14       call die_algos("OpenACC")
15 #endif
16       case(OMP_TARGET_ALGO)
17 #ifdef OMP_TARGET
18       if ( fsign > 0 ) then
19          !$omp target data use_device_ptr(box)
20          iErr = cufftExecZ2Z(plan, box, box, CUFFT_INVERSE)
21          !$omp end target data
22       else
23          !$omp target data use_device_ptr(box)
24          iErr = cufftExecZ2Z(plan, box, box, CUFFT_FORWARD)
25          !$omp end target data
26       end if
27 #else
28       call die_algos("OpenMP Target")
29 #endif
30    end select
```

```
 1    select case( mtxel_algo )
 2       case (OPENACC_ALGO)
 3 #ifdef OPENACC
 4          !$acc parallel loop private(bidx) present(g_comp,g_index,vec,box) async(queue)
 5          do iii=1, Ng
 6
 7             bidx(1:3) = g_comp(1:3, g_index(iii)) + 1
 8
 9             if (g_comp(1,g_index(iii)) < 0) bidx(1) = Nfft(1) + bidx(1)
10             if (g_comp(2,g_index(iii)) < 0) bidx(2) = Nfft(2) + bidx(2)
11             if (g_comp(3,g_index(iii)) < 0) bidx(3) = Nfft(3) + bidx(3)
12
13             box(bidx(1),bidx(2),bidx(3)) = vec(iii) * alpha
14          end do
15          !$acc end parallel
16 #else
17          call die_algos("OpenACC")
18 #endif
19          case(OMP_TARGET_ALGO)
20 #ifdef OMP_TARGET
21          !$omp target teams distribute parallel do private(bidx)
22          do iii=1, Ng
23
24             bidx(1:3) = g_comp(1:3, g_index(iii)) + 1
25
26             if (g_comp(1,g_index(iii)) < 0) bidx(1) = Nfft(1) + bidx(1)
27             if (g_comp(2,g_index(iii)) < 0) bidx(2) = Nfft(2) + bidx(2)
28             if (g_comp(3,g_index(iii)) < 0) bidx(3) = Nfft(3) + bidx(3)
29
30             box(bidx(1),bidx(2),bidx(3)) = vec(iii) * alpha
31          end do
32          !$omp end target teams distribute parallel do
33 #else
34          call die_algos("OpenMP Target")
35 #endif
36       end select
```

Fig. 2. For the `MTXEL` kernel shown is the portability layer between OpenACC and OpenMP-target for the (left) complex-to-complex FFT function `cufftExecZ2Z` of the cuFFT library and (right) the `PUT` function of the `MTXEL` kernel.

The porting of the `MTXEL` kernel (see Fig. 1) to OpenMP-target was straightforward to adapt from our previous OpenACC port. This kernel, for each of the

N_{Eqp} quasiparticle state, loops over all bands/wavefuntions N_B in the calculations and performs a series of simple operations between FFTs. The FFT is executed on the GPU using the complex-to-complex FFT function `cufftExecZ2Z` of the cuFFT library for both OpenACC and OpenMP-target. As an example, Fig. 2 shows the OpenACC/OpenMP-target portability layer for the FFT call and the `PUT` function. Host↔GPU data transfer is only performed before/after the `PUT` and `GET` for vector data type, without the need to copy large FFT boxes.

The Si-214 benchmark has values of $N_{Eqp} = 2$ and $N_B = 6,397$, corresponding to ≈1,600 bands per MPI task/GPU. To avoid hitting the memory limit on the GPU, the N_B loop is thus performed over batches (batch size ≈ 20 − 40). Since this version of the NVIDIA compiler did not support the `nowait` clause on the `target` construct, no asynchronous scheduling of batches is used in our OpenMP-target port. Our benchmarks show this lack of asynchronous scheduling in the OpenMP-target port has negligible performance impact compared to the OpenACC port of the `MTXEL` kernel for the Si-214 benchmark (see Table 1).

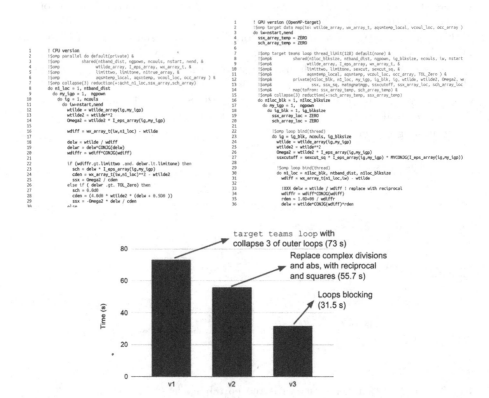

Fig. 3. Top-Left, OpenMP (multi-threaded) Fortran source code of the GPP kernel, isolated to be ported to OpenMP-target. Top-Right, OpenMP-target (v3) GPP kernel. Bottom, improvements in kernel performance (time to solution) for the various optimization step of the OpenMP-target GPP kernel.

For the GPP kernel, a straightforward conversion of the OpenACC port to OpenMP-target was unsuccessful. The code was non-trivial and implemented many optimizations. This made it hard to understand whether the OpenMP-target port failed because of programmer error or compiler error. In order to make progress, we reverted back to a simplified OpenMP multi-threaded CPU version of the kernel, ported this to OpenMP-target, and iteratively optimized. Figure 3 represents the CPU version, which closely matches the pseudo-code in Fig. 1.

To port this simplified GPP kernel to OpenMP-target, it was necessary to move the innermost iw loop outside the kernel since double-complex array reductions are not currently supported in this version of the NVIDIA compiler. The first version (v1) of the OpenMP-target port used a target teams loop combined construct and collapsed all three loops using the collapse(3) clause. Default assignment for either shared or private variables in the kernel was not correctly supported and, to ensure correctness of results, it was necessary to explicitly specify the data-sharing attributes. The target teams distribute parallel do combined construct compiled but failed at runtime, necessitating usage of the target teams loop construct; the converse case was found for the simple PUT/GET and multiply functions in the MTXEL kernel. The reason for the difference is that the NVIDIA compiler uses a different code generation path for the loop construct. Neither code generation path is mature in the 20.11 compiler. We have since found that these issues have been resolved in the 21.3 compiler.

Once the baseline (v1) implementation was working, we optimized the performance of the GPP kernel in a two-step procedure. A summary of the performance improvements in terms of time to solution for the kernel is given at the bottom of Fig. 3. As a first step (v2), long latency instructions, such as complex division and absolute values, were replaced by reciprocals and squares, yielding a 25% improvements in time to solution (1.3× speedup).

The greatest improvements came from the final set of optimizations (v3). We see in (v3) Fig. 3, the outermost (n1_loc) and innermost (ig) loops are blocked, and each block is executed sequentially by each thread via stride loops. To ensure that the innermost two loops are executed sequentially by each thread we added the bind(thread) clause. This prevents the NVIDIA compiler auto-parallelizing these two loops over threads. We could have also disabled auto-parallelization with the compiler option -mp=noautopar. Improvements in time to solution here come from (i) reducing re-computation in the innermost part of the kernel and (ii) improving cache reuse and data locality [27]. This optimization is not applied automatically by the compiler, although it could be once compilers implement the OpenMP-5.1 tile directive.

The final v3 version of the GPP kernel has a runtime of 43% of the v1 baseline implementation (2.3× speedup), and it compares favorably with the optimized OpenACC version (see Table 1). Both OpenACC and OpenMP-target versions lie within ≈10% in time to solution compared to the CUDA version. This discrepancy is due to the additional levels of optimization implemented in the CUDA version and not applied to the OpenACC and OpenMP-target versions. These

Table 1. Runtime comparison (in seconds) of the various kernels of `sigma` on Cori GPU (4 GPUs + 16 cores) at NERSC for Si-214 benchmark system.

	MTXEL	GPP	Total
CPU OpenMP	62	1235	1311
GPU CUDA	1.7	27.3	34.5
GPU OpenACC	3.2	30.2	43.4
GPU OpenMP-target	3.5	31.5	45.9

include (i) further blocking of the `n1_loc` loop, each block assigned to an independent CUDA stream allowing for multiple GPP kernels to run simultaneously on the GPU increasing occupancy, (ii) *ad hoc* implementation of the reduction, partially on GPU and finalized on host and (iii) use of non-blocking point to point MPI communication on the host which overlaps with the GPP kernel execution on the GPU. More details can be found in ref. [12].

3.1.5   Challenges and Lessons Learned

The majority of our OpenMP target offload porting experience used NVIDIA HPC SDK 20.11, the first NVIDIA compiler supporting OpenMP target offload to NVIDIA GPUs. In a relatively short period of time, even with the compiler issues, we were able to port most of the BerkeleyGW `sigma` module to OpenMP target offload and achieved comparable performance to our previous OpenACC port. Some of our workarounds for NVIDIA HPC SDK 20.11 included

- Switching between `target teams distribute parallel do` and `target teams loop` compute directives on certain loops to avoid application run time errors.
- Explicitly specifying the data sharing attributes of all variables used in an OpenMP target region.
- Explicitly mapping all variables used in OpenMP target region data reductions.

One of the keys to our success over the years has been the use of BerkeleyGW mini-apps. Having mini-apps that accurately capture the computational motifs without the various library dependencies and a small data footprint (data set fits in memory of single compute node) was helpful for sharing with vendors for independent assessment [4]. Another critical component of our GPU porting workflow has been the creation of OpenMP-target and OpenACC builds in our Buildbot continuous integration suite running on Amazon Web Services (AWS). These builds run all GPU-accelerated kernels through the full BerkeleyGW regression test suite for every pull request. Thanks to this we have been able to include the OpenMP-target features developed in this work into BerkeleyGW mainline and released in the 3.0 version of the software package.

Despite not being an issue of the OpenMP standard itself, we found that true portability is hampered by library API issues. In fact, we have found that it is necessary to include compiler-dependent preprocessor statements into the OpenMP-target code base to handle differences between vendor offload implementations of "standardized" APIs like BLAS/LAPACK[3]. This is only exacerbated for library calls where no standardized API is supported by multiple vendors, such as batched linear algebra and FFT operations.

During the development process, the NVIDIA compiler flag `-Minfo` was particularly useful since it provides informational messages about the compilation process, notably parallelization, vectorization, and GPU offloading. We found the following runtime environment variables helpful: `OMP_TARGET_OFFLOAD=MANDATORY` to make sure code runs on GPU and `NVCOMPILER_ACC_NOTIFY=3` to show kernel launch configurations as well as data transfers. Two profiling tools were used for the BerkeleyGW runs on the NVIDIA GPUs. Nsight Systems has a relatively small overhead ($\approx$2–4$\times$) for our OpenMP-target and OpenACC runs. We used it to visually inspect the kernel performances of OpenMP offload and OpenACC implementations. HPCToolkit has a much higher overhead ($\approx$20$\times$) because it samples the Program Counter (PC). We gained a 12% performance improvement when a single line of complex division in a nested loop was found as a top hotspot and replaced with reciprocals.

We plan to use OpenMP target offload as our portable solution across DOE machines in the coming years. We are confident that OpenMP compilers will meet BerkeleyGW requirements, as multiple vendors are committed to supporting a common subset of OpenMP features on accelerators [21].

3.2   WDMApp

The goal of the DOE Exascale Computing Project (ECP) Whole Device Model Application (WDMApp) project is high-fidelity simulation of magnetically confined fusion plasmas for future fusion reactors [7]. This involves coupling the gyrokinetic codes in different domains of the reactor, e.g., core region vs edge region. The gyrokinetic code, XGC, models the edge plasma regime [20].

3.2.1   Application Overview

XGC is a modern edge gyrokinetic particle-in-cell (PIC) code [8]. One of the key kernels is the computation of Coulomb collisions. XGC employs a non-linear collision operator [17].

XGC is a Fortran 90 code employing OpenMP (intranode) and OpenACC (intranode, GPU) for parallelism. There has been a recent effort to convert XGC to C++ from Fortran; consequently, the collision kernel has been converted to C++ and uses Kokkos [14] to run on GPUs.

3.2.2   Application Motif

This work focuses on the XGC collision operator. The computational grid is essentially a torus and consists of 2D planes (discretized by 2D unstructured

---

[3] No such differentiation is normally needed for CPU/multicore builds.

triangular elements) in the toroidal direction. The collision operator is calculated at each vertex in the grid.

XGC includes a standalone collision kernel. This collision standalone proxy application or "mini-app" is written in C++ and employs Kokkos to run on GPUs, and is the focus of this work.

3.2.3   OpenMP Parallelization Strategy

The XGC Collision mini-app was already GPU-enabled using Kokkos with the Kokkos CUDA backend. A performance profile showed that the application made poor use of GPU hardware. This was because the parallelization strategy only exploited parallelism on coarse-grained outer loops, as is common in many CPU-only applications. At the hackathon [25] we decided to experiment with a fine-grained parallelization strategy to make better use of GPU hardware. We could have done the experimentation in Kokkos, however, we chose to create a hybrid Kokkos+OpenMP target offload mini-app to quickly prototype different parallelization strategies with OpenMP target offload.

Our hackathon strategy relied on OpenMP compilers supporting the use of CUDA-allocated data in OpenMP target regions. Listing 1.1 shows how the is_device_ptr clause was used to access CUDA-allocated data in the OpenMP target region. The parallelization strategy is identical to the Kokkos implementation, where the function E_and_D_s_omptarget is executed by every single GPU thread.

```
1  #pragma omp target teams distribute \
2              parallel for is_device_ptr(...)
3  for (int idx=0; idx<col_f_nvrm1_nvzm1; idx++)
4    E_and_D_s_omptarget(...);
5
6  void E_and_D_s_omptarget(...) {
7    // ... user code
8    for (index_ip = 0; index_ip<nvzm1; index_ip++) {
9      for (index_jp = 0; index_jp<nvrm1; index_jp++) {
```

Listing 1.1. XGC v1: Coarse-grained parallelism + OpenMP-4.0 compute constructs

We modified the original, poorly performing, code by moving the outer loop into E_and_D_s_omptarget function. We parallelized and workshared this outer loop with **teams distribute** and the inner two loops with **parallel for collapse(2)**. The inner loops additionally required an OpenMP reduction over 5 scalar variables. Listing 1.2 shows the original fine-grained implementation.

```
1  void E_and_D_s_omptarget_v2(...) {
2  #pragma omp target teams distribute is_device_ptr(...)
3    for (int idx=0; idx<col_f_nvrm1_nvzm1; idx++) {
4      // ... user code
5  #pragma omp parallel for collapse(2) reduction(+:...)
6      for (index_ip = 0; index_ip<nvzm1; index_ip++) {
7        for (index_jp = 0; index_jp<nvrm1; index_jp++) {
```

Listing 1.2. XGC v2: Fine-grained parallelism + OpenMP-4.0 compute constructs

The original fine-grained code has a benefit and a downside. The benefit is that parallelism is now exploited on the innermost loops making it more suitable for execution on GPUs. The downside is that our implementation uses an inner **parallel** construct that is not strictly nested inside a **teams** region. This is a performance concern because there is a fork-join point, which itself has over-head, and the possibility that the code in the target region cannot be safely executed by each GPU thread as Single Program Multiple Data (SPMD). Pub-lications have reported significant slowdowns when using the pattern shown in Listing 1.2 [9,10]. As an alternative, the NVIDIA compiler has a tuned implemen-tation of the OpenMP-5.0 `loop` construct to avoid these performance concerns. The `loop` construct specifies that loop iterations may be executed concurrently and has restrictions that help compilers generate high performance code. List-ing 1.3 shows our OpenMP-5.0 `loop` implementation. The `bind` clause specifies the threads that may execute the `loop` region. Our outer loop has an implicit `bind(teams)` clause and the inner loops have an explicit `bind(parallel)` clause. This usage instructs the NVIDIA compiler to workshare the outer loop itera-tions over CUDA thread blocks and the inner loop iterations over CUDA threads when generating code for the GPU.

```
void E_and_D_s_omptarget_v3(...) {
#pragma omp target teams loop is_device_ptr(...)
  for (int idx=0; idx<col_f_nvrm1_nvzm1; idx++) {
    // ... user code
#pragma omp loop bind(parallel) collapse(2) reduction(+:..)
    for (index_ip = 0; index_ip<nvzm1; index_ip++) {
      for (index_jp = 0; index_jp<nvrm1; index_jp++) {
```

Listing 1.3. XGC v3: Fine-grained parallelism + OpenMP 5.0 `loop` construct

3.2.4   Results
We compiled the XGC collision mini-app with NVIDIA HPC SDK 21.5 and executed an XGC test problem with 100 mesh nodes on Cori GPU. The results are shown in Table 2.

Table 2. XGC collision time spent in seconds in the dominant two functions. Runs performed on Cori-GPU, which has NVIDIA V100 GPUs.

	v0 (Kokkos)	v1	v2	v3
E_and_D_ab	0.95	0.94	0.50	0.17
E_and_D_s	0.68	0.44	0.22	0.19

The results show that the fine-grained parallelism approach with the OpenMP `loop` directive (v3) compiled with the NVIDIA HPC SDK 21.5 com-piler gave a 5.6x and 3.6x improvement over the original Kokkos implementa-tion. We plan to backport this fine-grained parallelism approach into the original Kokkos mini-app. We also plan to assess the performance of the mini-app using the Kokkos OpenMP target offload backend. This backend is a work in progress, however, performance observations from this code and other codes have influ-enced the placement of OpenMP constructs in Kokkos to enable SPMD execution [5].

3.2.5   Challenges and Lessons Learned

Our lessons learned are as follows: **Profile the Application.** We had written high quality OpenMP target offload code that considered every single message printed by the `-Minfo=mp` compiler diagnostic to ensure that the OpenMP target region was mapped to the GPU kernel in exactly the way we expected. Yet, at runtime, our initial performance with an older version of the compiler (NVIDIA HPC SDK 20.11) was very poor. It was only by profiling the code with the NVIDIA Nsight-systems and Nsight-compute tools that we found that the NVIDIA OpenMP runtime was launching the dominant GPU kernel with only 8 OpenMP teams (CUDA thread blocks).

Leverage Compiler Experts. We were unable to reproduce the issue of 8 OpenMP teams in a simple standalone code to report an NVIDIA compiler bug. It was only by having NVIDIA compiler engineers present at the hackathon that they could rationalize about the cause of the issue and fix the issue in subsequent versions of the compiler. The results in this paper used the 21.5 compiler. This should be a reminder that today's applications are often sufficiently complicated that the standard model of application developers reporting simplified reproducers is not always possible.

Need for Streamlining the Performance Analysis Process. The XGC collision kernel mini-app is a Kokkos-based application with minimal library dependencies (BLAS and LAPACK); however, as the mini-app is built through the build system of the main XGC application, the mini-app has inherited many redundant dependencies (e.g. PETSc, CABANA, FUSIONIO, HDF5, FFTW). Consequently, it is unwieldy for experimentation with different compilers as these dependencies need to be satisfied across all compiler stacks. For comparing performance across compilers, it would be more efficient if the redundant dependencies inherited by the mini-app were eliminated by additional logic in the build system. It would also help us if there were pre-packaged compatible math libraries with all compilers, e.g. the NVIDIA HPC SDK provides LAPACK-/BLAS libraries.

We continue our application experiences with GAMESS, GESTS, and Grid-Mini in Part II.

References

1. BerkeleyGW. http://www.berkeleygw.org. Accessed 25 July 2021, 06:48:38
2. BerkeleyGW CUDA version. https://gitlab.com/NESAP/berkeleygw/berkeleygw-cuda. Accessed 25 July 2021, 06:48:38
3. BerkeleyGW development mainline. https://github.com/BerkeleyGW. Accessed 25 July 2021, 06:48:38
4. BerkeleyGW kernels and miniapps. https://gitlab.com/NESAP/berkeleygw/berkeleygw-kernels. Accessed 25 July 2021, 06:48:38
5. Kokkos Pull Request #3808. https://github.com/kokkos/kokkos/pull/3808. Accessed 25 July 2021, 06:48:38

6. OLCF Summit. https://www.olcf.ornl.gov/summit/. Accessed 25 July 2021, 06:48:38

7. WDMApp. https://www.exascaleproject.org/research-project/wdmapp. Accessed 25 July 2021, 06:48:38

8. XGC1. https://hbps.pppl.gov/computing/xgc-1. Accessed 25 July 2021, 06:48:38

9. Daley, C., Ahmed, H., Williams, S., Wright, N.: A case study of porting HPGMG from CUDA to OpenMP target offload. In: Milfeld, K., de Supinski, B.R., Koesterke, L., Klinkenberg, J. (eds.) IWOMP 2020. LNCS, vol. 12295, pp. 37–51. Springer, Cham (2020). https://doi.org/10.1007/978-3-030-58144-2_3

10. Davis, J.H., Daley, C., Pophale, S., Huber, T., Chandrasekaran, S., Wright, N.J.: Performance assessment of OpenMP compilers targeting NVIDIA V100 GPUs. In: Seventh Workshop on Accelerator Programming Using Directives (WACCPD-2020) (2020)

11. Del Ben, M.: BerkeleyGW Si214 Benchmarks (2021)

12. Del Ben, M., Yang, C., Li, Z., Jornada, F.H.d., Louie, S.G., Deslippe, J.: Accelerating large-scale excited-state *GW* calculations on leadership HPC systems. In: Proceedings of the International Conference for High Performance Computing, Networking, Storage and Analysis. SC '20. IEEE Press (2020)

13. Deslippe, J., Samsonidze, G., Strubbe, D.A., Jain, M., Cohen, M.L., Louie, S.G.: Berkeleygw: a massively parallel computer package for the calculation of the quasiparticle and optical properties of materials and nanostructures. Comput. Phys. Commun. **183**(6), 1269–1289 (2012)

14. Edwards, H.C., Trott, C.R., Sunderland, D.: Kokkos: enabling manycore performance portability through polymorphic memory access patterns. J. Parallel Distrib. Comput. **74**(12), 3202–3216 (2014). Domain-Specific Languages and High-Level Frameworks for High-Performance Computing

15. Giannozzi, P.: Quantum espresso: a modular and open-source software project for quantum simulations of materials. J. Phys. Cond. Matter **21**(39), 395502 (2009)

16. Gonze, X., et al.: ABINIT: First-principles approach to material and nanosystem properties. Comput. Phys. Commun. **180**(12), 2582–2615 (2009)

17. Hager, R., Yoon, E., Ku, S., D'Azevedo, E., Worley, P., Chang, C.: A fully non-linear multi-species Fokker-Planck-Landau collision operator for simulation of fusion plasma. J. Comput. Phys. **315**, 644–660 (2016)

18. Hybertsen, M., Louie, S.G.: First-principles theory of quasiparticles: calculation of band gaps in semiconductors and insulators. Phys. Rev. Lett. **55**(13), 1418 (1985)

19. Hybertsen, M.S., Louie, S.G.: Electron correlation in semiconductors and insulators: band gaps and quasiparticle energies. Phys. Rev. B **34**(8), 5390 (1986)

20. Ku, S., et al.: A fast low-to-high confinement mode bifurcation dynamics in the boundary-plasma gyrokinetic code XGC1. Phys. Plasmas **25**(5), 056107 (2018)

21. Kwack, J., et al.: OpenMP roadmap for accelerators across DOE Pre-Exascale/Exascale machines. In: Presentation at the ECP 2021 Annual Meeting on Apr 15 2021 (2021)

22. OpenMP.org: OpenMP Application Programming Interface version 4.5 (2015)

23. Rohlfing, M., Louie, S.G.: Electron-hole excitations and optical spectra from first principles. Phys. Rev. B **62**, 4927–4944 (2000)

24. Soler, J.M., et al.: The SIESTA method for ab-initio order-N materials simulation. J. Phys.: Conden. Matter **14**(11), 2745–2779 (2002)

25. SOLLVE and NERSC: January 2021 ECP OpenMP Hackathon by SOLLVE and NERSC (2021 [Online]), the event happened on 22, 27, 28, 29 Jan 2021. https://sites.google.com/view/ecpomphackjan2021. Accessed 7 Apr 2021

26. Tancogne-Dejean, N., et al.: Octopus, a computational framework for exploring light-driven phenomena and quantum dynamics in extended and finite systems. J. Chem. Phys. **152**(12), 124119 (2020)
27. Yang, C.: 8 Steps to 3.7 TFLOP/s on NVIDIA V100 GPU: Roofline Analysis and Other Tricks (2020). https://arxiv.org/abs/2008.11326

Outcomes of OpenMP Hackathon: OpenMP Application Experiences with the Offloading Model (Part II)

Barbara Chapman[5], Buu Pham[1], Charlene Yang[2], Christopher Daley[3],
Colleen Bertoni[4], Dhruva Kulkarni[3], Dossay Oryspayev[5], Ed D'Azevedo[6],
Johannes Doerfert[4], Keren Zhou[7], Kiran Ravikumar[8], Mark Gordon[1],
Mauro Del Ben[3], Meifeng Lin[5], Melisa Alkan[1], Michael Kruse[4],
Oscar Hernandez[6], P. K. Yeung[8], Paul Lin[3], Peng Xu[1(✉)], Swaroop Pophale[6],
Tosaporn Sattasathuchana[1], Vivek Kale[5], William Huhn[4],
and Yun (Helen) He[3]

[1] Iowa State University, Ames, IA, USA
{buupq,mgordon,alkan,pxu,tsatta}@iastate.edu
[2] NVIDIA Corporation, Santa Clara, CA, USA
charleney@nvidia.com
[3] Lawrence Berkeley National Laboratory, Berkeley, CA, USA
{csdaley,dkulkarni,mdelben,paullin,yhe}@lbl.gov
[4] Argonne National Laboratory, Lemont, IL, USA
{bertoni,jdoerfert,mkruse,whuhn}@anl.gov
[5] Brookhaven National Laboratory, Upton, NY, USA
{mlin,vkale}@bnl.gov
[6] Oak Ridge National Laboratory, Oak Ridge, TN, USA
{oscar,pophaless}@ornl.gov
[7] Rice University, Houston, TX, USA
keren.zhou@rice.edu
[8] Georgia Institute of Technology, Atlanta, GA, Georgia
kiran.r@gatech.edu,pk.yeung@ae.gatech.edu

Abstract. This paper reports on experiences gained and practices adopted when using the latest features of OpenMP to port a variety of HPC applications and mini-apps based on different computational motifs (BerkeleyGW, WDMApp/XGC, GAMESS, GESTS, and Grid-Mini) to accelerator-based, leadership-class, high-performance supercomputer systems at the Department of Energy. As recent enhancements to OpenMP become available in implementations, there is a need to share the results of experimentation with them in order to better understand their behavior in practice, to identify pitfalls, and to learn how they can be effectively deployed in scientific codes. Additionally, we identify best practices from these experiences that we can share with the rest of the OpenMP community.

Supported by Exascale Computing Project (ECP) OpenMP Hackathon hosted by SOL-LVE and NERSC [29].

© Springer Nature Switzerland AG 2021
S. McIntosh-Smith et al. (Eds.): IWOMP 2021, LNCS 12870, pp. 81–95, 2021.
https://doi.org/10.1007/978-3-030-85262-7_6

Keywords: OpenMP · Device offload · Application experiences

1   Introduction

In this paper we continue the exploration of OpenMP usage in HPC applications (GAMESS, GESTS, and GridMini) in Sect. 2. We conclude in Sect. 3 and provide acknowledgments in Sect. 4.

2   Application Experiences

2.1   GAMESS

2.1.1   Application Overview

GAMESS is a general electronic structure software package comprising of a variety of quantum mechanical (QM) methods [6]. GAMESS is primarily written in Fortran and parallelized using both pure MPI [12,14] and hybrid MPI/OpenMP [23,24]. A high-performance C++/CUDA library, namely LibC-Chem, has been recently developed to accelerate GAMESS on GPUs. Alternatively, GAMESS Fortran is directly offloaded to GPUs using OpenMP. In this section, offloading strategies of the Hartree-Fock (HF) method, which is an essential step of *ab initio* methods, will be discussed.

2.1.2   Application Motif

A HF computation requires i) evaluation of N^4 electron repulsion integrals (ERIs) as shown in eq. (1), ii) formation of N^2-element Fock matrix, iii) Fock matrix diagonalization for eigen energies and vectors. Here, N is the system size, usually represented by the number of Gaussian basis functions $\phi_\mu(r)$. In GAMESS, a basis function can be characterized by a few parameters, including the so-called angular momentum, which is an integer starting from 0 upwards, used here for sorting ERIs.

$$(\mu\nu|\lambda\sigma) = \iint dr_1 \, dr_2 \phi_\mu^*(r_1)\phi_\nu(r_1)r_{12}^{-1}\phi_\lambda^*(r_2)\phi_\sigma(r_2), \tag{1}$$

To provide the optimal performance for ERI evaluation, three different integral algorithms have been implemented in GAMESS, including a) Rotated-axis [1,21,25,28], b) Electron repulsion Integral Calculator (ERIC) [13], and c) Rys quadrature [11,19,27]. Depending on the characteristics of basis functions, different ERI algorithms are selected at runtime (Fig. 1a).

In this work, we focus on i) offloading the Rys quadrature kernel from full GAMESS package, ii) examining OpenMP offloading compiler support using a Fortran mini-app of rotated-axis integral code, and iii) analyzing performance of a C++ integral kernel from GAMESS-LibCChem. The first two efforts were carried out on Ascent/Summit, while the latter was performed on NERSC's CoriGPU.

2.1.3   OpenMP Parallelization Strategy

In the OpenMP HF implementation targeting CPUs [2,22], there is a large workload imbalance between threads. This imbalance is handled by using dynamic loop scheduling and loop collapsing (c.f. lines 2 and 3, Figure 1a). To adapt this code to the SIMT architecture in GPUs, the ERI codes were restructured based on their optimal algorithms as discussed in [4]. However, this code can be improved by sorting the integrals with respect to basis function angular momentum and the inherent permutational symmetry of the integrals into different classes (e.g. R 1112, R 1121 in Fig. 1c). In this study, a particular class, the 1121-kernel is presented in Fig. 1d and for further optimization see Fig. 1e. The main bottleneck of the 1121-Rys kernel is to contract calculated ERIs (line 6 of Fig. 1d) with density for six Fock matrix elements using atomic operations (lines 12 − 14). To reduce such synchronization overhead, in Fig. 1e, ERIs are evaluated in chunk (lines 4 − 7), which are then contracted with density to update the Fock matrix in a separated GPU parallel region (lines 10 − 17). Data exchange between quartet evaluation and Fock update are managed by the target data directive (lines 1 and 18).

2.1.4   Results

Relative timing of the new (Fig. 1e) and the original (Fig. 1d) offloading schemes for the 1121-kernel is studied using water cluster of 16 − 128 molecules. The cc-pVDZ basis set is used for all water clusters introducing 54 − 570K quartets for computation and Fock digestion. The 1121-kernel wall time of $(H_2O)_{64}$ is recorded while varying the number of quartets computed concurrently, which is NSIZE*80 * 128, the number of teams (NTEAMS) and threads per team (NTHREAD). The optimal wall time is usually achieved with a small number of threads, large number of team and medium value of chunk size (Fig. 2).

Table 1. Wall time (s) and speedup of new offloading implementation (Fig. 1e). relative to the original one (Fig. 1d)

	NQUART	Scheme 1d	Scheme 1e	Speedup
$(H_2O)_{16}$	54, 274	0.30	0.41	0.73
$(H_2O)_{32}$	263, 075	0.73	0.51	1.43
$(H_2O)_{64}$	1, 256, 691	2.94	1.00	2.94
$(H_2O)_{80}$	2, 095, 639	4.82	1.75	2.75
$(H_2O)_{96}$	3, 118, 724	6.97	2.56	2.72
$(H_2O)_{112}$	4, 322, 306	9.49	3.69	2.57
$(H_2O)_{128}$	5, 727, 489	12.40	4.80	2.58

Stacking optimal series, i.e., those contain minimum wall time data point, showing that the 1121-kernel can be evaluated in 1.00 (s) with medium chunk size

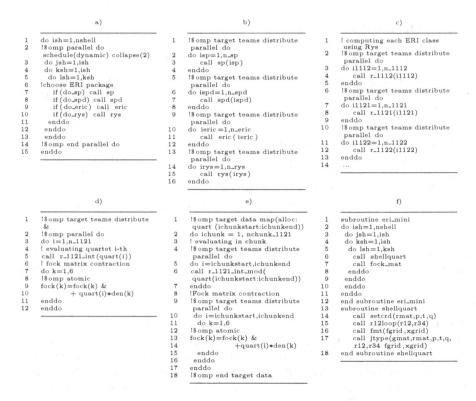

Fig. 1. (a) CPU OpenMP implementation, (b) refactoring ERI codes based on optimal algorithm, (c) further sorting for the Rys quadrature algorithm, (d) detail of 1121-Rys kernel; and (e) separation of ERI evaluation and digestion, f) Fortran mini-app ERI code and its SHELLQUART kernel.

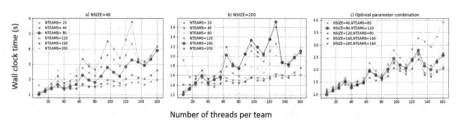

Fig. 2. a,b) variation of the 1121-kernel wall time with respect to NTEAMS, NTHREAD and NSIZE. Optimal series for each chunk size is in bold green; c) stacking of optimal series extracted from various chunk sizes.

NSIZE 80, NTEAMS 160, and NTHREAD 8. In comparison with the original algorithm, separating atomic updates introduce a speedup of 2.5× (Table 1).

2.1.5 Fortran Mini-App

A Fortran mini-app was extracted from the rotated-axis algorithm (Fig. 1f) to be portable to a variety of computer clusters and explore GPU compilers from different vendors. This Fortran mini-app has been compiled on various hardware and compilers (Table 2). The explicit interface is not required for the offloading region for IBM compiler, while it was needed for NVIDIA's HPC SDK 21.2 compiler. However this issue was resolved with HPC SDK 21.3. Despite the fact that the ERI code was well modularized and worked well on CPU, using compilers for offloading to GPU with the automatic inlining option (e.g., using `-qinline`) did not show noticeable performance improvements. On the other hand, manually inlining implementation greatly improves the performance. A noteworthy observation was made that a runtime out-of-memory on the device was encountered, which was resolved by moving some subroutine arguments to modules (e.g., STCRD, R12LOOP, FMT, and JTYPE).

Table 2. Summary of various compilers used for the mini-app.

Compiler	Systems	Declare target for external subroutine	Compiler flags
IBM NVIDIA HPC	Ascent	No clause	`-qsmp=omp -qoffload -O2|`
SDK 21.2	CoriGPU	Explicit interface	`-Mextend -tp=skylake -Mcuda=cc70 -ta=tesla:cc70 -fast -mp=gpu`

2.1.6 C++-mini-app

A C++ mini-app was extracted from LibCChem and ported to GPU using CUDA and OpenMP. The kernel was wrapped into a Google Benchmark [15] application that is configured using CMake [20]. Google Benchmark can adjust the number of iterations depending on single kernel execution time and measurement noise to output a reliable result. CMake and preprocessor provide flags handling of the compiler required for C++, CUDA, or OpenMP in a single source directory with multiple build directories, one for each compiler.

Table 3. Mini-Mini-App performance results in seconds.

Language	Compiler	Variant	CPU Kernel	GPU Kernel
CUDA	Nvcc		2003.0	43.0
CUDA	Nvcc	Localmem	1934.0	50.8
OpenMP	Clang		2657.0	54.3
OpenMP	CCE		2023.0	75.7
OpenMP	Gcc		5885.0	2054.9
OpenMP	Nvc		*Error*	

For the Cori GPU system, Table 3 shows the Google Benchmark CPU time per iteration (including waiting for results to arrive in the CPU) and the GPU kernel-only time as measured by NVIDIA's nvprof. The CUDA version has a "localmem" variant which uses temporary `__shared__` arrays containing copies of the working set of a single block, but otherwise calls the same (inlined) kernel. The OpenMP source does not have an equivalent to the localmem variant because required data-initialization of team-local memory in OpenMP are incompatible with clang's SPMD-mode and would cause a major performance penalty. For OpenMP, Clang performed the best, slightly behind the CUDA version, followed by CCE. The execution time when compiled with gcc was not competitive. NVIDIA's HPC SDK 21.3 compiler (formerly PGI) either failed with a compiler error or produced a crashing executable (`-O0` or `-O1`).

2.1.7   Challenges and Lessons Learned

To adapt the GPU SIMT model, the Hartree-Fock code was restructured so that integrals of the same class are computed concurrently. The bottleneck was found to be atomic updates in the Fock matrix contraction (Fig. 1d), which were further optimized by using them in a separate target region (Fig. 1e), in which data exchange between parallel regions are retained on GPU and governed by the target data directive. The kernel performance was also found to vary strongly with respect to the number of teams, threads per team and amount of data loaded to GPU for computation. The results show that utilizing NTEAMS=160 and NTHREAD=8 to be processed at a time yields desirable performance. The rotated-axis mini-app was offloaded with the basic target constructs and tested on various systems, and shown that "out-of-memory" runtime error can be resolved by using modules. The C++ mini-app was ported to GPU using CUDA and OpenMP, with the kernel wrapped into a Google Benchmark application configured using CMake. It was found that gcc-compiled OpenMP kernel did not show competitive timing. NVIDIA's HPC SDK 21.3 compiler either failed with a compiler error or produced a crashing executable.

2.2   GESTS

2.2.1   Application Overview

GESTS (GPUs for Extreme Scale Turbulence Simulations) is a pseudo-spectral Direct Numerical Simulation (DNS) code used to study the fundamental behavior of turbulent flows [17]. The presence of disorderly fluctuations over a wide range of scales in three-dimensional (3D) space and time poses stringent resolution requirements [30], especially if localized events of high intensity [31] must be captured accurately. However, large scale pseudo-spectral simulations are dominated by communication costs, which become an even greater burden versus computation when codes are ported to heterogeneous platforms whose principal strengths are in computational speed.

In recent work on Summit, we addressed these challenges by developing a batched asynchronous algorithm [26] to enable overlapping computations, data copies and network communication using CUDA, which enabled problem sizes as large as 6 trillion grid points.

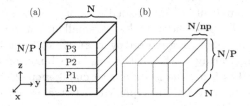

Fig. 3. Left/(a): Decomposition of an N^3 solution domain among P MPI processes into *slabs* of data of size $N \times N \times N/P$. Right/(b): Further decomposition of a slab into np smaller sub-volumes, each of size $N \times N/np \times N/P$.

Here we discuss the development of a portable implementation using advanced asynchronous OpenMP features on the GPUs, in order to enable even larger problem sizes using newer exascale architectures like Frontier.

2.2.2   Application Motif

We focus on three-dimensional Fast Fourier Transforms (3D FFT) which are crucial to the GEST code. To benefit from the architecture of emerging platforms with large CPU memory and multiple accelerators we use a one-dimensional (*slabs*) domain decomposition as shown in Fig. 3a. This helps reduce communication costs as fewer MPI processes are involved [26] although point-to-point message sizes are larger. Within each plane in a slab, 1D FFTs in two directions (here x and y) are performed readily using highly optimized GPU libraries (cuFFT or rocFFT), while the FFT in the third (z) direction requires an all-to-all global transpose that re-partitions the data into, say, $x - z$ planes. However if N is very large (up to 18,432 in [26]) a complete slab may not fit into the smaller GPU memory. We address this by dividing each slab into np smaller *sub-volumes*, as in Fig. 3b. In effect, batches of data formed from the sub-volumes are copied to the GPU, computed on, and copied back; while operations on different portions may overlap with one another. For example, as the code proceeds from left to right, GPU computation on a sub-volume colored in blue, host-to-device copy for another in red (or device-to-host in green) and non-blocking all-to-all on another in brown can occur asynchronously.

2.2.3   OpenMP Implementation Strategy

In the "batched" scheme described above, when FFTs in y need to be computed, a sub-volume of data consisting of $N \times N/P$ lines of size N/np need to be copied. Essentially, for each value of y (between 1 to N) and z (between 1 to N/P) a copy needs to be performed for N/np elements in the innermost dimension (x) of length N. Efficient strided data transfers between the CPU and GPU are thus important. Simple approaches such as packing on the host prior to transfer, or performing multiple copies one line at a time are inefficient, because of an extra data-reordering operation on the CPU and the overhead of numerous smaller copies respectively [26]. Instead, we make use of two different approaches depending on the complexity of the strided memory accesses.

For simple strided copies where strides are small and in the innermost dimension only, we can use `omp_target_memcpy_rect` which copies a specified subvolume inside a larger array on the host to a smaller buffer on the device or vice versa. This OpenMP 4.5 routine is similar to `cudaMemcpy2d` but asynchronous execution will be supported only in OpenMP 5.1. We are using OpenMP tasks as a workaround.

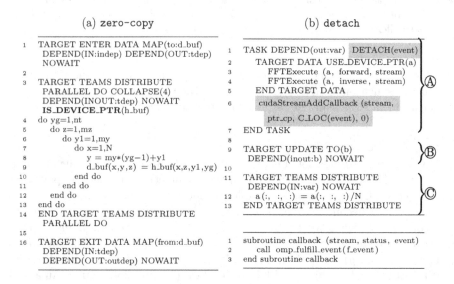

Fig. 4. (a) Asynchronous OpenMP implementation of the `zero-copy` kernel for unpacking data from the pinned host array (`h_buf`) to the device array (`d_buf`). Here for an N^3 problem $my = mz = N/nt$ where nt is MPI process count. (b) Interoperability between non-blocking FFT libraries and OpenMP *tasks* using `DETACH` while ensuring correct asynchronous execution.

For more complex stride patterns, like those in unpacking operations where strided read and write memory access are required to transpose data in the second and third dimension as shown in line 9 of Fig. 4a, a `zero-copy` kernel [3] is appealing. In this approach, GPU threads are used to initiate many small transfers between pinned memory on the host and the device memory. The array on the host is made device accessible using the `IS_DEVICE_PTR` clause. However, since using GPU compute resources for data copies may slow down other computations, we use the `zero-copy` approach only when complex stride patterns are involved.

In OpenMP, asynchronous execution can be achieved using the TASK clause for work on the host, NOWAIT for device kernels and data copies, and DEPEND to enforce the necessary synchronization between different *tasks*. However, when non-blocking libraries such as cuFFT or rocFFT are called from inside an OpenMP task, the desired asynchronism breaks down. Figure 4b illustrates the issue via a 1D FFT code fragment, in which Task A calls the non-blocking libraries to compute the transforms, Task B performs a host-to-device data copy, whereas Task C multiplies the result by a scalar. It is important to note here that the FFT library function is called from the host but device arrays need to be passed in to it. This is achieved using the USE_DEVICE_PTR clause which tells the OpenMP runtime to pass the device pointer of the array, to the library call. In OpenMP 5.1 usage of the USE_DEVICE_PTR with a Fortran pointer is depreciated, but the USE_DEVICE_ADDR clause can be used equivalently instead. Without the highlighted gray lines, the host thread that is executing task A will launch the FFT kernels to the GPU. Since these library calls are non-blocking, control will return immediately to the host thread, which proceeds to end the task. As a result, the device kernels launched may not have completed, or even started running, when Task A is considered "complete". The subsequent release of dependency between Tasks A and C allows the latter to start prematurely, leading to incorrect answers.

Correct execution can be ensured using the OpenMP 5.0 DETACH clause, with cudaStreamAddCallback, as shown in Fig. 4b. Now as the host thread launches the FFTs, it introduces a callback function (where ptr_cb is a pointer to it) into the stream in which the FFTs are executing. The host thread then detaches itself from task A to proceed with other operations. Once the FFTs finish executing on the device, the callback function is invoked which "fulfills" the event and completes task A, releasing the dependency and thus allowing Task C to execute correctly with the intended data. We also understand that OpenMP interop clause introduced in the 5.1 standard can help overcome this issue as well. However, so far we have chosen to use DETACH as it is part of the 5.0 standard and is expected to be supported by the compilers earlier.

2.2.4 Summary and Future Work

We have briefly addressed some key challenges encountered in developing a portable implementation of extreme scale 3D FFTs using OpenMP to target GPUs. Efficient strided data copies are performed using Zero-copy kernels and omp_target_memcpy_rect. Although full compiler support for it is not yet available, the OpenMP 5.0 feature DETACH is expected to resolve an issue of interoperability between non-blocking GPU library calls and OpenMP tasks. Future work will include testing the DETACH approach and using it to develop a batched asynchronous 3D FFT code (and eventually pseudo-spectral simulation of turbulence) capable of problem sizes beyond that recently achieved on Summit. Timing data over a range of problem sizes will be reported separately when available.

2.3 GridMini

2.3.1 Application Overview

Lattice Quantum Chromodynamics (LQCD) [16] is a computational framework that allows scientists to simulate strong interactions between the subatomic particles called quarks and gluons. LQCD provide crucial theoretical input to nuclear and high energy physics research, but its high computational demand limits the precision of the numerical results it can obtain. LQCD software has been written and optimized for many different computer architectures, including many/multi-core CPUs [9] and NVIDIA GPUs [10], to access as many computing resources as possible. Recently there has also been significant effort getting some of the major LQCD code bases to run on Intel and AMD GPUs. Portable programming models and frameworks such as Kokkos, HIP and SyCL have been investigated [7,18], and implementations for production-grade software are under way. Here we evaluate use of OpenMP as a portable programming model for Grid [8], a new lattice QCD library written in modern C++. Since Grid is a fairly large library, with multi-level abstractions, we use a mini-app based on Grid, `GridMini`[1], to evaluate several OpenMP features that are needed to support LQCD computing, including the `target` directive and associated data management clauses.

2.3.2 Application Motif

LQCD is a cartesian-grid based application, with a four-dimensional hypercubic mesh representing space and time. Each grid point represents a quark field variable, while the links between grid points approximate the gluon field variables. The main computational algorithm in lattice QCD is Markov Chain Monte Carlo simulations that are used to generate ensembles of background gluon fields. These gluon field ensembles are then used to perform measurement calculations which then lead to physical results. In both the Monte Carlo ensemble generation and measurement calculations, high-dimensional complex sparse matrix inversions are needed, which are usually done through iterative linear solvers such as conjugate gradient (CG). In CG, the key computational kernel is high-dimensional matrix-vector multiplication, the so-called Dslash operator in LQCD. There are several variants of the discrete Dslash operator depending on the discretization schemes used, but in modern lattice QCD simulations, all of them are very large sparse matrices, on or larger than the order of $10^{10} \times 10^{10}$. The arithmetic intensity for the Dslash operator is about 1.7 flops per byte in double precision. Since we use red-black preconditioning for CG, the arithmetic intensity is even lower, reduced to 0.85 flops per byte. Therefore LQCD computation is highly memory bandwidth bound, and the on-node performance of LQCD code depends on achieving as much memory bandwidth as possible on the given architecture. Grid has been highly optimized for many-core and multi-core CPUs with efficient SIMD vectorization, so our work focuses on performance and portability on the GPUs.

---

[1] https://github.com/meifeng/GridMini.

2.3.3   OpenMP Parallelization Strategy

Grid and GridMini support different architectures at the low level through C++ preprocessor macros, which may invoke different implementations. Since LQCD parallelization is mostly done to the `for` loops that iterate through lattice sites, an `accelerator_for` macro is defined, along with function attribute macros that may expand to different architecture-dependent definitions. Different implementations are enabled through macros passed through the compiler flag `-D`. The OpenMP paralleization for CPUs uses the standard `omp parallel for` directive, while for accelerator offloading, `omp target` directives are used. A relevant code snippet is shown in Listing 1.1.

```
1  #define naked_for(i,num,...) for ( uint64_t i=0;i<num;i++) { __VA_ARGS__ } ;
2  #define accelerator_inline __attribute__((always_inline)) inline
3  #ifdef OMPTARGET
4  #define accelerator_for(iterator,num,nsimd, ... ) \
5  { _Pragma("omp target teams distribute parallel for num_teams(nteams) thread_limit(gpu_threads)") \
6        naked_for(iterator, num, { __VA_ARGS__ }); }
7  #elif defined (GRID_OMP)
8  #define accelerator_for(iterator,num,nsimd, ... )   _Pragma("omp parallel for") naked_for(iterator, num, { __VA_ARGS__
   });
9  #endif
10
11 //other code omitted
12 accelerator_for(ss,me.size(),1,{
13            me[ss] = eval(ss,expr);
14            })
```

Listing 1.1. C++ macros that define the loop-level computation in GridMini.

A more tricky issue is the memory management, as Grid uses deeply nested data structures. In the CUDA implementation, `cudaMallocManaged` is used as the default dynamic memory allocator, so it is unnecessary to perform manual data management. Previously [5], we successfully used `cudaMallocManaged` together with OpenMP target offloading. But since it is CUDA specific, the code cannot run on other GPU architectures. Recently we have successfully replaced `cudaMallocManaged` with manual data management through OpenMP `map` clauses, but in order to do that, we have to explicitly expose the raw data pointer. An example of this is shown in Listing 1.2.

```
1  auto xv=x.View(); auto yv=y.View(); auto zv=z.View(); //x,y,z are arrays of SU(3) matrices
2  #pragma omp declare mapper(decltype(xv) x) map(x._odata[0:x.size()]) map(x)
3  extern uint32_t gpu_threads;
4  #pragma omp target enter data map(alloc:zv) map(to:xv) map(to:yv)
5  #pragma omp target teams distribute parallel for thread_limit(gpu_threads)
6  for(int64_t s=0;s<vol;s++) {
7        zv[s]=xv[s]+yv[s];
8  }
9  #pragma omp target exit data map (from:zv) map (delete:yv) map (delete:xv)
```

Listing 1.2. Manual data mapping in GridMini.

2.3.4   Results

We use the SU(3)×SU(3) benchmark (main computation is shown in Listing 1.2) to evaluate the GPU memory bandwidth, as this is highly indicative of the performance we can achieve on the GPUs since our application is memory-bandwidth bound. We compiled our code with LLVM/Clang++ built from the main LLVM repository on 01/17/2021, with the compiling options `std=c++14-g-fopenmp -fopenmp-cuda-mode-O3-fopenmp-targets=nvptx64-nvidia-cuda`. We used gcc/8.3.0 and cuda/11.0.3. The results for achieved GPU memory bandwidth of the NVIDIA V100 GPU on the NERSC's CoriGPU system as a function of the memory footprint are shown in Fig. 5, where we compare four different implementations. llvm map refers to the implementation with manual map clauses and malloc memory allocator. llvm managed uses cudaMallocManaged without any manual data mapping. llvm map+managed allocates memory with cudaMallocManaged, but also uses map to do data copying. nvcc managed is the reference CUDA implementation with cudaMallocManaged, compiled with the nvcc compiler.

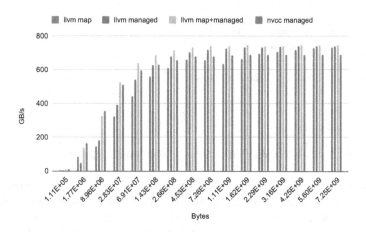

Fig. 5. Measured GPU memory bandwidth on NVIDIA V100 (Cori) with the SU(3)×SU(3) benchmark.

We find that the llvm map implementation generally performs a little worse than the llvm managed version. But if we combine the managed memory allocator with manual data mapping, in the llvm map+managed version, we obtain the best performance, which even outperforms the native CUDA implementation. In all these tests, 8 GPU threads per block is used, which gives the best performance compared to 16, 32 and up to 512 threads per block. This is probably due to the fact that the current data layout does not guarantee data coalescing.

3 Conclusions

The five applications presented in the paper(s) have different complexity and computational motifs. As seen in the BerkeleyGW application, some optimizations required line-level profiling information. It is therefore desirable for all OpenMP compilers to provide accurate symbolic debugging information without impeding compiler optimizations. For the WDMApp/XGC application, the main challenge was to tune a multi-level loop nest using OpenMP target offload constructs. Finding concurrency in applications and exploiting it using fine-grained parallelism is important for achieving good performance. With different vendor implementations, it becomes necessary for applications to be aware of equivalent OpenMP directives that may not be equally performant. For example, a parallel for construct was converted into a loop construct because this provided better performance with the NVIDIA OpenMP compiler.

The lessons learnt by the GAMESS team during the hackathon were the need to reduce overhead in atomic operations using chunks, strategies for target data and offloading blocks of code, and selecting the optimal number of threads per team. The GESTS application discussed some of the current challenges they are facing regarding the portable implementation of the extreme-scale 3D FFTs, a Fortran code, using OpenMP, and reported on efficient strided data copies. The detach clause is used to address the problem of synchronizing an OpenMP kernel that uses the depend clause with a prior asynchronous CUDA call. The GridMini application team has reported on their $SU(3) \times SU(3)$ benchmark in order to evaluate the GPU memory bandwidth, since the application is memory-bandwidth bound. They found that cudaMallocManaged allocators can be replaced with OpenMP unstructured maps for local host storage and that the use of cudaMallocManaged with OpenMP gave the best performance.

The more successful application teams had mini-apps to experiment with before porting the actual application. One major advantage of this approach is isolation of experimental changes for easy debugging and reproducibility. Having compiler experts at hand to help with ports is beneficial to applications, especially while resolving issues that appear in full-scale application runs but are not reproducible in mini-apps. Most applications also reported issues between OpenMP and vendor math libraries. It would be beneficial for applications if there were prepackaged compatible math libraries with all OpenMP compilers. Most of the applications were successfully able to use the OpenMP offload API as well as see speedup, which is very encouraging for OpenMP adoption by applications.

Acknowledgement. This research was supported by the Exascale Computing Project (17-SC-20-SC), a collaborative effort of two U.S. Department of Energy organizations (Office of Science and the National Nuclear Security Administration) responsible for the planning and preparation of a capable exascale ecosystem, including software, applications, hardware, advanced system engineering and early testbed platforms, in support of the nation's exascale computing imperative.

This research used resources of the Oak Ridge Leadership Computing Facility, which is a DOE Office of Science User Facility supported under Contract DE-AC05-00OR22725.

This research used resources of the National Energy Research Scientific Computing Center (NERSC), a U.S. Department of Energy Office of Science User Facility located at Lawrence Berkeley National Laboratory, operated under Contract No. DE-AC02-05CH11231.

This work was supported by the Argonne Leadership Computing Facility, which is a DOE Office of Science User Facility supported under Contract DE-AC02-06CH11357.

We'd like to thank all other mentors who volunteered their time and expertise during the hackathon.

References

1. Shimura, K., Nagase, S.: A new algorithm of two-electron repulsion integral calculations: a combination of Pople-Hehre and McMurchie-Davidson methods. Theor. Chem. Acc. **120**, 185–189 (2008). https://doi.org/10.1007/s00214-007-0295-5
2. Alexeev, Y., Kendall, R.A., Gordon, M.S.: The distributed data SCF. Comput. Phys. Commun. **143**(1), 69–82 (2002)
3. Appelhans, D.: Tricks, tips, and timings: the data movement strategies you need to know. In: GPU Technology Conference (2018)
4. Bak, S., et al.: OpenMP application experiences: porting to accelerated nodes. summitted
5. Bak, S., et al.: OpenMP application experiences: porting to accelerated nodes. Submitted to Parallel Computing (2020)
6. Barca, G.M.J., et al.: Recent developments in the general atomic and molecular electronic structure system. J. Chem. Phys. **152**(15), 154102 (2020)
7. Bi, Y.J., et al.: Lattice QCD package GWU-code and QUDA with hip. arXiv preprint arXiv:2001.05706 (2020)
8. Boyle, P., Yamaguchi, A., Cossu, G., Portelli, A.: Grid: A next generation data parallel c++ qcd library. arXiv preprint arXiv:1512.03487 (2015)
9. Boyle, P.A.: Machines and algorithms. arXiv preprint arXiv:1702.00208 (2017)
10. Clark, M.A., Babich, R., Barros, K., Brower, R.C., Rebbi, C.: Solving lattice QCD systems of equations using mixed precision solvers on GPUs. Comput. Phys. Commun. **181**, 1517–1528 (2010)
11. Dupuis, M., Rys, J., King, H.F.: Evaluation of molecular integrals over gaussian basis functions. J. Chem. Phys. **65**(1), 111–116 (1976)
12. Fedorov, D.G., Olson, R.M., Kitaura, K., Gordon, M.S., Koseki, S.: A new hierarchical parallelization scheme: generalized distributed data interface (GDDI), and an application to the fragment molecular orbital method (FMO). J. Comput. Chem. **25**(6), 872–880 (2004)
13. Fletcher, G.D.: Recursion formula for electron repulsion integrals over Hermite polynomials. Int. J. Quantum Chem. **106**(2), 355–360 (2006)
14. Fletcher, G.D., Schmidt, M.W., Bode, B.M., Gordon, M.S.: The distributed data interface In Gamess. Comput. Phys. Commun. **128**(1), 190–200 (2000)
15. Google: Google benchmark - a microbenchmark support library. https://github.com/google/benchmark
16. Gupta, R.: Introduction to lattice QCD: Course. In: Les Houches Summer School in Theoretical Physics, Session 68: Probing the Standard Model of Particle Interactions (1997)
17. Ishihara, T., Gotoh, T., Kaneda, Y.: Study of high Reynolds number isotropic turbulence by direct numerical simulations. Annu. Rev. Fluid Mech. **41**, 165–180 (2009)
18. Joó, B., et al.: Performance portability of a wilson dslash stencil operator miniapp using kokkos and SYCL. In: 2019 IEEE/ACM International Workshop on Performance, Portability and Productivity in HPC (P3HPC), pp. 14–25. IEEE (2019)
19. King, H.F., Dupuis, M.: Numerical integration using Rys polynomials. J. Comput. Phys. **21**(2), 144–165 (1976)
20. Kitware: Cmake. https://cmake.org/
21. McMurchie, L.E., Davidson, E.R.: One- and two-electron integrals over cartesian gaussian functions. J. Comput. Phys. **26**(2), 218–231 (1978)

22. Mironov, V., Alexeev, Y., Keipert, K., D'mello, M., Moskovsky, A., Gordon, M.S.: An efficient mpi/openmp parallelization of the hartree-fock method for the second generation of intel® xeon phi^{TM} processor. In: Proceedings of the International Conference for High Performance Computing, Networking, Storage and Analysis. SC 2017, Association for Computing Machinery, New York, NY, USA (2017)
23. Mironov, V., Moskovsky, A., D'Mello, M., Alexeev, Y.: An efficient MPI/OpenMP parallelization of the Hartree-Fock-Roothaan method for the first generation of Intel® Xeon phi^{TM} processor architecture. Int. J. High Perform. Comput. Appl. **33**(1), 212–224 (2019)
24. Pham, B.Q., Gordon, M.S.: Hybrid distributed/shared memory model for the RI-MP2 method in the fragment molecular orbital framework. J. Chem. Theor. Comput. **15**(10), 5252–5258 (2019)
25. Pople, J.A., Hehre, W.J.: Computation of electron repulsion integrals involving contracted gaussian basis functions. J. Comput. Phys. **27**(2), 161–168 (1978)
26. Ravikumar, K., Appelhans, D., Yeung, P.K.: GPU acceleration of extreme scale pseudo-spectral simulations of turbulence using asynchronism. In: Proceedings of The International Conference for High Performance Computing, Networking and Storage Analysis SC (2019), Denver, CO, USA. ACM, New York, NY, USA
27. Rys, J., Dupuis, M., King, H.F.: Computation of electron repulsion integrals using the Rys quadrature method. J. Comput. Chem. **4**(2), 154–157 (1983)
28. Schlegel, H.B.: An efficient algorithm for calculating ab initio energy gradients using s, p cartesian gaussians. J. Chem. Phys. **77**(7), 3676–3681 (1982)
29. SOLLVE and NERSC: January 2021 ECP OpenMP Hackathon by SOLLVE and NERSC (2021 [Online]), the event happened on 22, 27, 28, 29 Jan 2021. https://sites.google.com/view/ecpomphackjan2021. Accessed 7 Apr 2021
30. Yeung, P.K., Sreenivasan, K.R., Pope, S.B.: Effects of finite spatial and temporal resolution on extreme events in direct numerical simulations of incompressible isotropic turbulence. Phys. Rev. Fluids **3**, 064603 (2018)
31. Yeung, P.K., Zhai, X.M., Sreenivasan, K.R.: Extreme events in computational turbulence. Proc. Nat. Acad. Sci. **112**, 12633–12638 (2015)

An Empirical Investigation of OpenMP Based Implementation of Simplex Algorithm

Arkaprabha Banerjee[1], Pratvi Shah[1], Shivani Nandani[1], Shantanu Tyagi[1], Sidharth Kumar[2], and Bhaskar Chaudhury[1(✉)]

[1] Group in Computational Science and High Performance Computing, DA-IICT, Gandhinagar, India
bhaskar_chaudhury@daiict.ac.in
[2] University of Alabama at Birmingham, Birmingham, USA

Abstract. This paper presents a shared-memory based parallel implementation of the standard simplex algorithm. The simplex algorithm is a popular technique for linear programming used to solve minimization and maximization problems that are subject to linear constraints. The simplex algorithm reduces the optimization problem to a series of iterative matrix operations. In this paper we perform an empirical analysis of our algorithm and also study the impact of the density of the underlying matrix on the overall performance. We observed a maximum speedup of 10.2 at 16 threads and also demonstrated that our proposed parallel algorithm scales well over a range of matrix densities. We also make an important observation that the effect of increasing the number of constraints is more significant than the effect of varying the number of variables.

Keywords: Large-scale problems · Linear programming · Simplex · Parallel computing · Scalable algorithms · OpenMP

1 Introduction

Linear programming, also known as linear optimization, is a method to achieve the optimal outcome for a minimization or maximization problem, subject to a set of linear relationships. Among the various methods available for solving linear programming problems, simplex is the most widely used algorithm, both commercially and academically [1]. The storage and computational overhead make the standard simplex method an expensive approach for solving large linear programming problems. Apart from the computational cost, the standard simplex algorithm also requires the previous iteration to be completed before the new solution can be computed, thus restricting the scope of parallelization [2].

Even though the simplex algorithm is primarily sequential, several attempts have been made during the last decades to parallelize it. There are broadly two implementations for the Simplex Algorithm: The Standard Simplex Method and The Revised Simplex Method (RSM). The Standard Simplex method refers to

© Springer Nature Switzerland AG 2021
S. McIntosh-Smith et al. (Eds.): IWOMP 2021, LNCS 12870, pp. 96–110, 2021.
https://doi.org/10.1007/978-3-030-85262-7_7

the original algorithm proposed by George Dantzig [1]. RSM, on the other hand, seeks to efficiently implement the Standard Simplex algorithm by employing a host of Matrix operations specifically built to exploit the sparsity of matrices [3,4]. This means that the RSM is mathematically equivalent to the standard simplex method but differs in implementation. In RSM, instead of having to compute and store the full table in each iteration, it is only necessary to keep track of some of the information, reducing the redundancy, and use the matrix operations directly on the relevant data. This matrix-oriented approach allows for greater computational efficiency, as it exploits, the sparsity of the matrix using matrix inversion techniques optimized for sparse matrices. Apart from certain GPU-based implementations, RSM's optimizations strategies fall short for denser matrices. Furthermore, the steps employed have a limited scope for parallelization [1].

As we moved to the multi processor era, the importance shifted to running the standard algorithm on multiple cores. In 2000, Maros and Mitra presented a cooperative parallel version of the sparse implementation of the revised simplex method for linear programs on distributed memory multiprocessors [5]. Ploskas presented a parallel implementation of the standard simplex algorithm using a personal computer with two cores. Due to dense matrices and heavy communication, the ratio of computation to communication is extremely low and Ploskas' computational results show that a linear speedup is hard to achieve even with carefully selected communication optimization [3,5]. Later many other optimization strategies were proposed [6] such as using certain linear algebraic techniques necessary to exploit the dual block-angular structure of the problem or parallelizing the matrix inverse step based upon GPU implementations. Most of these improvements were primarily done on the revised simplex algorithm [5]. A parallel implementation based on combination of CPU and GPU was also proposed in 2016 [7].

In this paper, we analyze the performance gains of an efficient parallel implementation of the Standard Simplex Algorithm over the sequential version, using a shared-memory architecture. The standard simplex version has been chosen over the revised method owing to known issues of scalability for denser matrices. Here, we define the density of a matrix as the ratio of non-zero elements to the total elements in the matrix. Our study revolves around the following parameters which will help in effective understanding of the parallel implementation of the Standard Simplex Algorithm proposed in this paper:

- Explore the scalability of the algorithm over a range of densities
- Explore the effect on varying the number of constraints
- Explore the effect on varying the number of variables
- Effectively exploiting the SIMD units to update the matrix.

We have analyzed the most important aspects of the algorithm based on the above parameters and the underlying hardware architecture, which to the best of our knowledge, have not been explored and reported in the existing literature. The state-of-the-art implementation does not talk about the performance of the algorithm on varying the density of the matrices. The code has been run on shared-memory architecture systems. All processors share a single view of data and the communication between them can be as fast as memory accesses to a particular location with a lot of intra-node parallelisms to exploit and our implementation is designed specifically for this purpose.

2   Serial Algorithm

Any linear programming (LP) problem can be modelled into the following standard form:

$$\text{maximize } \mathbf{Z} = \mathbf{CX}$$
$$\text{subject to } \mathbf{AX} = \mathbf{B} \qquad\qquad \text{where } X \geq 0$$

where A is the constraint matrix, B forms the constant vector matrix and C corresponds to the objective function coefficients. The objective function is the function whose value is to be either minimized or maximized subject to the given set of constraints given by Z. The X vector is the required solution to the LP problem. After the initial modifications, the problems are formulated in the above representation for solving via the Simplex Algorithm.

The simplex method is an iterative procedure for getting the most feasible solution. In this method, we keep transforming the value of basic variables to get the maximum value for the objective function. Within the current context the following assumptions have been made for the linear inequality problems:

- All problems are maximization problems. In the event of a minimization problem, the objective function is multiplied by -1.
- All problems are to be initially considered in the form of less than or equal ($\leq$) inequalities.

$$AX \leq B$$

The following steps illustrate the working of the serial simplex algorithm.

1. Introduce Slack Variables to convert inequality to equality constraints ($AX = B$). The slack variables are known as basic variables and the original ones as non-basic. All slack variables have a zero coefficient in the objective function.
2. Create an initial table[1] consisting of n non-basic variables and m-basic variables. The table consists of the coefficient of the linear constraint variables and the coefficients of the objective function. The slack variables form the initial basis.

		C_j	C_1	C_2	$\cdots$	0	0			
C_B	X_B	B	x_1	x_2	$\cdots$	x_{n+1}	x_{n+2}	$\cdots$	Min Ratio	Row Operations
C_{n+1}	X_{n+1}	B_1	A_{11}	A_{12}	$\cdots$	1	0	$\cdots$		
C_{n+2}	X_{n+2}	B_2	A_{21}	A_{22}	$\cdots$	0	1	$\cdots$		
$\vdots$	$\vdots$	$\vdots$	$\vdots$	$\vdots$	$\vdots$	$\vdots$	$\vdots$	$\vdots$		
$Z_j - C_j$		ans	$-C_1$	$-C_2$	$\cdots$	$\cdots$	0	0		

---

[1] **Note:** The table mentioned in Step 2 is not in the block-structured notation. The sample table has been employed in order to effectively explain the serial algorithm.

3. The value of the objective function with respect to every variable (Z_j) at that instant can be calculated by summing up the product of the objective function coefficients of the variable in the basis and the coefficient associated to other variables in the same row of the table.

4. Calculate $Z_j - C_j$ for all the variables. C_j represents the coefficient of the variable in contention in the objective function. The column with the maximum value (< 0) represents the entering variable for the basis in the next iteration. This column is known as the pivot column. If all values of reduced cost ($Z_j - C_j$) are ≥ 0 then the optimal solution has been reached.

5. Calculate the ratio of the elements of B with the corresponding coefficients of the pivot column. The row representing the minimum positive value of the ratio represents the variable that will leave the basis in the next iteration. This row is known as the pivot row. If all the values of the replacement ratio are either negative or infinite, then it represents a case of unbounded solution.

6. The intersection value of the Pivot row and Pivot column gives the value of the pivot coefficient. Divide the pivot row with the pivot coefficient. Subtract all the other rows from the new modified pivot row by a multiplier such that all the other values in the pivot column apart from the pivot coefficient become zero. In order to prepare for the next iteration, swap the entering and leaving variables along with all the other associated values.

7. Go to step 3. Repeat until the algorithm ends.

An example of the above-mentioned algorithm can be seen in Appendix A.

3   Parallel Algorithm

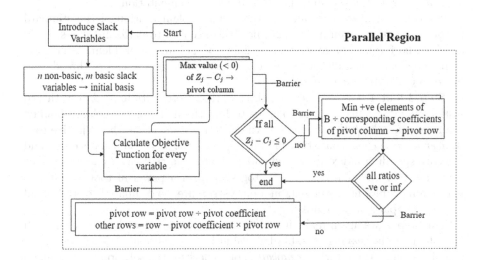

Fig. 1. Flowchart for the parallel implementation. Nodes with an overlying boundary in the background represent regions where multiple threads work concurrently.

Researchers till now have stated that the serial time complexity of the simplex algorithm is generally a polynomial, but for the worst case, the time complexity tends to increase exponentially [6]. The execution time depends on two factors: time taken for each iteration and secondly, the number of iterations which will be equal to the number of pivots that need to be traversed in order to reach the optimal point in the n-dimensional space which satisfies the given constraints [8]. The latter factor makes the evaluation of time complexity a highly involved task, as every problem depending on the density and the structure of the constraint matrix gives rise to a novel situation.

Efforts to effectively modify the algorithm, by evaluating the different cases, are being carried out in order to generalize the time complexity expression [6]. From a generic standpoint, one can assume that the time complexity increases with the number of equations or the number of variables, however, this is not guaranteed. For certain cases, it tends to the worst exponential time complexity, leading to an exceptionally large number of iterations to obtain a solution, even for relatively smaller problem sizes [9].

In order to understand how the serial algorithm can be parallelized, the time distribution among various steps of the naive serial version (Sect. 2) is analyzed. The results show that Step 6 constitutes the major portion of the run time with more than 99.5% contribution followed by Steps 3 and 4 (or Step 7), with Step 5 taking the least time.

3.1   Implementation

In this Section we provide a methodology for parallel implementation using OpenMP which optimizes its serial counterpart mentioned in Sect. 2. Figure 1, gives an overview of the steps involved in the implementation.

Steps 1 and 2 are the same as the serial implementation of the standard simplex algorithm given in Sect. 2, since it is essential to perform these steps in a sequential format before solving the linear programming problem. After these steps, we create a parallel region and define the required number of threads and move to OpenMP implementation.

Step 3 and 4 now uses all the threads that were initialized. Every thread works among a defined set of columns to find the index of the column holding the maximum absolute value among the negative elements in the objective row. A *user-defined class* consisting of the values of the maximum data entry and the corresponding index are stored and evaluated via the *reduction* clause. This class notation and reduction clause together form a powerful tool to evaluate maximum or minimum elements in a data structure, as compared to traditional explicit comparison mechanisms.

For Step 5, we again make use of the *reduction* clause with the user-defined class to find the leaving variable by evaluating the Minimum Ratio row-wise. Finally, a single thread with a *nowait* clause checks if the solution is unbounded or not present, and exit the parallel region if the solution satisfies the unbounded constraints.

In Step 6, the pivot row is now updated concurrently among the threads. Once the pivot row has been updated, all the remaining rows are updated. The rows are evaluated via the *pragma for* construct, while the iterations among columns has also been vectorized via the *simd* construct. Simultaneous modifications are possible because there are no dependencies among columns or rows.

Steps 3 and 4 (as Step 7), are again performed in the parallel region with the mechanism mentioned above. A single thread finally updates all iteration-specific local variables. Finally, the loop continues until a solution reached, or an exit clause is triggered for 'Unbounded Solution/No Possible solution'.

The above steps are implemented using a block-structured matrix notation having dimensions $(m + 1) \times (n + m + 1)$ (where m is the number of constraints and n, the number of variables) as proposed in the case of the Standard Simplex method of Dantzig [1]. The same is given as $\begin{bmatrix} A & B \\ -C & 0 \end{bmatrix}$ where A is an $m \times n$ matrix, B is an $m \times 1$ vector, and C is an $1 \times n$ matrix.

Algorithm 1. Parallel Implementation of Simplex Algorithm

```
1   //Get the dimension of the table
2   Rows(R)= m + 1,
3   Columns(C) = m + n + 1
4   Initialize  & load the data in table
5   Algorithm time starts from here
6
7   # pragma omp parallel <shared variables>
8   {
9   //Step 3 & 4
10  # pragma omp for <schedule> <reduction>
11  for(int j=0;j<C;j++){
12      find max negative value (max_value)
13      from reduced cost row
14  }
15
16  Corresponding index=max_index
17  & column=Pivot Col
18
19  #pragma omp single nowait
20  max_value=0
21
22  do{
23      // Step 5
24      #pragma omp for <schedule><reduction>
25      for(int j=0;j<R;j++) {
26          find the min value
27          (min_value) from Min Ratio column
28          do count++ for negative values
29      }
30
31      #pragma omp single nowait
32      {
33          if count == R
34              there is unbounded/no solution
35              flag=False break
```

```
36          else
37              Row corresponding to
38              min_value is the
39              Pivot row with index= min_index
40      }
41
42      // Step 6
43      pivot = table[min_index][max_index]
44      #pragma omp barrier
45
46      #pragma omp parallel for
47      for(int i=0;i<C;i++)
48          update Pivot Row
49      #pragma omp parallel for
50      for(int i=0;i<C;i++)
51          #pragma omp simd
52          for(int i=0;i<R;i++)
53              update all elements except
54              that of Pivot row
55      }
56
57      //Step 3 & 4 repeated
58      #pragma omp for <schedule> <reduction>
59          for(int i=0;i<C;i++)
60              find the new reduced cost values
61              for updated table
62              countNegative++ for negative values
63
64      #pragma omp single
65          Update the initial conditions
66      }while(countNegative and flag)
67  }
68
69  //Algorithm time ends here
70  Solution = table[Rows][Columns]
```

3.2   Optimization Strategies

After analyzing the time bifurcation and identifying the steps which take significant amount of time we conducted experiments to optimize the code. The following methodologies were explored to make the algorithm more efficient.

Optimal Scheduling Clause and Load Balancing: As shown in Fig. 2, for larger problem sizes, the performance for static scheduling clauses is possibly hampered when some threads take more time to complete their share of work. Even for dynamic scheduling, with a completely random thread allocation, enhanced performance may require guided scheduling. Thus, guided scheduling mechanisms were used to effectively tackle the load balancing problem.

Optimal SIMD Units: In order to find the SIMD units for vectorization in Step 6 above, multiple values of SIMD units ranging from 2 to 8 were considered. The optimal SIMD length was found to be 4 for our implementation, just half of the total number of lanes. We assume that the use of all SIMD lanes generates excessive overhead for using additional SIMD units, and the use of fewer than half the SIMD lanes under-utilizes a SIMD unit's resources (Fig. 3).

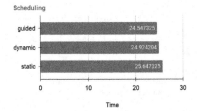

Fig. 2. Scheduling on 512×512 dataset of 0.5 density

Fig. 3. Variation of simdlen()

3.3   Algorithm Analysis

In this section the algorithm is analyzed to provide a basis for drawing out conclusions.

Cache Miss Analysis Assume that the number of rows is 'r' and the number of columns is 'c', while the matrix is stored in row-major format in the memory. Theoretical analysis of each step led to the following expression: The steps mentioned below are the corresponding steps in the Serial Algorithm mentioned in Sect. 2.

   Steps 3 and 4 access the matrix row wise (considering a cache line of 64 bytes and double data-type): c/8 misses

   Step 5 requires us to access the matrix column-wise: r misses

   Step 6 update almost the entire matrix : $\frac{r*c}{8}$. Thus Miss ratio in a single iteration of the overall loop would be

$$MissRatio = \frac{\frac{c}{8} + r + \frac{r*c}{8}}{r + c + r*c} \approx \frac{1}{8}$$

In order to verify the above miss ratio, profiling was performed via **Valgrind** using the memcheck and callgrind tools on BENCH2 for a 256×256 problem of density 0.5. The cache simulator simulates a computer with a split L1 cache (separate instruction I1 and data D1), which is backed up by a single second-level cache (L2). This is consistent with the architecture of most modern machines' caches. The reads/writes and respective misses recorded after profiling for L1 data and L2 unified cache are (Table 1):

Table 1. D refs (Data cache memory reads), D1 misses (D1 cache data misses but found in L2), LLd misses (L2 cache data misses but found outside it), LL refs (Combined L2 cache references), LL misses (Combined L2 cache misses)

	D refs	D1 misses	LLd misses	D1 miss rate	LL refs	LL misses	LL miss rate
Serial	39,028,802,003	66,529,666	28,606	0.1705%	66,547,316	31,020	0.0466%
openMP	44,301,959,277	66,980,319	29,457	0.1512%	66,998,585	32,331	0.0483%

The key observations to be made here is that that the D1 cache miss rate has gone down in the parallel (OpenMP) version as compared to the serial version. Furthermore, the cache miss rate is significantly less than what is expected theoretically. This can be explained by the fact that instead of bringing in cache blocks one by one, the compiler automatically optimizes this procedure based on the repetitive access patterns that it finds with every iteration. One such compiler optimization is pre-fetching. Pre-fetches are possible only if the memory addresses can be determined ahead of time. However, for extremely small table sizes, the cache miss rate is much higher on account of ineffective compiler optimizations and follows the standard expected values.

Analyzing the Nature of the Algorithm. The serial implementation of the simplex algorithm, Sect. 2, was evaluated for understanding the nature of the algorithm, in particular, whether the algorithm is CPU-bound or memory-bound. In our algorithm we consider m as the number of constraints and n as the number of variables. So, the size of the table will be $(m + 1) \times (n + m + 1)$, and let $a = m + 1$ and $b = n + m + 1$.

Now, let's consider a single iteration of the **do** loop, as this represents the most granular as well as comprehensive segment of this iterative algorithm. An analysis of its steps will provide a basic picture of the algorithmic operation. We obtained the following expression after analyzing the number of computations and memory access counts:

$$\texttt{Computations} = 3a + b + a + 2ab + 6b$$
$$\texttt{Memory Access} = 2a + b + a + 2ab + 2b$$

The above figures will be multiplied by the total number of pivots which is a constant factor, depending upon the problem. So, barring that factor, we can state that our implementation of the simplex algorithm has more computations in comparison to memory access and thus, being CPU-bound it will be more suitable to be parallelized on a shared-memory architecture.

4   Experimental Results and Observations

We have implemented our algorithm on two systems with the following hardware architecture.

Specifications	BENCH1	BENCH2
Model Name	Intel(R) Xeon(R) Silver 4214R CPU @ 2.40 GHz	Intel(R) Xeon(R) CPU E5-2640 v3 @ 2.60 GHz
Core(s) per socket	12	8
Socket(s)	2	2
L1d cache	768 KB	32 KB
L2 cache	24 MB	0.256 MB
L3 cache	33 MB	20.48 MB
GNU GCC version	9.3.0	10.2.0

The primary motivation for using two different hardware architectures was to understand the performance of this algorithm on different hardware cores with large and small L1 caches and large and small L2 caches per core. The above data represents the total cache of the system in consideration. BENCH1 has 1MB L2 cache per core while BENCH2 has 256KB of L2 cache per core. L3 cache is shared in both cases.

We have compared certain selected results with the current state-of-the-art algorithm implementation which was implemented on a system with four AMD Opteron 6376 processors with 16 cores, totalizing 64 cores, 768KB L1 and 16MB L2 individual caches per core, and 16Mbytes L3 caches per socket, running Ubuntu 16.04.2 LTS [5].

For reproducibility, we have made use of the standard NETLIB LP dataset[2], which comes in the specific mps format, consisting of all the necessary variables and their respective coefficients. In addition to the Netlib dataset, we made use of a computationally generated dataset of specific dimensions and density [10]. The generated datasets do not guarantee a finite solution, and hence, some anomalies might arise in the analysis of those datasets, but they are not relevant to the behavior of the algorithm. The results have been verified using standard reference codes, and the answer is consistent over multiple thread configurations.

Keeping into consideration the configuration of our machines and the fact that in the worst case the Simplex algorithm can take exponential time to solve, we limit our observations to the maximum number of variables to 4096 and the number of constraints as 512 in the primal formulation. We have also analyzed their dual counterpart. For most of the cases we have either fixed variables to 256 and varied the number of constraints or vice versa, as this allowed us to efficiently exploit the different levels of the underlying memory hierarchy of the system.

---

[2] http://www.netlib.org/.

All mean execution times have been measured in seconds. All standard graphs have been plotted with respect to the run time on the BENCH1 unless mentioned otherwise.

4.1   NETLIB Dataset

In this section we evaluated the standard Netlib dataset using our serial and parallel code.

From Fig. 4 we observed that the speedup for all the datasets remained within the linear upperbound and we could also see that for smaller datasets the speedup for large number of threads was very low due to the synchronisation overhead. The decrease in speedup after certain problem size is due to fetching of the data from L3 cache as we have 1MB per core L2 cache and the size of dataset exceeds that limit.

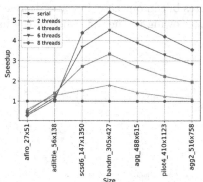

Fig. 4. Speedup for standard netlib datasets (performed on BENCH 1)

4.2   Variation of the Number of Variables

In this section, we examine LP problems of 256 constraints and variables varying from 256 to 4096 with a density of 0.5. We can verify from the hardware architecture that the data with this large problem size would be fetched from the L2 or L3 cache. This lead to an increase in fetching time and overhead incurred due to the necessity to maintain consistent copies of the data across all the processors.

In Fig. 5 (256 constraints) it is observed that the speedup for each thread size increases (up to a point at mid-size) and then decreases. Peak values for large thread counts occur at larger problem sizes. At the largest problem size, the reduction in the peak performance is greatest for small thread counts (1, 2 and 4) and smallest for the largest thread counts (8,12 and 16).

We could observe superlinear speedup in the case of 2 and 4 threads for certain problem sizes. Due to *pragma omp for*, there is coarse parallelization, whereas the use of *simd* enables finer parallelization within each thread and specifying the vector length in *simdlen()* can give us control over the extent of parallelization needed/supported by the system. Thus, the superlinear speedup can be attributed to this increased parallelization within each thread.

From Fig. 6 we see that the speedup achieved in the BENCH2 is similar to the one achieved in the BENCH1, till the problem size fits in the L1 and L2 cache of the respective systems. After that, we witness a drop in the speedup. In the case of BENCH2, when the work allocated per thread (in terms of the size of the table) exceeds the L2 cache size and results in data being continuously fetched from the L3 cache, an increase in the mean execution time occurs. BENCH1 had larger L1 and L2 cache sizes leading to higher speedup for its simulation.

Our implementation observes a maximum speedup of 10.2 with 16 threads for 256×2048 which is comparable to the maximum speedup of ≈ 10 for a problem size of 256×4096 with 16 threads in a state-of-the-art implementation, shown in [5]. Secondly, we see that in the state-of-the-art implementation, although the relative trend is similar, the speedup increases till 16 threads for all problem sizes but in our case, it starts decreasing from 4 to 8 threads for smaller problem sizes owing to the difference in the hardware architecture.

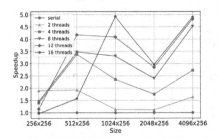

Fig. 5. Speedup (256 constraints)

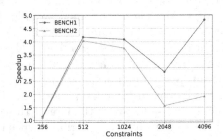

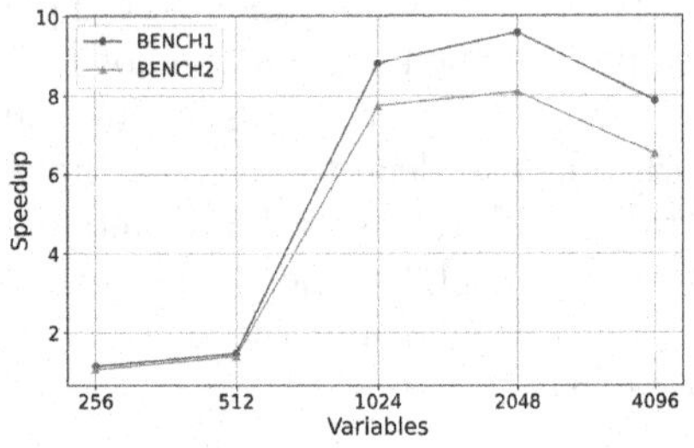

Fig. 6. Speedup (256 constraints and 12 threads)

4.3   Variation of the Number of Constraints

In this section, we examine LP problems for 256 variables and constraints varying from 256 to 4096 with a density of 0.5.

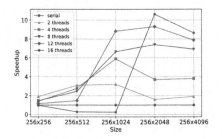

Fig. 7. Speedup (256 variables)

Fig. 8. Speedup (256 variables and 12 threads)

On increasing the constraints for 256 variables, the speedup increases faster (because of the number of iterations increase), as compared to when the number of variables increased. As a result of this, the drop in speedup on increasing threads, which occurred in the previous section for 256 constraints(Fig. 5), now happens at a lower threshold and is evident from Fig. 7 and Fig. 8. For 2048 constraints with 256 variables the problem size is about 36 MB which exceeds the L3 cache limit for the BENCH1. Thus we observe a drop. We observe a temporary increase for 4096 × 256 since the problem has no solution and has a very low execution time.

As compared to the state-of-the-art implementation, for problems with 256 variables, we see that in both the implementations, the speedup increases for larger problem size as threads increase to 16 and vice versa is seen for smaller problem sizes where the speedup first increases and then decreases as the threads increase to 16. We see smaller speedup values, in general, as compared to the state-of-the-art implementations. This can be attributed to the smaller cache architecture for L2 and L3 levels.

4.4   Variation in Matrix Density

The standard Simplex Algorithm for OpenMP was initially proposed in [5] primarily for dense matrices. In this section, we attempt to explore its scalability to lower densities. We have considered 512 × 512 matrices with densities varying from 0.1 to 1 in steps of 0.1. These experiments were performed on BENCH1.

Sparse problems often take fewer number of iterations to be solved, as compared to dense matrices, owing to their inherent matrix structure and the number of manipulations involved. Therefore, the synchronization overhead has a greater precedence, and speedup is reduced. Hence from a generic standpoint, sparse matrices may have a slightly less speedup as compared to dense matrices in this algorithm. The final result however depends on the actual problem structure. We can see from Fig. 9, that the speedup in all the cases remains almost constant or increases a little when the density of the matrices increases. Hence, the parallel algorithm is scalable in that nature.

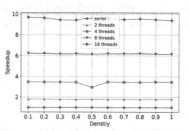

Fig. 9. Speedup vs Matrix Density

4.5   Discussion

As the number of threads increase, the problem partitioning also increases. Since every iteration needs to modify the entire table, using more threads increases the synchronization overhead, while using a lower number of threads reduces the parallelization. We achieve an optimal limit on the number of threads somewhere in between. We could also conclude that there exists a critical problem size for each thread where the nature of the speedup changes from increasing to decreasing on either side of that critical number. This critical value is achieved at a larger problem size when using a larger thread count.

We observed that smaller problems performed better with a lower number of threads as the overhead associated with a larger number of threads significantly increases the run-time. This overhead is mainly attributed to two factors:

synchronisation overhead amongst the threads, and false sharing when there are multiple threads working on the same cache line(primarily in step 6). However, on increasing the problem size, the synchronization overhead takes less precedence as the scope for parallelization increases leading to higher speedups.

In general, efficiency decreases with an increase in the number of threads. At large problem sizes with high thread counts, even though the absolute speedup is high, the efficiency is quite low. This can be verified from Fig. 10. For larger problems with higher iteration counts, we need to maintain synchronization even among a single iteration, highlighted by *pragma omp barrier* constructs in the parallel implementation. This is why the synchronization overhead plays a major role.

As compared to the state-of-the-art implementation, for problems with 256 constraints, we see similarity for smaller number of variables where efficiency decreases as threads increases for a given number of variables. The comparison for 2 threads is not valid due to their assumption that the time for serial implementation is double that of using 2 threads while we did not make that assumption.

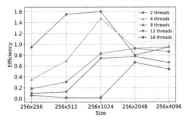

Fig. 10. Efficiency (256 constraints)

5   Conclusion

The theoretical understanding of the standard simplex algorithm supported by the experimental observations from our OpenMP based parallel implementation on two different architectures for a variety of problem sizes enabled us to critically analyze the problem. In our CPU based parallel implementation, vectorization contributes significantly towards improving the performance, however, this is constrained by the hardware properties of the system as well as the problem structure. Our parallel algorithm proved to be fairly scalable, in terms of relative speedup, for the matrices of varying densities (in range of 0.1 to 1).

We could also conclude that the number of constraints has a greater factor of proportionality while determining speedup in comparison to the number of variables. This is because the problem size or the number of computations increases more with the increase in the number of constraints in comparison to the number of variables. This can also be explained using two types of overhead, synchronization overhead and/or the overhead due to completely filled cache leading to delayed memory access. Increasing the number of constraints for the chosen problem sizes lead to cache fulfillment hence the drop in the performance, whereas on increasing variables, the synchronisation overhead incurred due to false sharing, dominates and in a bid to maintain consistent values, in the shared L3 cache and higher memory units, we incurred a drop in the performance. The source code pertaining to this work is being made publicly available under a permissive open source licence at Github https://github.com/arkaprabha10/Simplex-Algorithm.

A Appendix: Serial Algorithm - Working Example

This example illustrates the standard simplex algorithm steps mentioned in Sect. 2. Steps 1 to 7 are the basic steps of the algorithm, whereas steps 8 and onward are for a second iteration.

Suppose, $Z = 3x_1 + 4x_2$
Subject to,
$x_1 + 2x_2 \leq 4$
$3x_1 + 2x_2 \leq 6$
$x_1, x_2 \geq 0$

1. Introduce slack variables to get,
   $Z = 3x_1 + 4x_2 + 0x_3 + 0x_4$
   Subject to,
   $x_1 + 2x_2 + x_3 + 0x_4 = 4$
   $3x_1 + 2x_2 + 0x_3 + x_4 = 6$
   $x_1, x_2 \geq 0$

2. Table of coefficients is made with slack variables as basic variables.

		Ci	3	4	0	0	Min Ratio	Operation
Cb	Xb	b	a1	a2	a3	a4		
0	x3	4	1	2	1	0		
0	x4	6	3	2	0	1		
Zj - Cj								

3. The $Z_j - C_j$ differences are evaluated.

4. The smallest value (-4 here) for x_2 is determined. It becomes the new entering variable and the corresponding column becomes the pivot column.

		Ci	3	4	0	0	Min Ratio	Operation
Cb	Xb	b	a1	a2	a3	a4		
0	x3	4	1	2	1	0		
0	x4	6	3	2	0	1		
Zj - Cj		0	-3	-4	0	0		

5. The min ratios are determined and the smallest value (2) is set for x_3 variable, which becomes the leaving variable, and the corresponding row becomes the pivot row.

		Ci	3	4	0	0	Min Ratio	Operation
Cb	Xb	b	a1	a2	a3	a4		
0	x3	4	1	2	1	0	2	
0	x4	6	3	2	0	1	3	
Zj - Cj		0	-3	-4	0	0		

6. The pivot row is divided by the pivot coefficient (2).

		Ci	3	4	0	0	Min Ratio	Operation
Cb	Xb	b	a1	a2	a3	a4		
4	x2	2	1/2	1	1/2	0		R1' = R1'/2
0	x4	2	2	0	-1	1		R2' = R2 - 2R1'
Zj - Cj								

7. Now we have the new basis variables as x_2 and x_4. We again evaluate $Z_j - C_j$ values.

8. The smallest value for differences is -1, and is set in x_1, which is the new entering variable, with the corresponding column set as the pivot column.

		Ci	3	4	0	0	Min Ratio	Operation
Cb	Xb	b	a1	a2	a3	a4		
4	x2	2	1/2	1	1/2	0		
0	x4	2	2	0	-1	1		
Zj - Cj		8	-1	0	2	0		

9. The min ratios are determined and the smallest value (1) is set in x_4, which becomes the leaving variable, and the corresponding row becomes the pivot row.

		Ci	3	4	0	0	Min Ratio	Operation
Cb	Xb	b	a1	a2	a3	a4		
4	x2	2	1/2	1	1/2	0	4	
0	x4	2	2	0	-1	1	1	
Zj - Cj		8	-1	0	2	0		

10. The pivot row is divided by the pivot coefficient (2).

		Ci	3	4	0	0	Min Ratio	Operation
Cb	Xb	b	a1	a2	a3	a4		
4	x2	3/2	0	1	3/4	-1/4		R1' = R1 - R2'
3	x1	1	1	0	-1/2	1/2		R2' = R2/2
Zj - Cj								

11. Now we have the new basis variables as x_2 and x_1. We again evaluate all $Z_j - C_j$ values. All values are ≥ 0 and we terminate the algorithm with: $x_1 = 1$, $x_2 = \frac{3}{2}$, and $Z = 9$

References

1. Dantzig, G.B.: Origins of the simplex method. In: A History of Scientific Computing, pp. 141–151. Association for Computing Machinery, New York (1990). https://doi.org/10.1145/87252.88081
2. Borgwardt, K.H.: A Probabilistic Analysis of the Simplex Method. Springer, Heidelberg (1986). https://doi.org/10.1007/978-3-642-61578-8
3. Ploskas, N., Samaras, N., Margaritis, K.: A parallel implementation of the revised simplex algorithm using OpenMP: some preliminary results. In: Migdalas, A., Sifaleras, A., Georgiadis, C., Papathanasiou, J., Stiakakis, E. (eds.) Optimization Theory, Decision Making, and Operations Research Applications. Springer Proceedings in Mathematics & Statistics, vol. 31. Springer, New York (2013). https://doi.org/10.1007/978-1-4614-5134-1_11
4. Wagner, H.M.: A comparison of the original and revised simplex methods. Oper. Res. **5**(3), 361–369 (1957). https://doi.org/10.1287/opre.5.3.361
5. Coutinho, D., Souza, S.X., Aloise, D.: A scalable shared-memory parallel simplex for large-scale linear programming (2018). https://arxiv.org/pdf/1804.04737v1.pdf
6. Goldfarb, D.: On the Complexity of the Simplex Method. In: Gomez, S., Hennart, J.P. (eds.) Advances in Optimization and Numerical Analysis. Mathematics and Its Applications, vol. 275. Springer, Dordrecht (1994). https://doi.org/10.1007/978-94-015-8330-5_2
7. Mamalis, B., Perlitis, M.: A hybrid parallelization scheme for standard simplex method based on CPU/GPU collaboration. In: Proceedings of the 20th Pan-Hellenic Conference on Informatics (PCI 2016), Article 12, pp. 1–6. Association for Computing Machinery, New York (2016). https://doi.org/10.1145/3003733.3003757
8. Fearnley, J., Savani, R.: The complexity of the simplex method. In: Proceedings of the Forty-Seventh Annual ACM Symposium on Theory of Computing (STOC 2015), pp. 201–208. Association for Computing Machinery, New York (2015). https://doi.org/10.1145/2746539.2746558
9. Klotz, E., Newman, A.M.: Practical guidelines for solving difficult linear programs. Surv. Oper. Res. Manag. Sci. **18**(1–2), 1–17 (2013). https://doi.org/10.1016/j.sorms.2012.11.001. ISSN 1876–7354
10. Ketabchi, S., Moosaei, H., Sahleh, H., Hedayati, M.: New methods for solving large scale linear programming problems in the windows and linux computer operating systems (2012). https://doi.org/10.12785/amis/070440

Task Inefficiency Patterns for a Wave Equation Solver

Holger Schulz[1]([✉]), Gonzalo Brito Gadeschi[2], Oleksandr Rudyy[3],
and Tobias Weinzierl[1]

[1] Department of Computer Science, Durham University, Durham, UK
{holger.schulz,tobias.weinzierl}@durham.ac.uk
[2] NVIDIA GmbH, Munich, Germany
gonzalob@nvidia.com
[3] High Performance Computing Center Stuttgart (HLRS), University of Stuttgart,
Stuttgart, Germany
oleksandr.rudyy@hlrs.de

Abstract. The orchestration of complex algorithms demands high levels of automation to use modern hardware efficiently. Task-based programming with OpenMP 5.0 is a prominent candidate to accomplish this goal. We study OpenMP 5.0's tasking in the context of a wave equation solver (ExaHyPE) using three different architectures and runtimes. We describe several task-scheduling flaws present in currently available runtimes, demonstrate how they impact performance and show how to work around them. Finally, we propose extensions to the OpenMP standard.

Keywords: OpenMP 5.0 · Task-based parallelism · Assembly-free task graph · Dynamic tasking · Message queue · Shared memory

1 Introduction

Modern high-performance computing (HPC) architectures exhibit unprecedented hardware parallelism [1,6]. The potential of which must be harnessed on the software side. As traditional loop-based parallelism and, in particular, the bulk-synchronous (BSP) paradigm increasingly struggle to achieve this alone, task-based programming promises to come to the programmers' rescue. Task graphs [2] allow the programmer to oversubscribe the system logically, i.e. to write software with a significantly higher concurrency than the hardware provides. Once task graphs are translated to task-based source code, a threading runtime can efficiently map this code onto the actual hardware, as the oversubscription provides the scheduler with the freedom to utilise all resources. Despite the promise and flexibility it offers, tasking as a low-level parallelisation paradigm, i.e. for tiny work units [5], often yields inferior performance compared to more traditional parallelisation.

Our work orbits around the second installment of the code ExaHyPE [20], which can solve hyperbolic equation systems in the first-order formulation. We

© Springer Nature Switzerland AG 2021
S. McIntosh-Smith et al. (Eds.): IWOMP 2021, LNCS 12870, pp. 111–124, 2021.
https://doi.org/10.1007/978-3-030-85262-7_8

focus on its patch-based Finite Volume schemes realising block-structured adaptive mesh refinement (AMR) [7]. This application requires a high degree of concurrency in order to smooth out the imbalances introduced by dynamic AMR, consecutive solver steps that are drastically different in their compute characteristics, and bandwidth limitations due to a flurry of MPI activity. We orchestrate all that with a task formalism on top of classic domain decomposition. Despite its complexity, the code's execution time is dominated by bursts of similar computational steps applied to a large set of unknowns. For example, the application of the same compute kernel to a large number of cells. This pattern is likely archetypical for many HPC codes.

Our demonstrator code ExaHyPE uses a parallelisation strategy consisting of MPI and OpenMP [12]. We note that, with current OpenMP runtimes, our implementation that uses *native* OpenMP task parallelisation yields an inferior time-to-solution compared to plain BSP-style parallelism. Further, the task-based formalism struggles to compete with traditional data decomposition. Our analysis identifies two primary reasons for this behaviour in the OpenMP runtimes and versions that we studied.

BSP task subgraphs are treated as critical paths. If the runtime encounters an imbalance, idle times are not used to swap in further ready tasks from the non-BSP region. Instead, we busily wait for the completion of the BSP subgraph.

The creation of massive numbers of ready tasks is likely to lead to the suspension of currently active tasks. We observe the runtime to prioritise the execution of descendent tasks before resuming the primarily active ones—even if there are no dependencies.

The aforementioned shortcomings of OpenMP task runtimes lead us to reject the hypothesis that task-based parallelism helps mitigate load imbalances and sequential program phases introduced by classic BSP-style parallelism. We identify causal properties and propose wrappers around existing OpenMP calls to mitigate these flaws. The patterns studied in this work are not exclusive to ExaHyPE. The ideas presented are therefore of broader interest for the supercomputing community working with task graphs.

The remainder of the text is organised as follows: We sketch our application in Sect. 2 with a particular emphasis on two distinct task graphs produced by two different solver implementations. After introducing the test platform (Sect. 3), these task patterns are analysed. We highlight shortcomings encountered with current runtimes, and outline tweaks to the OpenMP port of our application. This Sect. 4 is the main part of our contribution. A brief summary and an outlook (Sect. 5) close the discussion.

2   Case Studies

We use the patch-based Finite Volume (FV) solver on adaptive Cartesian meshes [7] that comes with the second generation of the ExaHyPE engine [16]. The mesh consists of squares (dimension $d = 2$) or cubes ($d = 3$). Each *cell* hosts a patch of N^d d-dimensional volumes. Each *volume* carries a piece-wise constant representation of the solution, and an additional halo-layer of d-dimensional volumes surrounds each patch.

Once per time-step, our FV solvers evolve all patches in time by computing the underlying Riemann problem with a Rusanov scheme [10] supplemented by volumetric source terms (right-hand side). The Rusanov scheme requires the halo layer mentioned above to evolve the cells at the patch boundary. After the temporal evolution, the FV solvers *reduce* the maximal eigenvalue of the solution over all cells. This eigenvalue determines the largest time-step that satisfies the CFL condition [10]. Before the next time-step, each patch writes $4N$ ($d = 2$) or $6N^2$ ($d = 3$) boundary cells into a face buffer. Each cell has its own halo. This enables us to separate the halo updates into a "project onto faces" epilogue of the patch solve, and a "write halo" preamble to a patch update, ultimately allowing the patches to be *independently* advanced in time.

Solver 1: Plain BSP-Style Adaptive Time-Stepping. Our baseline code splits the computational domain into non-overlapping segments along a space-filling Peano curve (SFC) [21]. Several adjacent segments along the SFC are deployed to each MPI rank. Per time-step, each rank maps its local SFC segments onto an OpenMP `taskloop` [12]. The programming paradigm is classic SPMD on the MPI side, followed by a BSP-style traversal of the local subdomains per rank. Equivalent code using a `parallel for` construct with dynamic scheduling yields the same performance.

Every time the task encounters a cell, it writes the halo, updates the cell, determines the next permissible time-step size, and stores the new halo data in the faces. The computation of the permissible time-step size is a per-cell operation and is therefore fused with the actual cell update, meaning that one large BSP section per time-step is sufficient.

The underlying load balancing problem is a chains-on-chains problem [14]. We operate with an SFC subpartition count that is close or equal to the number of available cores. Due to the AMR, boundary handling and administrative overhead, the individual subpartitions are not perfectly balanced per thread. We obtain a classic BSP-style task graph (Fig. 1), where the bulk is not perfectly balanced.

Solver 2: Enclave Tasking. In contrast to the plain domain decomposition scheme, this solver traverses the mesh twice per time-step, and it classifies cells as either skeleton (those adjacent to partition boundaries or AMR resolution transitions) or enclave cells (all others) [4]. As soon as the primary traversal encounters a skeleton cell, it updates it and thereby determines the new local solution, the permissible time-step size and the new value as required by adjacent cells in the next time-step. This data has to be interpolated or restricted, sent via MPI, or copied over locally to another logical subpartition.

If the thread-local traversal hits an enclave cell, it maps this local cell update onto a task. At the end of this primary grid sweep, we exchange the partition boundary data. The secondary grid traversal waits for its task to terminate, weaves the task outcome into the solution representation, and reduces the

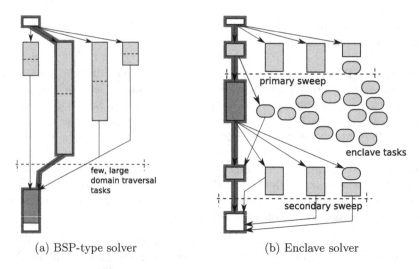

(a) BSP-type solver   (b) Enclave solver

Fig. 1. Anatomy of a time-step. a): Plain domain decomposition yields one BSP-type graph per MPI rank with a warm up phase per time-step (white) where we determine the time-step size and global variables. Each local SFC subpartition is processed by one thread (light grey). A quasi-serial bit of code handles the MPI boundary exchange (dark grey). b): In our enclave solver, the rank-local domain traversal is split into two BSP-type traversals. The first bulk produces small enclave tasks (rounded corner), while skipping local computations within the subdomain. It is faster than the plain counterpart and immediately triggers the boundary data exchange. Once completed, it spawns another bulk which weaves in the enclave task outcomes before completing the time-step. The producer-consumer dependencies are shown for one enclave task only. The critical path is highlighted in red. (Color figure online)

permissible time-step size per rank. A final, brief serial phase launches the global time-step size reduction and finalises all MPI data exchanges.

Our enclave tasking (Fig. 1) is realised as a sequence of two `taskloop` constructs per time-step (Algorithm 1). In contrast to the plain implementation, the first `taskloop` acts as a producer of tasks. It does not synchronise with the spawned enclave tasks, as the `nogroup` first eliminates all implicit barriers and the `taskwait` then waits for the direct children of the master thread only. Despite the elimination of this barrier we continue to refer to this as task group. The local domain decomposition remains invariant and generates only a few relatively large tasks. The stark contrast to the plain variant is that we create a plethora of tiny enclave tasks per primary sweep.

We use a simple hashmap for the bookkeeping of our task outcomes: Enclave tasks are assigned a unique number at the point of their creation. Upon completion, they reduce their permissible time-step size and enter the new time-step data of their associated patch in the hash map.

The busy waits in the secondary traversals of Algorithm 1 incorporate simulation outcomes into the computational mesh. This is required to allow updating

---

Algorithm 1. Schematic layout of the time-stepping in our enclave tasking.

```
 1: function TIMESTEP(dt)
 2:     #pragma omp taskloop nogroup
 3:     for rank-local partition do                    ▷ Primary traversal (large task)
 4:         for local cell do
 5:             if cell is skeleton then
 6:                 update cell
 7:             else
 8:                 #pragma omp task                   ▷ Spawn enclave task
 9:                 update cell
10:             end if
11:         end for
12:     end for
13:     #pragma omp taskwait                           ▷ Wait only for traversal tasks
14:     Realise domain boundary exchange
15:     #pragma omp taskloop nogroup
16:     for rank-local partition do                    ▷ Secondary traversal (large task)
17:         for local cell do
18:             if cell is enclave then
19:                 busy-wait for enclave task outcome          ▷ With taskyield
20:             end if
21:         end for
22:     end for
23:     #pragma omp taskwait                           ▷ Implicitly wait for all tasks
24: end function
```

---

the patch halo and synchronising the patches with their neighbours. In our baseline OpenMP implementation, this is realised by busy waiting: The code polls the hash map repeatedly. As long as the hash map does not yet contain the required task outcome, the polling code releases the semaphore and issues a `taskyield` before it polls again. This constitutes a naïve implementation of the consumer in a producer-consumer pattern.

3   Test Environment

We work with three different test systems (Table 1), each using a different compiler: A GNU compiler, the Intel compiler, and the new LLVM-based Intel compiler. This allows use to make qualitative statements. *Quantitative* comparisons are beyond the scope of this work. All tasking code is based on OpenMP 5.0. `OMP_PROC_BIND` is set to `close`.

We simulate compressible Euler equations in a unit-square domain with periodic boundaries, hosting 59,049 patches. An initial high-density peak in the domain serves as a causal agent for spreading waves. We use FV with a patch size of 63×63 per cell such that the face count (Riemann problems) per patch along each coordinate axis equals a power of two. The computational simplicity

Table 1. Test systems

Test system	Hamilton	HPE Hawk	Cosma
CPU	Intel Xeon E5-2650V4	AMD EPYC 7742	Intel Xeon Gold 5218
Name	Broadwell	Rome	Cascade Lake
Cores	2×14	2×64	2×16
NUMA domains	2	2×4	2
Baseline freq.	2.4 GHz	2.25 GHz	2.3 GHz
L2/L3	256 kB/30 MB	512 kB/16 MB	1 MB/22 MB
Compiler	icpc (ICC) 19.1.3.304	g++ (GCC) 10.2.0	icpx (ICX) 2021.1 Beta

of Euler equations implies that the code is never compute-bound. Due to this characteristic, scheduling flaws become apparent immediately.

We limit our experiments to a single node but explicitly keep all management code for inter-node data exchange enabled, i.e. after each time-step, we run the routines that orchestrate multi-node and heterogeneous runs. Doing so eliminates interference with MPI. We further disable dynamic load balancing (cf. [13]) and instead rely on two static ways to split the domain along the Peano SFCs: For our first, *well-balanced* mode, we ensure that each core obtains one SFC-partition of the domain and that the partition sizes (cell counts) do not differ by more than 10%. When using a single core we end up with 58,564 enclave cells. Splitting the same domain over 24 cores yields a smaller *total* of 53583 enclave cells as we have more boundaries and therefore more skeletons. In our second, *ill-balanced* mode, we assign around half of the partition (26,244 cells) to the first core and then continue to iteratively cut the partition size in half for the remaining cores. Doing so yields a highly ill-balanced data decomposition with up to 20 partitions where the smallest partition consists of only one patch.

4   Benchmarking and Task Runtime Modifications

We first compare the performance of the BSP-style solver and the enclave solver *without* modifications of the OpenMP 5.0 runtime (referred to as "native" in the following). The baseline BSP-type code scales robustly only for the well-balanced domain decomposition (Fig. 2a). In the ill-balanced setup, BSP parallelisation (circles in Fig. 2b) maximally achieves a 2x-speedup (w.r.t. single-core), regardless of the number of cores and type of machine studied. The enclave algorithm arguably performs better than pure BSP. All measurements report time per time-step and patch.

The strength of enclave tasking is its ability to migrate computational work to underutilised cores. This migration pays off for an ill-balanced setup, but its impact in a well-balanced setup is small, as this (experimental) choice does not benefit from the flexibility of OpenMP tasking. Overall, the strong scaling regime exhibits limited efficiency which is, however, beneficial for our purposes as it makes all scheduling flaws immediately apparent.

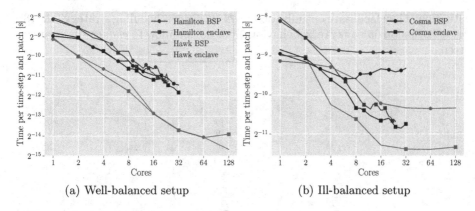

(a) Well-balanced setup   (b) Ill-balanced setup

Fig. 2. Baseline scaling, measuring the time per time-step and patch. Both the BSP and the enclave implementation use native OpenMP tasks.

4.1   Direct Translation of Enclave Tasking to OpenMP (native)

Busy Polling. In our baseline code, we map enclave tasks directly onto OpenMP tasks and realise the busy-wait in Algorithm 1 via polling: We check whether the task outcome is available and otherwise invoke `taskyield`. This implementation notoriously causes OpenMP runtimes to starve once the number of domain partitions exceeds the number of OpenMP threads: Those consumer threads of the `taskgroup` which have not yet hit the implicit barrier take turns waking up each other instead of an enclave task, thereby starving the latter.

Observation 1. `taskyield` *tends to switch between tasks within the same group. This pattern starves ready tasks outside the task loop. The OpenMP implementations tested are not "fair".*

To be formally correct, our implementation should introduce dependencies between the tasks instead of polling. We refrain from doing so as the additional bookkeeping would require complex rewrites over multiple classes distributed among multiple components. Some parallel algorithms, like our enclave tasking, are "starvation-free" yet require "fair" task scheduling to progress. If `taskyield` does not yield to other taskgroups, progress for these algorithms can be minimal or the code can starve. In contrast, non-fair scheduling switching between few ready tasks is advantageous in many situations as it avoids cache capacity misses.

Feature 1. *It is desirable to annotate* `taskyields` *with scheduling hints to allow it to also process tasks that are not direct descendants.*

Since we lack a cross-taskgroup yield, oversubscribing the machine threads with large traversal tasks is not an option. The flexibility that geometric load balancing offers is therefore limited [13]. More flexible scheduling (`KMP_TASK_STEALING_CONSTRAINT`) or untied task progression do not help in this situation: They facillitate optimisation *within* a given scheduling strategy (cf. [18] for a discussion on `taskyield` behaviour) but do not allow to *change* the strategy itself.

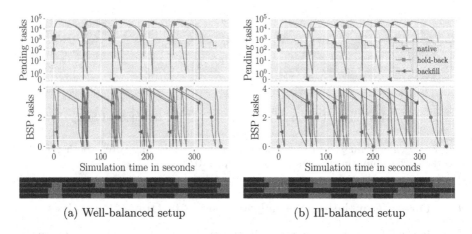

(a) Well-balanced setup   (b) Ill-balanced setup

Fig. 3. Analysis of five time-steps. Top: Number of pending enclave tasks for three different tasking realisations. The native OpenMP implementation prevents spawning more than 1,000 enclave tasks. Middle: Number of active BSP (producer/consumer) tasks. The two traversals per time-step are clearly visible. The native OpenMP implementation leads to the first traversal taking much longer than the second. For the other implementations, the behaviour is the opposite. Bottom: Core activities of the native implementation (brown: CPU time, red: spinning). The data show five time-steps of two runs on Hamilton utilising four cores. (Color figure online)

Task Execution Pattern. For the enclave tasking to have its desired effect, it is imperative to spawn a large number of tasks during the first traversal to have them pending for the *second* traversal. Our measurements (Fig. 3) clearly show that the native OpenMP implementation caps the number of tasks at about 1,000. The runtime processes pending tasks immediately. In doing so, the completion of the majority of the tasks coincides with the `taskwait` clause at the end of the primary traversal (Algorithm 1, line 13). All our OpenMP implementations use this scheduling point to process a significant amount of enclave tasks (ready by definition). Once the runtime progresses beyond the synchronisation point, in the native implementation, only a few enclave tasks (if any) remain. This implies that any idle time in the subsequent BSP-type traversal cannot be backfilled with further ready tasks. The resulting wait at the end of the secondary sweep causes the spin times in the traces measured. This behaviour leads to the first traversal lasting significantly longer than the second one, exactly the opposite of what enclave tasking requires. It should be noted that an ill-balanced domain partitioning amplifies the observed patterns. The following paragraphs describe how we circumvent these effects.

4.2 Manual Task Postponing (Hold-Back)

Thresholds that influence the task processing behaviour degrade the predictability of the runtime performance, and they destroy our code's efficiency: We create enclave tasks to compensate for imbalances once the primary taskloop has terminated. If OpenMP decides to suspend the task producer and instead launches tasks immediately, or OpenMP does not continue with the main control flow at the synchronisation point, the desired pay-off vanishes.

Observation 2. *OpenMP runtimes switch to immediate task processing if the number of ready tasks exceeds a threshold. This behaviour introduces the risk that these tasks are not available to mend subsequent imbalances. It also denies the programmer the opportunity to migrate expensive but not immediately required work to subtasks.*

Observation 3. *OpenMP's* `taskwait` *allows the runtime to switch to processing any ready tasks—not only the child tasks of the current task region—rather than continuing with the main control flow. That suspends the task producer thread.*

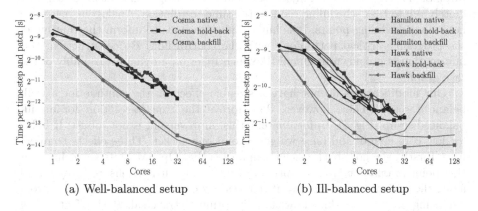

(a) Well-balanced setup   (b) Ill-balanced setup

Fig. 4. Three different enclave tasking strategies per machine: Native mapping onto OpenMP tasks, manually hold-back of spawned enclave tasks, and a manual backfilling of idling cores. We measure the time per time-step and patch.

Our code eliminates the immediate task processing by adding a manual queue: Instead of spawning OpenMP tasks, the BSP-type task regions queue their tasks in this helper container. They *hold back* the tasks manually. The busy polling checks whether a task outcome is available, otherwise processes one task from our manual queue, and then checks again. It implicitly realises a lazy task evaluation.

Our measurements show that such an additional, thin, user-defined tasking layer on top of OpenMP ensures that all enclave tasks remain pending while we continue to spawn tasks (Fig. 3). In contrast to the native implementation, we now see (Fig. 3, middle panel plots) that the primary traversal is very short compared to its secondary counterpart. The reason is that the manual queue *collects* all tasks instead of processing them. Consequently, the secondary traversal dominates the runtime thanks to the lazy evaluation. The secondary sweep's polling does not discriminate which tasks are spawned by which BSP-type task. It simply grabs the tasks one by one and automatically balances out the secondary BSP tasks. This advantageous behaviour is much more pronounced in the ill-balanced setup.

Feature 2. *It is desirable to manually control OpenMP's ready task thresholds or inform the runtime that many tasks will be spawned, and although they are ready, not to process them right away.*

Feature 3. *It is desirable to manually annotate OpenMP's scheduling points that the (serial) control flow in the code is part of the critical path.*

It is reasonable to introduce a threshold for ready tasks to avoid excessive bookkeeping overhead incurred by long task queues. However, we have an algorithm that suffers tremendously from immediate task processing as it relies on bursts of ready tasks to compensate for task ill-balancing in subsequent computational phases. In this case, injecting domain knowledge ("do not process immediately") into task scheduling reduces the time-to-solution. Analogous reasoning holds for scheduling points: It is hugely advantageous to inform the runtime of the program's critical path along with the control flow. By construction, this information is unknown to OpenMP, which relies on a dynamic assembly of the task graph.

Our modifications do not have a sizeable effect on the runtime for a well-balanced setup. They, however, do improve the time-to-solution for an ill-balanced setup (Fig. 4). Unfortunately, this improvement is not robust: It holds for low core counts and once we go beyond one socket. Three effects compete here: Firstly, the hold-back mechanism avoids that OpenMP hits a synchronisation point (`taskwait` after the primary sweep) and thereby ensures progression along the critical path. Secondly, it reduces any cache thrashing that arises from balancing out task workloads within the primary traversal. Both effects bring down the runtime of the BSP-type task production. Thirdly, the centralised task queue increases the coordination pressure (semaphore access) between the tasks.

4.3 Manual Backfilling (Backfill)

Manual task postponing (holding back) and the native OpenMP task processing behaviour materialise two extreme cases of task scheduling: They either process tasks relatively early (around the synchronisation point) or very late due to our lazy mechanism.

It is not immediately clear which approach is more beneficial. On the one hand, making `taskwait` work through the set of ready tasks as aggressively as possible reduces the bookkeeping overhead, and for many codes, we may assume that any ready task will spawn further tasks. Discovering this early reveals more fragments of the final task graph. This approach yields high throughput. If, on the other hand, we make `taskwait` busy poll its siblings instead of processing further tasks, we prevent situations where the BSP-type subgraph terminates, but the runtime does not immediately continue with the source code following the BSP-type section. This approach eliminates latency along the BSP-type subgraph.

Algorithm 2. Manual backfilling of a BSP-type task section.

1: $busyThreads \leftarrow max(\#threads, \#bsp\ tasks)$ ▷ Ensure all threads are used
2: **for** $i = 0..busyThreads - 1$ **do**   ▷ A `parallel for` would be equivalent
3:    `#pragma omp task shared(busyThreads)`
4:    {
5:    **if** $i < \#tasks$ **then**
6:       RUN($task[i]$)
7:    **end if**
8:    `#pragma omp atomic`
9:    $busyThreads \leftarrow busyThreads - 1$
10:    **while** $busyThreads > 0 \wedge busyThreads < \#threads$ **do**   ▷ Second clause
11:       PROCESSPENDINGTASKS   ▷ avoids deadlocks
12:    **end while**
13:    }
14: **end for**
15: `#pragma omp taskwait`

Our code requires a compromise between high throughput and low latency, as any delay along the control flow with the BSP section will introduce imbalances and delays later down the line. We, therefore, augment the postponed scheduling with a manual task backfilling (Algorithm 2): Enclave tasks created within the task group (BSP-style) are enqueued using a container as before. They are not handed over to OpenMP. Once a BSP-type task terminates, it decrements a global counter of active BSP tasks ($busyThreads$). If there are fewer active BSP-type tasks than logical threads, and not all BSP-type tasks have terminated yet, we grab tasks from the local task queue and process them immediately. This is the actual backfilling, which is in essence a conservative form of work-stealing [11].

The backfilling ensures that our latency-sensitive BSP-subgraph realisation does not let threads idle. Therefore, the backfilling robustly outperforms a native OpenMP task implementation, as long as we utilise only one socket (Fig. 4—one socket means 14 cores for Hamilton, 16 cores for Cosma, 64 cores for Hawk). If we have a well-balanced setup, the backfilling does not kick in. We, however, benefit from the payoffs of the hold-back strategy, which automatically balances partitions with different numbers of enclave tasks. These tasks differ, even if the partitions all have similar cell count. If we have an ill-balanced setup, backfilling outperforms a native OpenMP version, as we benefit from the hold-back mechanisms but do not let cores idle. The benefits disappear as soon as we use both sockets or the problem gets too small. The program suffers from cache thrashing and synchronisation overhead, and is therefore outperformed by the hold-back strategy.

Feature 4. *It would be beneficial if a* `taskwait` *or implicit BSP synchronisation could be annotated whether throughput or latency (immediate continuation) take priority.*

Our backfilling wraps around OpenMP's BSP constructs (`taskloop`), and makes it latency-aware: The implementation works well if the BSP-graph section is aligned with the task graph's critical path, and thus latency-critical. However, it does not prioritise latency above all else. Instead, it tries to process enclave tasks—but only if other tasks are still busy with the BSP section. It is thus *weakly* latency-aware.

5   Evaluation and Conclusion

Our studies start from the observation that a plain taskification of source code with OpenMP does not necessarily reduce the time-to-solution for sophisticated codes. If a code is intrinsically BSP-style, we should map it onto BSP constructs. If we add tasking on top of these BSP regions, we quickly suffer from poor performance. The reason for this is not solely rooted in tasks of low arithmetic intensity, but also stems from the fact that OpenMP runtime characteristics impede performance as soon as we go beyond a pure tree-based task-graph layout.

We propose extensions of tasking runtimes and their API. They can be summarised as a proposal to allow the programmer to inform OpenMP about the criticality and characteristics of tasks (implying statements on the arithmetic intensity and task type homogeneity) as well as to facilitate balancing manually between throughput- and latency-prioritisation. Some of this information is available in approaches with a priori, i.e. static task graph assembly [9,17] or can be mapped onto OpenMP's task priorities, though the latter is not fully implemented in the OpenMP runtimes that we used. Our approach goes beyond sole prioritisation and does not require a static task graph assembly. Instead, we wrap task APIs to include more domain knowledge about the long-term knock-on effects of scheduling decisions. We are confident that this idea is of value for many codes that exhibit more of a consumer-producer tasking pattern. It is worthwhile to discuss how to make these concepts available within OpenMP.

It is safe to assume the performance gain from our techniques will be significantly higher if the queues and scheduling are directly integrated into the runtime. Different to state-of-the-art queue implementations, our queue is not distributed and thus suffers from congestion if many threads check it simultaneously. Different to high-level frameworks like Kokkos [8] and RAJA [3,15] it also lacks any affinity knowledge [19] and thus stresses the caches.

Acknowledgments. Holger's and Tobias' work is sponsored by EPSRC under the ExCALIBUR Phase I call through the grants EP/V00154X/1 (ExaClaw) and EP/V001523/1 (Massively Parallel Particle Hydrodynamics for Engineering and Astrophysics). Both appreciate the support from ExCALIBUR's cross-cutting tasking theme (grant ESA 10 CDEL). The Exascale Computing ALgorithms & Infrastructures Benefiting UK Research (ExCALIBUR) programme is supported by the UKRI Strategic Priorities Fund. The programme is co-delivered by the Met Office on behalf of PSREs and EPSRC on behalf of UKRI partners, NERC, MRC and STFC. The present software [20] is part of a major rewrite of the original ExaHyPE code funded by the European Union's Horizon 2020 research and innovation programme under grant agreement No 671698 (ExaHyPE). Oleksandr's work motivating this research has received funding from the European Union's Horizon 2020 research and innovation programme under the project CoE POP, grant agreement No. 824080.

Our work made use of the facilities of the Hamilton HPC Service of Durham University, and it also made use of the facilities provided by the ExCALIBUR Hardware and Enabling Software programme, funded by BEIS via STFC grants ST/V001140/1 and ST/V002724/1, and hosted by the DiRAC@Durham Memory Intensive facility managed by the Institute for Computational Cosmology on behalf of the STFC DiRAC HPC Facility (www.dirac.ac.uk). The equipment was funded by BEIS capital funding via STFC capital grants ST/P002293/1, ST/R002371/1 and ST/S002502/1, Durham University and STFC operations grant ST/R000832/1. DiRAC is part of the UK's National e-Infrastructure.

This work was funded under the embedded CSE programme of the ARCHER2 UK National Supercomputing Service (http://www.archer2.ac.uk), grant no ARCHER2-eCSE04-2.

References

1. EuroHPC2020: EuroHPC supercomputer systems. European Commission (2021). http://eurohpc.eu/
2. Ayguade, E., et al.: The design of OpenMP tasks. IEEE Trans. Parallel Distrib. Syst. **20**(3), 404–418 (2009). https://doi.org/10.1109/TPDS.2008.105
3. Beckingsale, D.A., et al.: RAJA: portable performance for large-scale scientific applications. In: 2019 IEEE/ACM International Workshop on Performance, Portability and Productivity in HPC (P3HPC) (2021)
4. Charrier, D., Hazelwood, B., Weinzierl, T.: Enclave tasking for dg methods on dynamically adaptive meshes. SIAM J. Sci. Comput. **42**(3), C69–C96 (2020)
5. Demeshko, I., et al.: Tbaa20: taskbased algorithms and applications. doe report la-ur-21-20928 (2021). https://permalink.lanl.gov/object/tr?what=info:lanl-repo/lareport/LA-UR-21-20928
6. Dongarra, J., et al.: The international exascale software project roadmap 1. IJHPCA **25**, 3–60 (2011). https://doi.org/10.1177/1094342010391989
7. Dubey, A., et al.: A survey of high level frameworks in block-structured adaptive mesh refinement packages. CoRR **74**(12), 3217–3227 (2016)
8. Edwards, H.C., Trott, C.R., Sunderland, D.: Kokkos: enabling manycore performance portability through polymorphic memory access patterns. J. Parallel Distrib. Comput. **74**(12), 3202–3216 (2014). https://doi.org/10.1016/j.jpdc.2014.07.003, http://www.sciencedirect.com/science/article/pii/S0743731514001257. Domain-Specific Languages and High-Level Frameworks for High-Performance Computing

9. Haensel, D., Morgenstern, L., Beckmann, A., Kabadshow, I., Dachsel, H.: Eventify: event-based task parallelism for strong scaling. In: Proceedings of the Platform for Advanced Scientific Computing Conference (2020)
10. LeVeque, R.J.: Finite Volume Methods for Hyperbolic Problems. Cambridge Texts in Applied Mathematics, Cambridge University Press (2002). https://doi.org/10.1017/CBO9780511791253
11. Olivier, S.L., Porterfield, A.K., Wheeler, K.B., Spiegel, M., Prins, J.F.: OpenMP task scheduling strategies for multicore NUMA systems. Int. J. High Perform. Comput. Appl. **26**(2), 110–124 (2012). https://doi.org/10.1177/1094342011434065
12. OpenMP Architecture Review Board: OpenMP application program interface version 5.0 (2018). https://www.openmp.org/wp-content/uploads/OpenMP-API-Specification-5.0.pdf
13. Orland, F., Terboven, C.: A case study on addressing complex load imbalance in OpenMP. In: Milfeld, K., de Supinski, B.R., Koesterke, L., Klinkenberg, J. (eds.) IWOMP 2020. LNCS, vol. 12295, pp. 130–145. Springer, Cham (2020). https://doi.org/10.1007/978-3-030-58144-2_9
14. Pinar, A., Aykanat, C.: Fast optimal load balancing algorithms for 1D partitioning. J. Parallel Distrib. Comput. **64**(8), 974–996 (2004)
15. RAJA: RAJA performance portability layer (2021). https://github.com/LLNL/RAJA
16. Reinarz, A., et al.: ExaHyPE: an engine for parallel dynamically adaptive simulations of wave problems. Comput. Phys. Commun. **254**, 107251 (2020)
17. Schaller, M., Gonnet, P., Chalk, A.B.G., Draper, P.W.: Swift: using task-based parallelism, fully asynchronous communication, and graph partition-based domain decomposition for strong scaling on more than 100,000 cores. In: Proceedings of the Platform for Advanced Scientific Computing Conference. PASC '16. Association for Computing Machinery, New York (2016). https://doi.org/10.1145/2929908.2929916
18. Schuchart, J., Tsugane, K., Gracia, J., Sato, M.: The impact of Taskyield on the design of tasks communicating through MPI. In: de Supinski, B.R., Valero-Lara, P., Martorell, X., Mateo Bellido, S., Labarta, J. (eds.) IWOMP 2018. LNCS, vol. 11128, pp. 3–17. Springer, Cham (2018). https://doi.org/10.1007/978-3-319-98521-3_1
19. Terboven, C., et al.: Approaches for task affinity in OpenMP. In: Maruyama, N., de Supinski, B.R., Wahib, M. (eds.) IWOMP 2016. LNCS, vol. 9903, pp. 102–115. Springer, Cham (2016). https://doi.org/10.1007/978-3-319-45550-1_8
20. Weinzierl, T., et al.: ExaHyPE-an exascale hyperbolic PDE engine (2021). http://www.exahype.eu. http://www.exahype.eu
21. Weinzierl, T.: The peano software - parallel, automaton-based, dynamically adaptive grid traversals. CoRR arXiv:1506.04496 (2015)

Case Studies

Comparing OpenMP Implementations with Applications Across A64FX Platforms

Benjamin Michalowicz[1]([✉]), Eric Raut[1], Yan Kang[1], Tony Curtis[1],
Barbara Chapman[1,2], and Dossay Oryspayev[2]

[1] Institute For Advanced Computational Science, Stony Brook University,
Stony Brook, NY, USA
{benjamin.michalowicz,eric.raut,yan.kang,anthony.curtis,
barbara.chapman}@stonybrook.edu
[2] Computational Science Initiative, Brookhaven National Laboratory,
Upton, NY, USA
{bchapman,doryspaye}@bnl.gov

Abstract. The development of the A64FX processor by Fujitsu has created a massive innovation in High-Performance Computing and the birth of Fugaku: the current world's fastest supercomputer. A variety of tools are used to analyze the run-times and performances of several applications, and in particular, how these applications scale on the A64FX processor. We examine the performance and behavior of applications through OpenMP scaling and how their performance differs across different compilers both on the new Ookami cluster at Stony Brook University as well as the Fugaku supercomputer at RIKEN in Japan.

1 Introduction

The introduction of the A64FX processor by Fujitsu, and its use in the Fugaku supercomputer (Fugaku), has sparked the re-emergence of vectorized processors/programming and the birth of the next world's-fastest supercomputer[1]. This comes on top of the fact that the A64FX chip also brings an unprecedented co-design approach, impressive performance, and energy awareness that puts it at the top of all 5 major HPC benchmarks. In this paper, we will be analyzing OpenMP[2], a well-known shared memory/parallel programming model, from its scaling abilities on the A64FX processor to how it performs across different compiler toolchains.

The full list of current compilers that support OpenMP can be found at https://openmp.org[3]. Although there is one OpenMP specification, compiler support varies both in terms of specific OpenMP features and general performance.

---

[1] https://top500.org/.
[2] https://www.openmp.org/.
[3] https://www.openmp.org/resources/openmp-compilers-tools/.

© Springer Nature Switzerland AG 2021
S. McIntosh-Smith et al. (Eds.): IWOMP 2021, LNCS 12870, pp. 127–141, 2021.
https://doi.org/10.1007/978-3-030-85262-7_9

In the next two subsections we give a brief overview of the A64FX processor, followed by the paper's contribution and organization.

1.1 The A64FX Processor

The A64FX processor [13,18] is the processor specifically manufactured for Fugaku, which was made possible as part of the Japanese FLAGSHIP 2020 project as a co-design between RIKEN and Fujitsu. Currently, Fugaku is ranked number 1 on both Top500 and HPCG lists. The A64FX, is a general-purpose processor based on the Armv8.2-A architecture [18] and comes with 48 compute cores + 2/4 cores dedicated to OS activities.

The A64FX processor produced by Fujitsu has 4 core memory groups (CMG). In the FX700 chip, each CMG has 12 cores, while the FX1000 chip has 2-4 extra assistant cores. Ookami currently has the FX700 chips, with each core laid out sequentially: cores 0-11 make up CMG 0, 12-23 make up CMG 1, etc. [2].

1.2 Paper's Contribution and Organization

Although OpenMP support is available in many compilers, to the best of our knowledge, there were no studies of OpenMP's performance in various compilers (and specific versions) specifically for A64FX processors with the set of applications considered in this paper, and features of OpenMP they're using. To that end, the paper's contributions are as follows:

- We present and evaluate the single node performance of various applications using all available compilers on two systems that have A64FX processors, viz. Ookami and Fugaku.
- We present, evaluate, and compare the differences in performance on two different models of A64FX.
- We discuss our findings, and based on the results obtained, we summarize the maturity level of compilers available on these two systems to fully utilize the features of A64FX processors.

The rest of the paper is organized as follows. In Sect. 2 we present the details of the applications considered in this study, and of the systems and compilers used. In Sect. 3 we present and discuss the results obtained as well as inferences obtained from running applications through various profilers and performance analysis tools. In Sect. 4 we list related work and discuss their contributions and the contribution of our work. Finally, in Sect. 5 we summarize our findings and list some work to be performed in near future.

2 List of Applications and Experimental Setup

2.1 List of Applications

- PENNANT [4] - A mesh physics mini-app designed for advanced architecture research. PENNANT is dominated by pointer chasing and operates based on input files with different parameters. The larger the parameters, the larger the mesh. PENNANT can be run solely with MPI, OpenMP, or in a hybrid MPI+OpenMP fashion, and uses OpenMP's static scheduling feature.

- SWIM - a weather forecasting model designed for testing current performance of supercomputers. It is a Fortran code using OpenMP. Like PENNANT, it also uses static scheduling of OpenMP. It has been updated within SPEC CPU 2000 benchmark collections by Paul N. Swarztrauber [19].
- Minimod [9,15,16] - a seismic modeling mini-app that solves the acoustic wave equation using finite differences with a stencil. Minimod is developed by TotalEnergies and is designed as a platform to study the performance of emerging compilers and runtimes for HPC. In this paper we consider the OpenMP loop-based and task-based variants of the code [16].

2.2 Systems and Compilers

Fugaku is the world's fastest supercomputer, located at the RIKEN Center for Computational Science in Japan [17], and runs on the FX1000 A64FX, which provides extra cores for OS-communication. Its underlying TofuD interconnect is implemented as an interconnect controller (ICC) chip to allow for low latency and offloading [6].

Ookami is a cluster installed at Stony Brook University (SBU) in the middle of 2020. It contains 174 compute nodes, with another two set aside for quick experimentation. Ookami was funded through an NSF grant [11] as the first

Table 1. Compilers of Fugaku and Ookami.

Compiler family	Versions	
	Fugaku	Ookami
ARM	–	20.3
Cray	–	10.0.1
Fujitsu	4.3.0a, 4.4.0a	–
GCC	8.3.1, 10.2.1	8.3.1, 10.2.1, 11.0.0
LLVM	11.0.0	11.0.0, 12.0.0

A64FX cluster outside of Japan. It comes with an array of software modules, including GNU, LLVM, and Cray compilers, profilers, and MVAPICH/OpenMPI packages. Ookami uses a non-blocking HDR 200 switching fabric via 9 40-port Mellanox Infiniband switches in a 2-level tree, which allows for a peak bandwidth of 100 Gb/s between nodes. In addition, each node currently has 32GB of high-bandwidth memory with a peak memory bandwidth of 1 TB/s. Both systems' compiler toolchains are shown in Table 1.

2.3 Runtime Environment

Each benchmark was run on 1 compute node with 1 MPI rank/process to avoid shared memory operations that occur with 2 or more processing elements and over-subscription of threads to cores, which result in degraded performance. Threads are bound to cores using the OMP_PLACES environment variable.

Threads are assigned to specific cores (e.g. Thread 0 is assigned to Core 0) and divided equally among specific CMGs. For example, 32 threads are divided equally among the four CMGs on a single Ookami node (cores 0-8 in CMG 0, 12-19 in CMG 1, etc.) using

```
OMP_PLACES="{0}:8,{12}:8,{24}:8,{36}:8".
```

We ran experiments using 1, 2, 4, 8, 12, 16, 24, 32, 36, and 48 OpenMP threads. For every value up to 12, we placed all threads in one CMG. The 16-thread and 24-thread experiments were run on 2 CMGs, with each group having half the total thread values. The 32-thread and 48-thread experiments were run on all 4 CMGs on the A64FX chip, with 36 threads being run on 3 CMGs.

2.4   Compiler Options

For each compiler mentioned in Sect. 2.2, we turned on specific flags, maximizing thread optimization, SVE instruction generation, and execution speed while maintaining correctness of output. We also enabled fine-tuning for the A64FX

Table 2. Flags used for each compiler.

Compiler	Flags
Cray	-homp -hvector3 -hthread3
GCC	-mcpu=a64fx -Ofast -fopenmp
LLVM	-mcpu=a64fx -Ofast -fopenmp
Fujitsu-Traditional	-Nnoclang -Nlibomp -O3 -Kfast,-Kopenmp,ARMV8_2_A-KSVE,A64FX
Fujitsu-LLVM	-Nclang -Nlibomp -Ofast -Kfast,openmp -mcpu=a64fx+sve

processor and the ARM-8.2 architectures where possible. The flags are listed for each compiler/group are set as shown in Table 2. Note that GCC versions before version 9 do not support the mcpu=a64fx flag – for GCC 8, we compile directly on an A64FX node and use mcpu=native. These flags instruct the compiler to use auto-vectorization; we have not tested OpenMP's SIMD clauses.

3   Experimental Results

Our experiments analyzed runtime, relative speedup through OpenMP threads, and efficiency with respect to different compiler/compiler classes – Cray, ARM, GNU, and LLVM. Subsect. 3.1 contains all the results run on SBU's Ookami cluster, followed by Subsect. 3.2 containing results from Fugaku. For each application, we deemed three compilers as "best in class" (best runtime) for the families mentioned above: GNU-10.2.0 (gcc/g++/gfortran), ARM/LLVM-20.1.3 (armclang/armclang++/armflang), and Cray-10.0.1 (cc/CC/ftn), with the results for the other compilers explained in the following subsections. Preliminary results are showin in [10].

Our results are drawn from running our programs 5 times per OpenMP thread value requested (1, 2, 4, 8, 12, 16, 24, 32, 36, 48) and taking the arithmetic mean values from each set of runs. These experiments are limited to a single node.

3.1   Ookami

PENNANT. Runs were based on 2 medium-sized inputs whose memory constraints did not expend the A64FX's high bandwidth memory and swap space: **Leblancbig** and **Sedovbig**. These inputs both revolve around structured meshes with all square zones, but deal with considerably different mesh parameters, such as the number of elements in the respective mesh's zone adjacency lists and the number master/slave points/array sizes.

Figure 1(a) shows how, in every value given for `OMP_NUM_THREADS`, the Cray compilers vastly outpace every other compiler toolchain presented. It has a maximum runtime with **Leblancbig** of 1056 s on 1 OpenMP thread, and 28 s on 48 threads. Conversely, the generic LLVM compilers had the absolute worst runtime, running consistently around 2200 s on 1 OpenMP thread, nearing 70 s with 48 threads. Part of this is a result of how many SVE instructions are generated by each compiler when vector optimizations are turned on at the compilation stage. Cray generates the second largest amount of SVE instructions after the Fujitsu compilers, followed by the generic GNU and ARM compilers. Conversely, the generic LLVM compilers produce no SVE instructions at all, nor do they make use of the A64FX's `z[0-32]` registers.

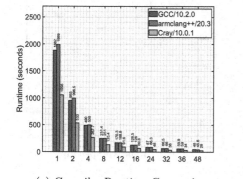

(a) Compiler Runtime Comparisons

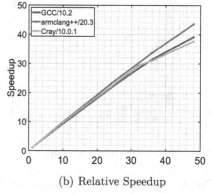

(b) Relative Speedup

Fig. 1. PENNANT/LeblancBig Input Results on Ookami; X-axes refer to number of OpenMP threads

In Fig. 1(b), we show the relative speedup observed between each of the "best in class compilers", measured by the amount of speedup at a given thread value compared to 1 OpenMP thread. While the `armclang` results from Fig. 1(a) show it having the slowest runtime, it has the largest and most linear relative speedup, with the Cray compilers having the smallest relative speedup. Because the Cray compiler is able to efficiently utilize SVE instructions, increasing the number of OpenMP threads will not necessarily guarantee a linear speedup.

Efficiency for these tests is measured as speedup divided by the number of threads used for a given result. We noticed that the ARM compilers are the most efficient when compared to the GNU and Cray compilers.

Profiling the **LeblancBig** input with CrayPat [3] and ARM Forge [1] on Ookami using 48 threads, we noticed that while the output remained the same with different values for `OMP_WAIT_POLICY`, different policies resulted in substantially different behaviors. An "active" wait policy showed that PENNANT spends 66.3% of its runtime in OpenMP regions, with the initial thread taking 66% more load on account for allocating all of the data before creating the mesh and performing computations. A "passive" wait policy shows sharply contrasting behavior: only 17.8% of **LeblancBig**'s runtime was spent inside these OpenMP regions, with the initial thread only taking 21.2% more of the load. The difference in time spent between computation and synchronization of threads is proportional to the number of threads requested at execution runtime, with very little time–under 30%– being used for thread synchronization.

Similar trends are seen with **Sedovbig**, with the fastest runtimes seen with the Cray compilers–its slowest runtime being 1387 s–and the slowest runtimes seen by the ARM-based LLVM compilers (2694 s)–in Fig. 2(a). The generic LLVM compilers, not shown in the graph, displayed runtimes as slow as 3000 s.

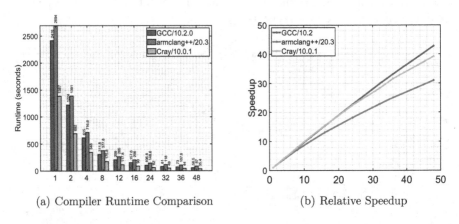

(a) Compiler Runtime Comparison   (b) Relative Speedup

Fig. 2. PENNANT/SedovBig Input Results on Ookami; X-axes refer to number of OpenMP threads

Unlike the results from Fig. 1(b), Fig. 2(b) shows the GNU compilers having the most linear/largest speedup, with the Cray compilers coming in relatively close until diverging at the 24-thread experiments. The armclang experiments deviate from the Cray and GNU experiments after 4 OpenMP threads.

SWIM was run with the default test problem, `swim.ref.in`. It sets up a 7701×7701 matrix running 3000 iterations. In our experiments, we tested 7 different compiler versions, but to avoid clutter and data overlap, we have chosen 3 representatives from the various compiler families: GNU, ARM's LLVM-based compiler, and Cray. We present results from these compilers in this section. The runtime results and speed-up plots are shown in Figs. 3(a) and (b):

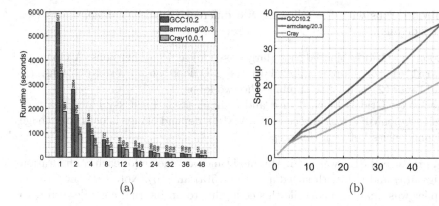

Fig. 3. (a) SWIM/Ookami Compiler Runtimes (b) SWIM/Ookami Relative Speedup

As shown in Fig. 3(a), it is clear that the Cray compiler has the best performance among all three compilers with SVE support enabled on the Ookami cluster. Cray obtained a 2.3x faster performance than `armclang` with a single thread. The ARM-based LLVM compiler generally has better performance than the ARM-based GNU compilers, which is also expected. The LLVM compiler has generated more SVE operations comparing with GNU compiler which leads to the better runtime performance.

In Fig. 3(b), we see that among all the compilers, the GNU compiler seems to have the greatest speed up. 48 threads achieve a 37x speed-up over 1 thread. Conversely, the Cray compiler only gives a 16x speedup between 1 and 48 threads shown in Fig. 3(b).

A clear result shows that the GNU compiler obtained the best efficiency among all these three compilers. On the contrary, the Cray compiler seems to have a much lower efficiency than GNU and ARM based compilers for all runs. For all three compilers the general trends are the similar. Clear drops are happening when using 2, 4, 8 and 12 OpenMP threads especially at 12 threads. It is also interesting that even though Cray compiler obtained the best runtime performance, there are still a lot more could be improved.

With profiling tools ARM MAP and CrayPat [3] on Ookami with 48 threads, SWIM has spent 70.2% runtime on OpenMP region which is understandable since it is a purely OpenMP benchmark. OpenMP generates a small amount of overhead: 28.5% was seen with this particular runs. Like with PENNANT, this indicates that more threads will spend more time communicating with each other and less overall time on performing computations.

Minimod runs with the following two different OpenMP configurations (see [16] for details):

- Loop xy: Grid is blocked in x (largest-stride) and y dimensions. A OpenMP `parallel for` loop is applied to the 2-D loop nest over x-y blocks. (A `collapse(2)` is used to combine the two loops).
- Tasks xy: Grid is blocked in x and y dimensions. Each x-y block is a task using OpenMP's *task* directive. OpenMP's `depend` clause is used to manage dependencies between timesteps.

A grid size of 512^3 was used. Minimod times are shown for each configuration in Figs. 4(a) and (b), with speedups in Fig. 5(a) and (b). Note that the Cray C compiler was unable to compile this code, due to an internal compiler error, so only GCC and Arm compiler results are shown.[4]

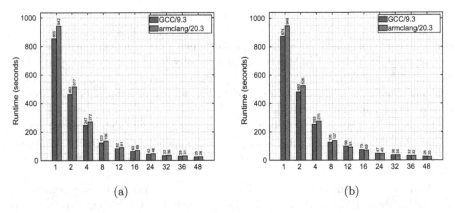

Fig. 4. (a) Minimod/Ookami/timing (loop xy) (b) Minimod/Ookami/timing (tasks xy)

In the GCC compilers, the loop-based configuration tends to outperform the task-based configuration. In LLVM compilers, however, the performance is similar between the two configurations.

We profiled Minimod using the ARM Forge Performance Report tool with 48 threads. We find that in both configurations, the application spends almost the entire runtime within OpenMP regions, and both have a high number of stalled cycles (76.5% and 80.7% of cycles for loop-xy and tasks-xy configurations respectively), indicating that the application is memory-bound. This makes the HBM2 memory of the A64FX processor potentially advantageous for this type of application.

---

[4] A Fortran version of Minimod was also evaluated using the Cray Fortran compiler. While this version was successfully compiled, the final numerical result was incorrect with optimization turned on.

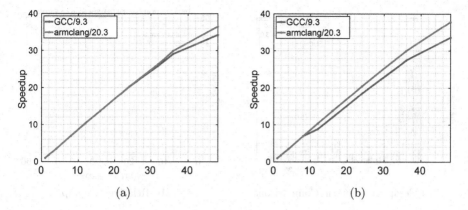

Fig. 5. (a) Minimod/Ookami/speedup (loop xy) (b) Minimod/Ookami/speedup (tasks xy)

3.2 Fugaku

With Fugaku's customized Linux kernel and its compute node's processors having 2 extra cores compared to Ookami, it was a slight challenge creating experiments whose environment matched the conditions set in the Ookami-based experiments. The Fujitsu compiler's ability to compile with either their traditional backend and an LLVM backend creates the ability to compare a compiler's performance with itself. In this section, we will break down and explain our results on the Fugaku supercomputer comparing results between GNU Compilers, and the Fujitsu compilers. Per the experiments in Sect. 2, we ran each application 5 times and took the average of their runtimes.

PENNANT. Of all the compilers mentioned in this subsection and in Sect. 3.1, those from Fujitsu resulted in the longest recorded runtimes for both the **LeblancBig** and **SedovBig** inputs. In particular, the single-threaded runtimes for both inputs had surprisingly large standard deviations (107 s as opposed to a fraction of a second). Conversely, both versions of GNU compilers on Fugaku, when applied to PENNANT, still maintained comparable runtimes to those on Ookami.

In Fig. 6(a), we noticed that the traditional backend options for the Fujitsu Compiler took substantially longer runtimes in 1-and 2-thread runs compared to the LLVM-backend (see Sect. 2.4). Profiling **LeblancBig** shows that the traditional Fujitsu compiler backend takes a longer runtime, yet executes a higher amount of GFLOPS, than the LLVM backend on the **LeblancBig** input. In particular, both backends show a better runtime at 24 OpenMP threads – 181 s on the LLVM backend and 186 s on the traditional backend – than at 48 OpenMP threads – 233 and 236 s for the LLVM and traditional backends, respectively. This appears to be caused by the increased communication between each of the

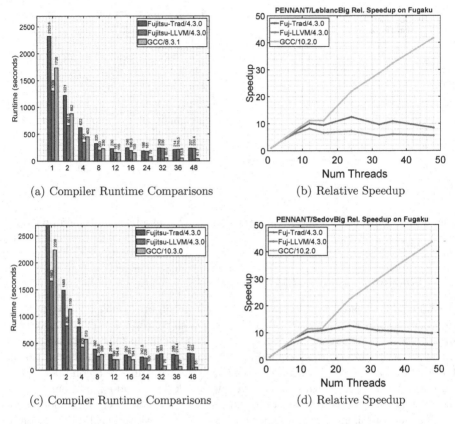

(a) Compiler Runtime Comparisons

(b) Relative Speedup

(c) Compiler Runtime Comparisons

(d) Relative Speedup

Fig. 6. (a)/(b): LeblancBig Input Results on Fugaku, (c)/(d): SedovBig Input Results on Fugaku; X-axes refer to number of OpenMP threads

CMGs on the A64FX processor, especially as the thread count and number of CMGs used increases.

Similarly, this results in observed reduced speedup for the Fujitsu compiler, especially after reaching 12 threads placed in 1 CMG (See Fig. 6(b)).

The GNU compilers across both the Ookami and Fugaku systems allow for reasonable speedup, and efficiency as well on top of this. All 3 compiler options first start off with similar trends, but once each compiled binary is run on more than twelve threads, we see a massive drop in efficiency with the Fujitsu compilers. One reason this may be the case is how the underlying communication between CMGs and how the Fujitsu compilers generate SVE instructions to rely more on MPI-based parallelism versus OpenMP/thread-based parallelism, especially if each process only takes 1 thread.

Similar cases occur with the **SedovBig** input. Here, we see that 1 CMG full of threads runs more quickly than 2 or more CMGs full of threads with **LeblancBig**, per in Fig. 6(c). The runtime for a single-OpenMP-thread run with the **SedovBig** input can take more than 3000 s on the Fujitsu-traditional backend, and over half as long as on the Fujitsu-LLVM backend. Similar trends in speedup are shown in Fig. 6(d).

In an experiment on Fugaku, we ran the "Fujitsu Instant Performance Profiler" (FIPP) [5] on **SedovBig** using 1 OpenMP thread, as adding more threads results in minimal runtime differences between runs of PENNANT compiled by both Fujitsu backends. Using the LLVM backend results in a shorter runtime (1662 s) and fewer GFLOPS (1.41) while having a higher bandwidth usage (1.69 GB/s). Conversely, the traditional backend results in nearly twice the runtime (3108 s), a larger GFLOP value (1.93), but just over half the bandwidth usage (0.8868 GB/s) of the LLVM-backend's run. Larger values of OpenMP threads using PENNANT compiled by either backend begins leveling off/converging once a user requests more than 12 OpenMP threads for their application, as per Fig. 6(c).

SWIM. With the Fugaku cluster, two compilers were used to test SWIM's capabilities: Fujitsu v4.4.0a and GNU-10.2.1. In contradiction with PENNANT results mentioned in Sect. 3.2, SWIM has gained a significant runtime improvement with Fujitsu compiler compared with best runtime performance with Ookami cluster as shown in Fig. 7(a). As for the GNU compiler, the runtime results are much comparable with runs made on Ookami. Note that the Fujitsu compilers do not support multiple backends for Fortran.

It is also worth mentioning that memory allocation across multiple CMGs running for thread parallelism is crucial for optimizing SWIM's runtime performance. The environment variable `XOS_MMM_L_PAGING_POLICY` is set to `demand:demand:demanddemand:demand:demand` for multiple CMGs in order to place data near the thread that has first touched it, and `prepage:demand:prepage` for a single CMG, as recommended.

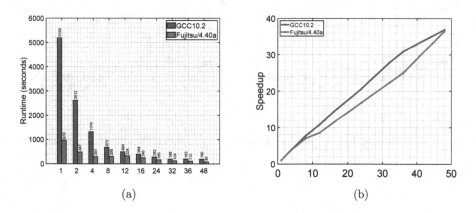

Fig. 7. (a) SWIM/Fugaku Timing (b) SWIM/Fugaku Relative Speedup

Although the Fujitsu compiler has better overall performance, as shown in Fig. 7(b), the GNU compiler seems to have a greater speed up than the Fujitsu compiler. GNU runs with 36 threads achieve a 32x speed-up over 1 thread, while he Fujitsu compiler only obtained 25x speed up with the same thread difference. The Fugaku-based runs show a drop in relative speedup starting at 8 OpenMP threads before leveling out at 12 threads. Our studies on relative compiler efficiency have further backed up our results in Fig. 7(b).

On Fugaku, with the Fujitsu Instant Performance Profiler, SWIM has shown a much better performance than all other compilers that we have tested previously on Ookami. It has achieved 31.20 GFLOPS with 48 threads, and overall faster runtimes compared to those made on Ookami. One reason might be the extreme high SVE operation rate. As shown in the profiling results, a 99.9% SVE operation rate has been obtained by Fujitsu compiler. Besides the impressive performance results, the rest are similar with Ookami profiling results. Most of the runtime went into the OpenMP region.

Minimod times are shown for each configuration in Figs. 8(a) (loop xy) and Fig. 8(b) (tasks xy), with speedups in Fig. 9(a) and (b). Because the traditional backend for the Fujitsu compiler supports OpenMP up to only version 3.0, it cannot compile the task-based version of Minimod, whereas the LLVM backend supports up through the latest OpenMP specification versions, per Figs. 8(b) and Fig. 9(b).

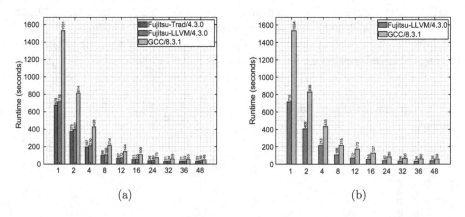

(a)   (b)

Fig. 8. (a) Minimod/Fugaku/timing (loop xy) (b) Minimod/Fugaku/timing (tasks xy)

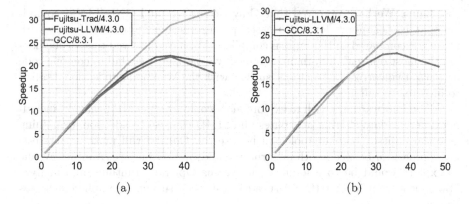

Fig. 9. (a) Minimod/Fugaku/speedup (loop xy) (b) Minimod/Fugaku/speedup (tasks xy)

Profiling of the Minimod application on Fugaku is currently in progress.

4   Related Work

In [12], a group from RIKEN reports their preliminary performance analysis of A64FX compared to the Marvell (Cavium) ThunderX2 (TX2) and Intel Xeon Skylake (SKL) processors based on 7 HPC applications and benchmarks. Some of the applications considered use only OpenMP and others use hybrid MPI + OpenMP for parallelization. The compilers used in this study are the Fujitsu Compiler 4.2.0 (under development) for A64FX, ARM-HPC Compiler 20.1 for TX2, and Intel Compiler 19.0.5.281 for SKL.

Another group [8] from EPCC at The University of Edinburgh, reports on their study of various complex scientific applications and mini-kernel benchmarks across multiple nodes, as well as on a single node on different production HPC platforms, which include Fujitsu A64FX processors, 3 Intel Xeon series – E5-2697 v2 (IvyBridge), E5-2695 (Broadwell), and Platinum 8260M (Cascade Lake)– and Marvell ThunderX2. Different compiler families, including several versions of some of them, like, Fujitsu, Intel, GCC/GNU, ARM/LLVM, and Cray, were used in their study. Also, they have considered various MPI implementations and scientific libraries.

Several recent works evaluated benchmark applications using multiple compilers on the A64FX processor; e.g., [7,14]. However, these works do not focus on OpenMP.

5   Conclusions and Future Work

In this paper, we have studied and observed the behavior of OpenMP implementations on the A64FX processor across several applications and several compiler toolchains. We have observed that Cray's compilers and GNU/LLVM compilers that have support for ARM-based processors appear to scale better with OpenMP compared to the Fujitsu compilers. We have observed that, while having the most optimal performance, the Cray Compilers may fail to compile code or generate incorrect instructions, such as with the Minimod application, leading to incorrect results.

Moving forward, we wish to explore more complex OpenMP behavior, including different data-sharing attributes and SIMD clauses. In addition, examining how the Fujitsu compiler toolchain behaves on Ookami will make an interesting comparison between both its structure and that on Fugaku. Another avenue to explore would be to examine serial versus OpenMP runtimes and analyze how much of an impact the overhead has in each runtime environment across compilers.

Acknowledgements. We would like to thank the NSF for supporting the Ookami cluster, and the ability to research the A64FX processor by Riken and Fujitsu, through grant OAC 1927880. We would like to thank the Riken Center for Computational Science for providing us with accounts to use the Fugaku supercomputer and conduct research on it. We would also like to thank Stony Brook University and the Institute for Advanced Computational Science for providing the resources to allow us to conduct our studies on Ookami. Finally, we would like to thank TotalEnergies Exploration and Production Research and Technologies for their support of experimentation using MiniMod.

References

1. ARM. Arm forge documentation. https://developer.arm.com/documentation/101136/2021/Performance-Reports
2. F. Corp. A64fx microarchitecture manual. https://github.com/fujitsu/A64FX/blob/master/doc/A64FX_Microarchitecture_Manual_en_1.3.pdf
3. H. P. Enterprise. Craypat documentation. https://pubs.cray.com/bundle/HPE_Performance_Analysis_Tools_User_Guide_S-8014_2012/page/CrayPat_Runtime_Environment.html
4. Ferenbaugh, C.R.: Pennant: an unstructured mesh mini-app for advanced architecture research. https://www.osti.gov/biblio/1079561-pennant-unstructured-mesh-mini-app-advanced-architecture-research
5. Fujitsu: Fujitsu instant performance profiler. https://www.fujitsu.com/global/about/resources/publications/technicalreview/2020-03/article07.html
6. Fujitsu: Icc: an interconnect controller for the tofu interconnect architecture. https://www.fujitsu.com/global/Images/20100824hotchips22_tcm100-933454.pdf
7. Graziano, V., Nystrom, D., Pritchard, H., Smith, B., Gravelle, B.: Optimizing a 3D multi-physics continuum mechanics code for the HPE APOLLO 80 system. In: Cray User Group (CUG) 2021, Virtual, May 2021
8. Jackson, A., Weiland, M., Brown, N., Turner, A., Parsons, M.: Investigating applications on the A64fx. In: 2020 IEEE International Conference on Cluster Computing (CLUSTER), Los Alamitos, CA, USA, September 2020, pp. 549–558. IEEE Computer Society (2020)

9. Meng, J., Atle, A., Calandra, H., Araya-Polo, M.: Minimod: a finite difference solver for seismic modeling (2020)
10. Michalowicz, B., Raut, E., Kang, Y., Curtis, T., Chapman, B., Oryspayev, D.: Comparing the behavior of OpenMP implementations with various applications on two different Fujitsu A64FX platforms. In: Proceedings of the Practice and Experience in Advanced Research Computing in Evolution Across All Dimensions, New York, NY, USA. Association for Computing Machinery (2021)
11. NSF. Ookami: a high-productivity path to frontiers of scientific discovery enabled by exascale system technologies. https://www.nsf.gov/awardsearch/showAward? AWD_ID=1927880
12. Odajima, T., Kodama, Y., Tsuji, M., Matsuda, M., Maruyama, Y., Sato, M.: Preliminary performance evaluation of the Fujitsu A64FX using HPC applications. In: 2020 IEEE International Conference on Cluster Computing (CLUSTER), pp. 523–530, September 2020
13. Okazaki, R., et al.: Supercomputer Fugaku CPU A64FX realizing high performance, high-density packaging, and low power consumption. Fujitsu Technical Review, November 2020
14. Poenaru, A., Deakin, T., McIntosh-Smith, S., Hammond, S., Younge, A.: An evaluation of the a64fx architecture for HPC applications. In: Cray User Group (CUG) 2021, Virtual, May 2021
15. Raut, E., Anderson, J., Araya-Polo, M., Meng, J.: Porting and evaluation of a distributed task-driven stencil-based application. In: Proceedings of the Twelfth International Workshop on Programming Models and Applications for Multicores and Manycores, PMAM '21, New York, NY, USA. Association for Computing Machinery (2021)
16. Raut, E., Meng, J., Araya-Polo, M., Chapman, B.: Evaluating performance of OpenMP tasks in a seismic stencil application. In: Milfeld, K., de Supinski, B.R., Koesterke, L., Klinkenberg, J. (eds.) IWOMP 2020. LNCS, vol. 12295, pp. 67–81. Springer, Cham (2020). https://doi.org/10.1007/978-3-030-58144-2_5
17. RIKEN. Fugaku project. https://www.r-ccs.riken.jp/en/fugaku/project
18. Sato, M., et al.: Co-design for a64fx manycore processor and "Fugaku". In: Proceedings of the International Conference for High Performance Computing, Networking, Storage and Analysis, SC 2020. IEEE Press (2020)
19. SPEC. Swim benchmark page. https://www.spec.org/cpu2000/CFP2000/171.swim/docs/171.swim.html

A Case Study of LLVM-Based Analysis for Optimizing SIMD Code Generation

Joseph Huber[1], Weile Wei[2(✉)], Giorgis Georgakoudis[3], Johannes Doerfert[4], and Oscar Hernandez[1]

[1] Oak Ridge National Laboratory, Oak Ridge, TN 37830, USA
{huberjn,oscar}@ornl.gov
[2] Lousiana State University, Baton Rouge, LA 70803, USA
wwei9@lsu.edu
[3] Lawrence Livermore National Laboratory, Livermore, CA 94550, USA
georgakoudis1@llnl.gov
[4] Argonne National Laboratory, Lemont, IL 60439, USA
jdoerfert@anl.gov

Abstract. This paper presents a methodology for using LLVM-based tools to tune the DCA++ (dynamical cluster approximation) application that targets the new ARM A64FX processor. The goal is to describe the changes required for the new architecture and generate efficient single instruction/multiple data (SIMD) instructions that target the new Scalable Vector Extension instruction set. During manual tuning, the authors used the LLVM tools to improve code parallelization by using OpenMP SIMD, refactored the code and applied transformation that enabled SIMD optimizations, and ensured that the correct libraries were used to achieve optimal performance. By applying these code changes, code speed was increased by 1.98× and 78 GFlops were achieved on the A64FX processor. The authors aim to automatize parts of the efforts in the OpenMP Advisor tool, which is built on top of existing and newly introduced LLVM tooling.

Keywords: OpenMP · SIMD · Compilers · Feedback · LLVM · HPC tools

1 Introduction

Program analysis tools are important in helping users understand, improve, and port their applications to new platforms. This is crucial for applications that need tuning and significant code restructuring to exploit new types of hardware devices, such as single instruction/multiple data (SIMD) units and accelerators. Compiler-based tools are crucially important for identifying opportunities to improve application codes as the compiler generates code for different architectures. In particular, the LLVM compiler is an open-source compiler that provides

© Springer Nature Switzerland AG 2021
S. McIntosh-Smith et al. (Eds.): IWOMP 2021, LNCS 12870, pp. 142–155, 2021.
https://doi.org/10.1007/978-3-030-85262-7_10

a set of tools for the static analysis and feedback of application code. Static program analysis information can be combined with dynamic information (profile-based) to filter the large amount of information produced by the compiler so that users can focus on the most frequently executed regions of their code.

This paper presents a methodology for using LLVM-based tools to tune an application to generate efficient SIMD instructions that target the new ARM A64FX processor, as well as describes what is required to achieve good performance.

2 Case Study: Porting DCA++ to Wombat

This section describes the authors' experiences in porting the DCA++ (dynamical cluster approximation) application to the Wombat[1] cluster, an ARM-based heterogeneous cluster at Oak Ridge National Laboratory. This section presents a methodology for using LLVM-based tools to tune the DCA++ application targeting the ARM A64FX and ThunderX2 processors. The goal is to describe what changes are required for the new architecture and generate efficient SIMD instructions that target the new Scalable Vector Extension (SVE) instruction set available in the A64FX processors based on LLVM-based tools information.

2.1 Evaluation Environment

The case study used the Wombat test bed with 24 compute nodes. Sixteen compute nodes are based on the Fujitsu A64FX processor with SVE and a theoretical peak performance of 3.3792 TFlops. Each A64FX node has one processor socket with 32 GB of second-generation High-Bandwidth Memory (HBM2). The A64FX-equipped nodes do not have additional Double Data Rate (DDR) memory. Eight compute nodes have two ThunderX2 processors with NEON vector instructions and a theoretical peak performance of 560 GFlops. The ThunderX2 nodes have 256 GB of DDR4 RAM and a 480 GB solid-state drive for node-local storage. All nodes are connected with Enhanced Data Rate InfiniBand (100 Gbit/s). The compilers on the system are the ARM 20.3 compilers and the Clang upstream compiler, which is based on Clang 12. The scientific libraries available on Wombat are the ARM Performance Libraries (APL) version 20.3.

2.2 DCA++

Quantum Monte Carlo (QMC) solver applications are popular tools essential to the US Department of Energy-supported scientific software. This paper studies one cutting-edge QMC application called the DCA++ algorithm. DCA++ [6] implements quantum cluster algorithms to solve quantum many-body problems in condensed matter physics. DCA++ is a highly scalable and performant scientific software written in modern C++ and has been ported to various high-performance computing architectures, including IBM Power9, x86_64, ThunderX2, and ARM A64FX [13]. The DCA++ software currently integrates three

---

[1] Wombat: www.olcf.ornl.gov/olcf-resources/compute-systems/wombat/.

different programming models—message passing interface (MPI), Compute Unified Device Architecture (CUDA), and High Performance ParalleX (HPX)/C++ threading—together with numerical libraries (e.g., Basic Linear Algebra Subprograms [BLAS], Linear Algebra Package [LAPACK], and MAGMA) to expose the parallel computation structure.

Wei et al. [13] reported that DCA++ with the HPX run time system [10] has produced a 20% run time speedup over the one with C++ standard threading support. The speedup is primarily due to the faster thread context switching and reduced scheduler synchronization overheads in the HPX run time. Moreover, Autonomic Performance Environment for Exascale (APEX) [8] is an in situ profiling and adaptive tuning framework to the HPX run time system that can capture operating system and hardware system performance data through various interfaces, such as Performance Application Programming Interface (PAPI) [12]. Because APEX is highly integrated into the HPX run time, for HPX-supported applications, users can easily capture PAPI counter information (e.g., level 2 data cache misses, vector/SIMD instructions, floating point instructions) through HPX function annotation. The overhead introduced by APEX profiling is as low as ~1% [5] compared with the overall application run time.

In DCA++, the QMC solver is the most computation-intensive unit that models strongly correlated electron systems [13]. Computation on the QMC solver is parallelized by using a multithreading scheme that comprises walker (i.e., producer) and accumulator (i.e., consumer) tasks. Each task runs on an independent thread. There are multiple walkers running concurrently. Each walker is responsible for a Monte Carlo (MC) update (sampling from the Markov chain), and then an accumulator is popped from the head of the accumulator waiting queue to compute an MC measurement from the walker. When each accumulator finishes its accumulation measurement, it is pushed back to the end of the queue. The walker-accumulator synchronization is managed by the synchronization primitives mutex and conditional_variable.

2.3 Baseline Performance

The following experiments compare DCA++'s performance on Wombat by using its A64FX and ThunderX2 nodes. The performance is measured using 48 accumulators and 48 walkers and using 100,000 measurements, which is a representative scientific simulation case in production. On A64FX, DCA++ is built with two different configuration settings: SVE vectorization and SVE-disabled. The SVE vectorization version of DCA++ means that DCA++ is built with SVE compiler flags enabled and vectorized loops, and it uses the APL optimized for SVE (i.e., LAPACK, BLAS, Fastest Fourier Transform in the West [FFTW]). The SVE compiler flags are set to "-DNDEBUG -fsimdmath -fopenmp -O3 -mcpu=a64fx" The SVE-disabled version means that DCA++ is built with original DCA++ code and open-source scientific libraries, including Netlib-LAPACK and FFTW. Similarly, on ThunderX2, DCA++ is built with two different configurations: with NEON and NEON disabled.

Figure 1 shows DCA++ execution time on A64FX and ThunderX2 architectures. On A64FX, the SVE vectorization version of DCA++ performs ∼2× faster than the SVE-disabled version. On ThunderX2, the NEON version of DCA++ is observed to be ∼1.66× faster than the NEON-disabled version. Noticeably, the SVE vectorization version of DCA++ on A64FX has ∼3.3× speedup over the NEON version on ThunderX2. Meanwhile, the NEON version on ThunderX2 is measured to have ∼27 GFlops, and the SVE vectorization version of DCA++ on A64FX reached ∼78 GFlops (∼2.8×).

Thes results show the performance gains of DCA++ due to the peak performance improvements of the A64FX processor (e.g., 500 GFlops for ThunderX2 vs. 2.5 TFlops for A64FX).

	vectorization	walltime (seconds) ± standard deviation	speedup	Gflop/s
A64fx	no	488.42±3.09	-	17
	yes	246.98±0.48	1.98	78
ThunderX2	no	1336.61±178.09	-	14
	yes	805.53±24.06	1.66	27

Fig. 1. DCA++ execution time.

Figure 2 shows the breakdown of DCA++ execution time into four categories: application, scientific libraries, HPX run time, and other activities. Each category only considers functions that have more than 1% overhead shown in the final profiling report generated from **perf**, a Linux built-in performance profiling tool. The application category includes custom modules developed in the DCA++ source code. The HPX run time category represents necessary scheduling and coordination efforts in HPX threads manager. The scientific libraries category captures routines from external numerical libraries, such as BLAS, LAPACK, FFTW, and math routines. The other activities category summarizes all other functions that have less than 1% overhead in the final profiling report.

Several observations were made from the timing breakdown shown in Fig. 2.

1. With SVE vectorization or NEON optimization, the dominant percentage of the overall execution time is shifted from the external scientific libraries to the application source code. For example, on A64FX, the percentage of application time in the SVE-disabled vectorization version of DCA++ is 26%, whereas the percentage of application time in the SVE version is 57%. A similar percentage shift is also observed on ThunderX2 comparisons. In other words, with APL (SVE vectorization on A64FX or NEON optimization on ThunderX2), less time is spent on scientific libraries because APL are particularly optimized on targeting platforms.
2. The HPX run time library imposes minimal overhead to the overall program execution. The overhead is primarily due to a lack of sufficient parallelism from the application so that some HPX worker threads in the kernel level are spinning and waiting for user-level tasks.

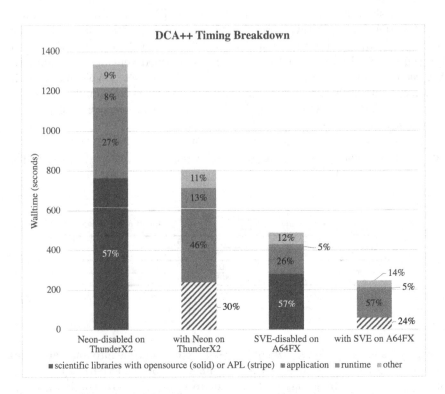

Fig. 2. DCA++ timing breakdown.

Accumulator	% total	L2_DCM	VEC_INS	TOT_CYC	FP_INS
no SVE	30.86	9.29E+09	6.05E+11	1.29E+13	2.73E+12
standard deviation	0.30	4.27E+07	0.00E+00	2.24E+10	0.00E+00
SVE vectorization	51.11	9.88E+09	6.53E+10	1.09E+13	2.62E+12
standard deviation	0.17	3.59E+07	0.00E+00	0.00E+00	0.00E+00
Walker	**% total**	**L2_DCM**	**VEC_INS**	**TOT_CYC**	**FP_INS**
no SVE	62.15	6.15E+10	3.99E+12	2.61E+13	8.37E+11
standard deviation	0.61	2.03E+08	0.00E+00	4.70E+10	0.00E+00
SVE vectorization	40.14	6.27E+10	5.05E+10	8.56E+12	3.45E+11
standard deviation	0.14	1.11E+08	0.00E+00	8.87E+09	0.00E+00
Total (Acc. + Walker)	**% total**	**L2_DCM**	**VEC_INS**	**TOT_CYC**	**FP_INS**
no SVE	93.00	7.08E+10	4.60E+12	3.90E+13	3.57E+12
standard deviation	0.90	2.46E+08	0.00E+00	6.94E+10	0.00E+00
SVE vectorization	91.25	7.26E+10	1.16E+11	1.95E+13	2.97E+12
standard deviation	0.31	1.46E+08	0.00E+00	8.87E+09	0.00E+00

Fig. 3. PAPI counter for DCA++ runs on A64FX.

Further investigation using hardware performance counters is shown in Fig. 3. Here, `hpx::annotated_function()` is used to wrap `accumulator` and `walker` tasks so that their activities (i.e., timing information and PAPI counters) can be distinguished in the final profiling report generated from the HPX-APEX profiling tool. Figure 3 shows that the total execution time of `accumulator` and `walker` takes the majority of the overall program execution time ($\sim$93.00% in the SVE-disabled version and $\sim$91.25% in SVE vectorization version). Several observations were made from Fig. 3.

1. The SVE-disabled version of DCA++ on A64FX has nearly $\sim$40$\times$ higher VEC_INC, 2$\times$ higher TOT_CYC, and 1.2$\times$ higher FP_INS than the SVE vectorization version, where VEC_INC is vector/SIMD instructions, TOT_CYC is total cycles, and FP_INC is floating point instructions. The authors noticed that by using the optimized libraries, the application uses less vector and floating point SVE instructions. Because SVE has wider 512 bit width, fewer vector instructions are needed in the computation than NEON, which has 128 bit width. Also, the SVE has a more powerful instruction set that uses fewer instructions for the same operation.
2. The L2_DCM (L2 data cache misses) does not change with the SVE optimized version because the SVE optimization does not impact overall memory access patterns. Access to HBM2 remained constant in both versions.
3. Using SVE vectorization on DCA++ shifts timing percentages between `accumulator` and `walker` in overall program execution. To perform efficient matrix-related operations, the implementation of `walker` extensively uses DGEMM routines, which are provided by the scientific libraries. The timing percentage of `walker` is 62.15% with the SVE-disabled version of DCA++ in overall program execution and is reduced to 40.14% with the SVE vectorization version. The percentage reduction of `walker` is similar to the percentage reduction of scientific libraries observed in Fig. 2.

The results show that to further improve the DCA++ application, the focus must be on tuning the application source code, particularly the accumulator code, to determine which loops need further optimization and which were successfully vectorized by the compiler. This requires significant interaction with the LLVM tools to understand the application hot spots and the opportunities for SVE optimizations.

3 An LLVM Tool Methodology to Generate Efficient Vectorization

A64FX performance is highly dependent on how well the source can be mapped to SVE instructions. It is important to determine which application loops are not being vectorized and their impact on the application's overall performance. The ARM C/C++ compiler is based on the LLVM/Clang compiler, which is also the basis for the authors' exploration and automation toward vectorizing the most important loops in an application.

Like most modern compilers, LLVM/Clang and its derivatives support profile guided optimization (PGO). The idea is that the compiler inserts profiling instructions into the target binary to collect information when the application is run. During application shutdown, profiling information is stored on the disk for later use. When the application is recompiled in the future, the collected profiling information is used to drive heuristics (e.g., to determine a suitable unroll count for loops). Such profiling also allows the compiler to approximate how much time was spent in a certain portion of code, also referred to as *code hotness*. The latter makes PGO especially interesting to filter optimization remarks because it allows users to only view remarks emitted for hot code regions. Thus, with PGO, users can be guided toward the loops that would benefit the most from vectorization and avoid overloading them with a plethora of uninteresting remarks.

The authors manually analyzed several loops in the DCA++ application by using the aforementioned method described to determine what was hindering loop vectorization. Some loops required a simple change in vectorization flags, and others required user intervention (e.g., vectorization directives, such as OpenMP SIMD) to assist the compiler. The authors also identified loops that required transformations to make the vectorization more efficient. The following sections present a brief discussion for four hot loops that the compiler was unable to vectorize without user intervention.

3.1   OpenMP SIMD

When optimizing any loops, the compiler's vectorization pass must preserve the semantics of the original source code. This usually requires static analyses to verify that the transformation is legal. However, it is not uncommon for a transformation to be correct but unable to be statically verified by the compiler. Since OpenMP 4.0, OpenMP has added support for the SIMD directive, which provides a cross-platform method for statically asserting information about the program's semantics to the compiler's vectorization pass [7]. In DCA++, various loops require additional information to be successfully vectorized.

Figure 4 shows a classical reduction loop. Because x_val is a floating point value, any reordering of the iterations (e.g., as part of vectorization) would break strict Institute of Electrical and Electronics Engineers (IEEE) floating point compliance and might introduce errors in the result. By default, LLVM/-Clang will not vectorize the loop but will instead emit a remark (lower part) that explains how *ffast-math* or vectorization pragmas can be used to overwrite the IEEE floating point semantics. The Clang pragmas are a less feature-rich variant of the cross-platform OpenMP SIMD directives, but both explicitly tell the compiler to allow vector execution for a loop. In the OpenMP variant, users should make the parallel reduction explicit. Additionally, the authors used the aligned clause to pass alignment information to the compiler, which can lead to improved performance due to specialized memory instructions.

In line 6 of Fig. 5, there is a noncontinuous memory load—a gather. ARM's SVE supports fast gathering operations; however, the compiler cannot vectorize

```
1   #pragma omp simd reduction(−:x_val) aligned(x_val, G_ptr : 64)
2   for (int i = 0; i < j; i++)
3     x_val −= x_ptr[i] * G_ptr[i];
```

remark: loop not vectorized: cannot prove it is safe to reorder floating−point operations; allow reordering by specifying '#pragma clang loop vectorize(enable)' before the loop or by providing the compiler option '−ffast−math'

Fig. 4. A loop performing a parallel reduction that is not vectorized automatically.

this loop without manual intervention because the accessed arrays M_ij_, M, config_left_ , and config_right_ might alias and hence overlap. In these situations, the compiler is often able to version the loop and generate a vectorized variant guarded by a run time alias check to verify that the accessed ranges of the arrays do not overlap at run time. However, the support for such run time alias checks in LLVM/Clang is limited to the case in which the accessed bounds are known statically [1]. Because the index into the M array is based on the values loaded from the configuration arrays, the access range cannot be bound statically. The compiler remark shown below the loop nest summarizes this discussion in a way that is difficult or impossible for application developers to understand. Using OpenMP SIMD effectively tells the compiler that there are no overlapping accesses, allowing the loop to be vectorized. Care must be taken to ensure that no aliasing actually occurs, otherwise this will result in incorrect results.

```
1   for (int j = start_index_right_ [orb_j]; j < end_index_right_[orb_j];  ++j) {
2     const int out_j = j − start_index_right_ [orb_j];
3     #pragma omp simd
4     for (int i = start_index_left_ [orb_i]; i < end_index_left_[orb_i];  ++i) {
5       const int out_i = i − start_index_left_ [orb_i];
6       M_ij_(out_i, out_j) = M(config_left_[i].idx, config_right_ [j].idx);
7     }
8   }
```

remark: loop not vectorized: Unknown array bounds

Fig. 5. A loop performing a memory gather that requires OpenMP SIMD to be vectorized by the ARM compiler.

3.2   Using the Correct Compiler Flags

Some loops require additional compiler flags to be vectorized. The code shown in Fig. 6 has two run time calls, line 5 and 6, which prevent the compiler from automatically vectorizing it. A function call usually requires an explicit vector version of the function and compiler support to allow vectorized execution. The ARM compiler provides an optimized math library that includes vector variants of common math functions. Users must explicitly enable such a vector library because it will disturb the precision of the result, similar to the floating point reordering. The ARM compiler provides the *fsimdmath* option to use its performance libraries, whereas standard Clang requires *fveclib* to be set to the desired vectorized library. *ffast-math* or *fno-math-errno* will allow the compiler to execute the loop out of order, but no vectorized math library is used. This means that the vector lanes are effectively unpacked before the call, and the math function is executed once per vector lane.

Another issue is that the application uses a custom matrix class that performs bounds checking by using assertions in the overloaded access operators. Although assertions are a good software engineering practice, their "complex" semantics must be preserved by the compiler. The problem is that no code is executed after a violated assertion. Thus, if assertions are enabled and present in a loop, the compiler must verify that the assertion cannot trigger to execute any side effects succeeding the assertion (e.g., from the next iteration). To disable assertions completely, *NDEBUG* can be defined during compilation; however this will cause a tension between "debug" and "release" builds that is often not desirable. For developers to identify issues that stem from assertions and other errors in handling code, the authors added a new remark to the LLVM vectorizer, which is shown below the code. For these experiments, the authors disabled assertions, provided a vectorized math library, and added OpenMP SIMD to allow vectorization, even in the presence of possibly aliasing accesses.

```
1   for (int j = 0; j < n_v; ++j) {
2   #pragma omp simd
3     for (int i = 0; i < n_w; ++i) {
4       const ScalarType x = configuration[j].get_tau() * w_[i];
5       T_[0](i, j) = std::cos(x);
6       T_[1](i, j) = std::sin(x);
7     }
8   }
```

remark: loop not vectorized: loop exit block contains control flow that does not return
remark: loop not vectorized: library call cannot be vectorized. Try compiling with −fno−math−errno, −ffast−math, or similar flags

Fig. 6. A code block using the math library functions *cos* and *sin*.

3.3   Loop Transformations

The loop in Fig. 7 contains gathers from memory at lines 11 and 18. More importantly, the code uses a column-major layout for all its matrices while this loop iterates across a row. This will require expensive scattering operations to distribute the stores to discontinuous memory addresses. This loop can be transformed to better exploit SIMD parallelism. Each iteration of this loop is independent, and the matrices are guaranteed to be square in the code, so this loop can safely be transposed to improve memory accesses. This transformation will also improve performance without vectorizing the loop.

```
1   for (int i = 0; i < Gamma.Rows(); i++) {      for (int j = 0; j < Gamma.Cols(); j++) {
2     for (int j = 0; j < Gamma.Cols(); j++) {      #pragma omp simd
3       int spin_idx_i = random_vertex_vector[i];    for (int i = 0; i < Gamma.Rows(); i++) {
4       int spin_idx_j = random_vertex_vector[j];      int spin_idx_i = random_vertex_vector[i];
5                                                      int spin_idx_j = random_vertex_vector[j];
6       if ( spin_idx_j < vertex_index) {
7         Real delta = (spin_idx_i == spin_idx_j)      if ( spin_idx_j < vertex_index) {
8                    ? 1.                                 Real delta = (spin_idx_i == spin_idx_j)
9                    : 0.;                                           ? 1.
10        Real N_ij = N(spin_idx_i, spin_idx_j );                   : 0.;
11        Gamma(i, j) =                                  Real N_ij = N(spin_idx_i, spin_idx_j );
12           (N_ij * exp_V[j] − delta) /                 Gamma(i, j) =
13           (exp_V[j] − 1.);                               (N_ij * exp_V[j] − delta) /
14      } else                                              (exp_V[j] − 1.);
15        Gamma(i, j) = G_precomputed(                 } else
16           spin_idx_i ,                                 Gamma(i, j) = G_precomputed(
17           spin_idx_j − vertex_index);                   spin_idx_i ,
18      if (i == j) {                                       spin_idx_j − vertex_index);
19        Real gamma_k = exp_delta_V[j];             }
20        Gamma(i, j) −=
21           (gamma_k) / (gamma_k − 1.);             Real gamma_k = exp_delta_V[j];
22      }                                            Gamma(j, j) −=
23    }                                                 (gamma_k) / (gamma_k − 1.);
24  }                                              }
```

remark: loop not vectorized: control flow cannot be substituted for a select
remark: loop not vectorized: cannot identify array bounds

Fig. 7. A loop requiring a source transformation and OpenMP SIMD (left) and its transformed version (right).

This loop contains conditional expressions that must be transformed into masks to be vectorized. This requires calculating the result of each branch and conditionally moving it into the final register by using a mask. In this case, the true condition of the loop at line 6 is much more computationally expensive than the false condition. If the result was not needed, then this will be calculated at each iteration of the loop, only to be thrown away. This problem is even worse for the final update across the diagonal at line 17, which will only be needed once every iteration of the inner loop but calculated every iteration. This conditional update can be hoisted from the loop to improve performance significantly.

Another issue is the division at line 14. This could cause a division-by-zero error that can block vectorization if regular error handling semantics are maintained. This can be disabled with fast math, but in some cases, the compiler is able to vectorize it by using masked division instructions. This would be a good application of the assume directive added in OpenMP 5.1 to assert to the compiler that the division will never cause an error.

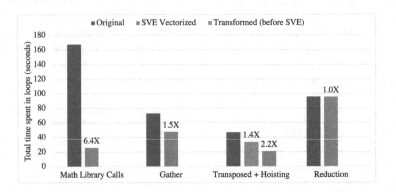

Fig. 8. The loops in Figs. 6, 5, 7, and 4, respectively, before and after the barriers to SVE execution were remedied. Performance is measured as the total time spent by all the threads in a run using 24 accumulators/walker threads over 100, 000 measurements.

3.4 Results

The overall impact of these transformations is shown in Fig. 8, which shows a significant speedup in most cases. The loop in Fig. 6 had the largest improvement when using ARM's vector math support. The reduction loop in Fig. 4 yielded no improvement. Upon further investigation, this was because the loop's trip count was very small in the average case, so the majority of the time was spent doing the final reduction, and work was rarely done in parallel. The other loops saw reasonable improvements, but their performance was limited by the gathering instructions required to vectorize them.

4   Automating the Process: The OpenMP Advisor

It is unrealistic but unfortunately still common practice to optimize code and add support for new platforms and features by manually inspecting and modifying the application. Given the increasing complexity when it comes to hardware and the requirement to support multiple heterogeneous platforms simultaneously, the authors must rethink their software engineering practices to ensure that the code is not only correct but also performant and portable. To automate this manual process and boost programmers' productivity, the authors began developing the OpenMP Advisor. Based on the portable OpenMP directive language, we hope to evolve the OpenMP Advisor over time into a valuable software engineering tool by using and extending LLVM capabilities. During the porting effort of the

DCA++ application described here, the authors experienced various issues that require interpretation to derive actionable advice. Using their experience, the authors began automating the parts of the process and improving the compiler remarks that were missing or misleading. As a result, the OpenMP Advisor the authors develop as part of the LLVM compiler framework will use optimization remarks from multiple optimization passes to report the most performance-critical problems in the code based on the available profiling data.

5   Related Work

There are several other tools that analyze source code or provide support for parallelization but with limited support that automatically inserts SIMD directives in the code. These include: CAPO [9] for automatic OpenMP work-sharing directives generation, which supports Fortran 77 and some F90 extensions; Appentra's Parallware [2], which focuses on parallelizing C/C++ applications by using OpenMP and OpenACC for multicores and accelerators; and Cray Reveal [4], which helps autoscope OpenMP variables and generate OpenMP work-sharing for Fortran and C/C++ for multicore and accelerators. Intel Inspector focuses on OpenMP semantic checking for data race detection. Foresys [11] and the Dragon Analysis tool [3] are legacy tools that supported the maintenance of Fortran code and help with parallelization with OpenMP.

6   Conclusion

Porting the DCA++ application to the A64FX processor requires the use of optimized scientific libraries and vectorizing the application hot spots. This process can be overwhelming to users, and tools are needed to automate this process. This work shows that by using LLVM tools, users can easily detect hot spots, determine why loops are not vectorized, and correct the issues by applying the correct compiler flags, transforming the code, or applying OpenMP directives.

Currently, authors are working an OpenMP Advisor tool that is built on top of existing and newly introduced LLVM tooling to automate this process. Ultimately, the authors want to enable application developers to navigate and handle compiler-generated information productively. Optimization reports should pinpoint important opportunities to tune the code (e.g., non-vectorized loops) and simultaneously provide sufficient information and suggestions to allow informed decisions without elaborate studies of compiler and programming language theory. The authors believe that tools can recommend portable annotations, such as OpenMP SIMD directives, when they inform users about the requirements for correctness. Furthermore, compiler analysis and optimizations can directly target the recently proposed OpenMP assume directive to request user feedback. In other words, OpenMP assume directives and the authors' implementation in the LLVM compiler will enable analyses and transformations to request high-level information from users naturally. The OpenMP Advisor will improve communication in the other direction to present users with important requests and remarks, together with information and examples that translate "compiler language" to "application language."

Acknowledgment. The authors would like to thank Manuel Arenaz (Appentra Solutions), Hartmut Kaiser (Louisiana State University), and Kevin Huck (University of Oregon) for their guidance and feedback on this work.

This work was supported by the Scientific Discovery through Advanced Computing (SciDAC) program funded by US Department of Energy, Office of Science, Advanced Scientific Computing Research (ASCR) and Basic Energy Sciences (BES) Division of Materials Sciences and Engineering. This research was also supported by the Exascale Computing Project (17-SC-20-SC), a collaborative effort of the US Department of Energy Office of Science and the National Nuclear Security Administration, in particular its subproject on Scaling OpenMP with LLVM for Exascale performance and portability (SOLLVE).

Notice: This manuscript has been authored by UT-Battelle, LLC, under contract DE-AC05-00OR22725 with the US Department of Energy (DOE). The US government retains and the publisher, by accepting the article for publication, acknowledges that the US government retains a nonexclusive, paid-up, irrevocable, worldwide license to publish or reproduce the published form of this manuscript, or allow others to do so, for US government purposes. DOE will provide public access to these results of federally sponsored research in accordance with the DOE Public Access Plan (http://energy.gov/downloads/doe-public-access-plan).

This work was performed under the auspices of the U.S. Department of Energy by Lawrence Livermore National Laboratory under Contract DE-AC52-07NA27344 (LLNL-CONF-819815).

References

1. Alves, P., et al.: Runtime pointer disambiguation. In: Proceedings of the 2015 ACM SIGPLAN International Conference on Object-Oriented Programming, Systems, Languages, and Applications, OOPSLA 2015, pp. 589–606. Association for Computing Machinery, New York (2015)

2. Arenaz, M., Martorell, X.: Parallelware tools: an experimental evaluation on POWER systems. In: Weiland, M., Juckeland, G., Alam, S., Jagode, H. (eds.) ISC High Performance 2019. LNCS, vol. 11887, pp. 352–360. Springer, Cham (2019). https://doi.org/10.1007/978-3-030-34356-9_27

3. Chapman, B., et al.: Dragon: an open64-based interactive program analysis tool for large applications. In: Proceedings of the Fourth International Conference on Parallel and Distributed Computing, Applications and Technologies, pp. 792–796 (2003)

4. DeRose, L., Poxon, H., Beyer, J., Hart, A.: A high level programming environment for accelerator-based systems. Procedia Comput. Sci. **29**, 1480–1490 (2014). 2014 International Conference on Computational Science

5. Diehl, P., et al.: Performance measurements within asynchronous task-based runtime systems: a double white dwarf merger as an application (2021)

6. Hähner, U.R., et al.: DCA++: a software framework to solve correlated electron problems with modern quantum cluster methods. Comput. Phys. Commun. **246**, 106709 (2020)

7. Huber, J.N., Hernandez, O.R., Lopez, M.G.: Effective vectorization with OpenMP 4.5, March 2017
8. Huck, K.A., et al.: An autonomic performance environment for exascale. Supercomput. Front. Innov. **2**(3), 49–66 (2015)
9. Ierotheou, C.S., Jin, H., Matthews, G., Johnson, S.P., Hood, R.: Generating OpenMP code using an interactive parallelization environment. Parallel Comput. **31**(10), 999–1012 (2005). OpenMP
10. Kaiser, H., et al.: HPX - the C++ standard library for parallelism and concurrency. J. Open Source Softw. **5**(53), 2352 (2020)
11. Pazat, J.-L.: Tools for high performance FORTRAN: a survey. In: Perrin, G.-R., Darte, A. (eds.) The Data Parallel Programming Model. LNCS, vol. 1132, pp. 134–158. Springer, Heidelberg (1996). https://doi.org/10.1007/3-540-61736-1_46
12. Terpstra, D., Jagode, H., You, H., Dongarra, J.: Collecting performance data with PAPI-C. In: Müller, M., Resch, M., Schulz, A., Nagel, W. (eds.) Tools for High Performance Computing 2009, pp. 157–173. Springer, Heidelberg (2010). https://doi.org/10.1007/978-3-642-11261-4_11
13. Wei, W., Chatterjee, A., Huck, K., Hernandez, O., Kaiser, H.: Performance analysis of a quantum Monte Carlo application on multiple hardware architectures using the HPX runtime. In: 2020 IEEE/ACM 11th Workshop on Latest Advances in Scalable Algorithms for Large-Scale Systems (ScalA), pp. 77–84. IEEE (2020)

Heterogenous Computing and Memory

Experience Report: Writing a Portable GPU Runtime with OpenMP 5.1

Shilei Tian[1]($\boxtimes$)(iD), Jon Chesterfield[3](iD), Johannes Doerfert[2](iD),
and Barbara Chapman[1](iD)

[1] Department of Computer Science, Stony Brook University, Stony Brook, USA
{shilei.tian,barbara.chapman}@stonybrook.edu
[2] Mathematics and Computer Science, Argonne National Laboratory, Lemont, USA
jdoerfert@anl.gov
[3] AMD, Milton Keynes, UK

Abstract. GPU runtimes are historically implemented in CUDA or other vendor specific languages dedicated to GPU programming. In this work we show that OPENMP 5.1, with minor compiler extensions, is capable of replacing existing solutions without a performance penalty. The result is a performant and portable GPU runtime that can be compiled with LLVM/Clang to Nvidia and AMD GPUs without the need for CUDA or HIP during its development and compilation.

While we tried to be OPENMP compliant, we identified the need for compiler extensions to achieve the CUDA performance with our OPENMP runtime. We hope that future versions of OPENMP adopt our extensions to make device programming in OPENMP also portable across compilers, not only across execution platforms.

The library we ported to OPENMP is the OPENMP device runtime that provides OPENMP functionality on the GPU. This work opens the door for shipping OPENMP offloading with a Linux distribution's LLVM package as the package manager would not need a vendor SDK to build the compiler and runtimes. Furthermore, our OPENMP device runtime can support a new GPU target through the use of a few compiler intrinsics rather than requiring a reimplementation of the entire runtime.

Keywords: OpenMP · LLVM · Portability · Target offloading · Runtimes · Accelerator

1 Introduction

In this paper, we describe how we ported the LLVM OPENMP device runtime library to OPENMP 5.1 using only minor extensions not available in the standard. The OPENMP device runtime provides the OPENMP functionalities to the user and implementation code on the device, which in this context means on the GPU. As an example, it provides the OPENMP API routines as well as routines utilized by the compiler e.g., for worksharing loops.

© Springer Nature Switzerland AG 2021
S. McIntosh-Smith et al. (Eds.): IWOMP 2021, LNCS 12870, pp. 159–169, 2021.
https://doi.org/10.1007/978-3-030-85262-7_11

Our work replaced the original LLVM OPENMP device runtime implemented in CUDA to allow for code reusibility between different targets, e.g. AMD and Nvidia. It further lowers the bar to entry for future targets that only need to provide a few target specific intrinsics and minimal glue code.

The OPENMP device runtime library can now be shipped with pre-built LLVM packages as they only need LLVM/Clang to build it; neither a target device nor vendor SDKs are required, which lowers the barrier to entry for OPENMP offloading. This work is a proof of concept for writing device runtime libraries in OPENMP, with identical functionality and performance to that available from CUDA or HIP compiled with the same LLVM version.

The remainder of the paper is organized as follows. We discuss background and motivation in Sect. 2. Section 3 presents our approach, which is followed by an evaluation in Sect. 4. Finally, we conclude the paper in Sect. 5.

2   Background

When compiling from one language to another, there are usually constructs that are straightforward in the former and complicated or verbose in the latter. For example, a single OPENMP construct `#pragma omp parallel for` is lowered into a non-trivial amount of newly introduced code in the application, including calls into a runtime that provides certain functionality, like dividing loop iterations. In this work, the input is OPENMP target offloading code, that is the OPENMP target directive and the associated code, and the output is ultimately Nvidia's PTX or AMD's GCN assembler.

2.1   Device Runtime Library

The LLVM OPENMP device runtime library contains the various functions the compiler needs to implement OPENMP semantics when the target is an Nvidia or AMD GPU. The original implementation in LLVM was in CUDA [8], compiled with Nvidia's NVCC to PTX assembler which was linked with the application code to yield a complete program. The source was later adapted to compile alternatively as HIP, which is close enough to CUDA syntax for the differences to be worked around with macros. Prior to this work the device runtime was hence comprised of sources in a common and target dependent part. In order to let the target dependent compiler recognize the code, target dependent keywords (such as `__device__` and `__shared__` in CUDA) are replaced with macros (DEVICE and SHARED), and the header where these macros are defined will be included accordingly depending on the target. The basic idea is visualized in Listing 1.

```
// Common part
DEVICE void *__kmpc_alloc_shared(uint64_t bytes);
SHARED int shared_var;
// CUDA header
#define DEVICE __device__
#define SHARED __shared__
```

```
// AMDGCN header
#define DEVICE __attribute__((device))
#define SHARED __attribute__((shared))
```

Listing 1. Macros in current device runtime.

This strategy works. For Nvidia offloading the source is compiled as CUDA, for AMDGPU offloading it is compiled as HIP. Both produce LLVM bitcode but with different final targets, Nvidia's PTX and AMD's GCN respectively. However, if a programming model does not adequately resemble CUDA, such as OpenCL or Intel's DPC++ [3], the approach will become less straight forward.

What's more, this setup requires vendor SDKs (such as CUDA Toolkit or ROCm Developer Tools) to compile the device runtime, which creates a barrier for the package managers of Linux distributions. In practice that means the LLVM OPENMP installed from Linux distributions does not support offloading out of the box because the package would require a dependence on the CUDA or ROCm package, among other things.

2.2 Compilation Flow of OPENMP Target Offloading in LLVM/Clang

The compilation of an OPENMP program with target offloading directives contains the following two passes (as shown in Fig. 1):

Host Code Compilation. This pass includes the regular compilation of code for the host and OPENMP offloading code recognition as preparation for the second pass. Offloading regions are replaced by calls to the corresponding host runtime library functions (e.g. `__tgt_target` for the directive `target` in LLVM OPENMP) with suitable arguments, such as the kernel function identifier, base pointers of each captured variables and the number of kernel function arguments. In addition, a fallback host version of the kernel function will be emitted in case target offloading fails at runtime.

Device Code Compilation. This pass utilizes the recognized OPENMP target offload regions, as well as related functions and captured variables, and then emits target dependent device code. This includes one entry kernel function per target region, global variables (potentially in different address spaces), and device functions, as well as some target dependent metadata. As part of this compilation the OPENMP device runtime library is linked into the user code as an LLVM bitcode library (`dev.rtl.bc` in the Fig. 1).

In addition to the `target` construct (as well as its combined variants), OPENMP provides the `declare target` directive which specifies that variables and functions are mapped onto a target device, and should hence be usable in device code. The `declare variant` directive can be used to specify a context, e.g., the compilation for a specific target, in which a specialized function variant should replace the base version.

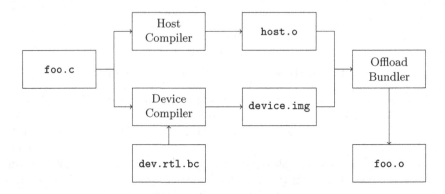

Fig. 1. Compilation flow of an OpenMP program with target offloading.

2.3 Motivation

While the OpenMP device runtime library can be implemented in any language it should be linked into the application in LLVM bitcode format for performance reasons. This setup, shown in Fig. 1, allows to optimize the runtime together with the application, effectively specializing a generic runtime as needed.

Given that the base language is irrelevant as long as we can compile to LLVM bitcode, OpenMP comes to mind as a portable and performant way to write code for different accelerators. As almost the entire device library can be interpreted as C++ code, rather than a CUDA or HIP code base, the compilation as OpenMP is feasible, in particular because LLVM/Clang is a working C++ and OpenMP compiler already.

Since OpenMP 5.1 all conceptually necessary building blocks are present in the language specification:

- The `declare target` directive can be used to compile for a device, hence to generate LLVM bitcode that is targeting Nvidia's PTX or AMD's GCN. As we do not need a host version at all, we can even use the LLVM/Clang flag `-fopenmp-is-device` to invoke only the device compilation pass described in Sect. 2.2.
- The `declare variant` directive can be used if a target requires a function implementation or global variable definition different from the default.
- The `allocate` directive provides access to the different kinds of memory on the GPU.

For an additional target architecture, the work done in the compiler backend to emit code for that architecture will allow one to retarget an OpenMP implemented device runtime almost without any additional effort. The incremental development cost is reduced from (re)implementing the device runtime in a language that can be compiled to the new architecture to providing a few declare variant specialisations.

Finally, if the port uses compiler intrinsics instead of CUDA or HIP functions for the small target dependent part, it can be compiled without a vendor specific SDK present. This unblocks shipping offloading as part of Linux distributions.

3   Implementation

In this section, we describe the new LLVM OPENMP device runtime implemented with OPENMP 5.1. First, we talk about the common part, and then discuss how target dependent parts are implemented and why extensions were necessary. Only AMD and Nvidia platforms are discussed as other GPU architectures cannot be targeted by the community LLVM version at this time.

3.1   Common Part

Device Code
Using the `declare target` directive around all source files causes all functions and data to be emitted for the target device. Macros to indicate that functions or globals are for the device, as shown in Listing 1, are not needed.

Global Shared Variables
The implementation of the device runtime maps an OPENMP team to a thread block[1] on the target device. Therefore, a shared variable visible to all threads in the same thread block is equivalent to a variable that can be accessed within the same OPENMP team. The `allocate` directive specifies how to allocate variables in different memory spaces. Uses with an `allocator(omp_cgroup_mem_alloc)`[2] we can place global variables in local shared memory, the equivalent of the CUDA `__shared__` shown in Listing 1.

In contrast to shared CUDA or HIP variables, C++ specifies that global variables are default initialized. While we can technically do this for global shared variables defined with OPENMP, it is not supported by LLVM/Clang at this time. Furthermore, the performance is likely to suffer as the device runtime is designed to initialize these variables explicitly on demand. To this end, we extended LLVM/Clang with a variable attribute for this work: `loader_uninitialized` [1]. The effect is that annotated variables will not have a default initialized value but instead be uninitialized like the CUDA or HIP shared variables are as well.

Listing 2 shows device code and global shared variable declaration as it is used in our OPENMP device runtime.

```
#pragma omp begin declare target

// Function declaration
extern __kmpc_impl_threadfence();
```

---

[1] We are using CUDA terminology here. For AMD platforms it is *wavefront*.

[2] The implementation currently uses `allocator(omp_pteam_mem_alloc)` which is equivalent given the current mapping of parallelism.

```
// Function definition
void __kmpc_flush(kmp_Ident *loc) {
  __kmpc_impl_threadfence();
}
// Global variable
int global_var;
// Shared variable
int shared_var;
#pragma omp allocate(shared_var).          \
        allocator(omp_pteam_mem_alloc)
// Shared variable declaration
extern int other_shared_var;
#pragma omp allocate(other_shared_var)     \
        allocator(omp_pteam_mem_alloc)

#pragma omp end declare target
```

Listing 2. An example of new device runtime code.

Atomic Operations

The device runtime uses five atomic operations, add, inc, max, exchange, and cas, implemented in target dependent parts with LLVM/Clang builtin functions.

OPENMP 5.1 [4] introduces the compare clause, which supports conditional update statements. When combined with the capture clause, all of these atomic operations except inc can be implemented via OPENMP, as shown in Listing 3. We implemented the support of the compare clause and its combination with the capture clause for LLVM/Clang but the it has not been merged into the community version yet. With the updated requirements for flush[3], which we also implemented for this work, our OPENMP versions of atomic operations can generate LLVM-IR that is identical to the original target dependent implementation via compiler intrinsics.

```
uint32_t atomic_add(uint32_t *X, uint32_t E) {
  uint32_t V;
#pragma omp atomic capture seq_cst
  { V = *X; *X += E; }
  return V;
}
uint32_t atomic_max(uint32_t *X, uint32_t E) {
  uint32_t V;
#pragma omp atomic compare capture seq_cst
  { V = *X; if (*X < E) { *X = E; } }
  return V;
}
uint32_t atomic_exchange(uint32_t *X, uint32_t E) {
  uint32_t V;
```

---

[3] OPENMP 5.1 removes the requirement for a flush operation at the entry and exit of an atomic operation if write, update, or capture is specified and the memory ordering is seq_cst.

```
#pragma omp atomic capture seq_cst
  { V = *X; *X = E; }
  return V;
}
uint32_t atomic_cas(uint32_t *X, uint32_t E, uint32_t D) {
  uint32_t V;
#pragma omp atomic compare capture seq_cst
  { V = *X; if (*X == E) { *X = D; } }
  return V;
}
```

Listing 3. Atomic operations implemented in OPENMP 5.1.

The missing atomic operation is `inc`. According to the CUDA specification [2], inc implements:

```
{ v = x; x = x >= e ? 0 : x + 1; }
```

and returns v. This atomic operation can not be represented in a form that OPENMP 5.1 supports because OPENMP 5.1 requires that the order operation be either < or >, and the alternative statement of the conditional expression statement must be x itself. Therefore, we still keep it in the target dependent part implemented with LLVM intrinsics as shown in Listing 4.

3.2 Target Specific Part

Target dependent global functions and variables are currently declared in a header and implemented in target dependent source files which are only compiled for the specific target, either as CUDA or HIP. A drawback of this method is that the creation of a device runtime for a new target might require us to remove a function from the common part and insert it into the target specific part if the existing (common) implementation is not suited for the new device.

Since OPENMP 5.0, the `declare variant` directive declares a specialized variant of a base function and specifies the context in which that specialized variant is used. It supports various context selector with the `match` clause, one of which is `device` selector. For example, with `match(device={arch(arch_name)})`, the code wrapped in a `begin/end declare variant` region will be only generated if the target architecture *matches* the `arch_name`.

Listing 4 shows how the atomic `inc` function is implemented with target dependent compiler intrinsics selected via the `begin/end declare variant` directive for both Nvidia and AMD GPU targets.

Note that we use the `match_any` extension for Nvidia platforms as we support two distinct architectures, `nvptx` and `nvptx64`, but we do not want to distinguish between them in the device runtime. While this can be handled by duplicating the code, our new context selector changes the semantic of the matching to produce a match if *any* architecture in `arch(nvptx, nvptx64)` is targeted. By default a match would require all architectures to be targeted. In addition to `match_any` we extended LLVM/Clang with other useful context selectors, e.g., `match_none` and `allow_templates`[4].

```
#pragma omp declare target
// Fallback version, which raises a compilation error
uint32_t atomic_inc(uint32_t *X, uint32_t E) {
  error("target dependent implementation missing");
}
// AMDGCN implementation
#pragma omp begin declare variant                          \
            match(device={arch(amdgcn)})
uint32_t atomic_inc(uint32_t *X, uint32_t E) {
  return __builtin_amdgcn_atomic_inc32(X, E,
                                        __ATOMIC_SEQ_CST, "");
}
#pragma omp end declare variant
// NVPTX implementation
#pragma omp begin declare variant                          \
            match(device={arch(nvptx,nvptx64)},            \
                implementation={extension(match_any)})
uint32_t atomic_inc(uint32_t *X, uint32_t E) {
  return __nvvm_atom_inc_gen_ui(X, E);
}
#pragma omp end declare variant
#pragma omp end declare target
```

Listing 4. Atomic `inc` implementation with the `match_any` clause.

Other target dependent functions are required to handle synchronization, thread hierarchy, etc. These are implemented via compiler intrinsics, function calls to the corresponding native runtime library, or inline assembly.

4   Evaluation

In this section, we evaluated our proposed method in three ways: code comparison, functional testing, and performance evaluation.

4.1   Code Comparison

The previous implementation compiled CUDA to LLVM-IR, and HIP to LLVM-IR, while our proposed method compiles OPENMP to LLVM-IR for both platforms. The accuracy of the port to OPENMP was assessed by comparing the emitted LLVM IR of the library before and after changing over to OPENMP. If the text forms were identical, we would be certain the language change made no difference. This was not quite the case. The differences were in semantically unimportant metadata, symbol name mangling for variant functions, and the order of inlining as preferred by the language front end which had minor reordering effects on PTX and GCN generation.

---

[4] See: https://clang.llvm.org/docs/AttributeReference.html#pragma-omp-declare-variant.

4.2 Functional Testing

There are a number of OPENMP test suites and applications in use for checking the behaviour of the compiler, including SOLLVE V&V [7], and Ovo [5]. All ran identically with the new OPENMP runtime as they had using the previous device runtime.

4.3 Performance Evaluation

Systems Configuration. We evaluate the performance of our method experimentally on the SUMMIT supercomputer. Each SUMMIT node contains two IBM POWER9 processors and six Nvidia Volta V100 GPUs (only one was used in this paper). CUDA 10.1.243 was used, which is the version loaded by default.

Benchmarks. The SPEC ACCEL benchmark suite V1.3 was used to evaluate the new device runtime. Because support for Fortran is still in progress, we chose those benchmarks written in C. There are 15 OPENMP enabled benchmarks in SPEC ACCEL. Seven of them are in C, namely 503.postencil, 504.polbm, 514.pomriq, 552.pep, 554.pcg, 557.pcsp, and 570.pbt. 557.pcsp can not be compiled[5], therefore we only ran the other six benchmarks. We also chose a C++ proxy application, miniQMC [6].

-O2 compiler flag was used when compiling the benchmarks and application. Each test case was executed five times, and the execution time was averaged. miniQMC was measured through the miniqmc_sync_move benchmark executed as follows: miniqmc_sync_move -g "2 2 1".

Results. Figure 2 compares the execution time when the original device runtime is used with the execution time obtained using our proposed new device runtime. We can see that the execution times are almost identical, and for those cases where they are not same, the variance is less than 1% and assumed to be noise.

The proxy application benchmark miniqmc_sync_move contains two target regions, evaluate_vgh and evaluateDetRatios. They are executed multiple times. Table 1 shows the profiling results (execution time) of each target region from Nvidia's profiler nvprof. There is no performance difference between the two versions.

All the results above demonstrate that our proposed portable OPENMP device runtime can provide the same performance as the current CUDA-like version on the Nvidia platform. Based on the code comparison, functional testing and some AMD internal performance testing results, the portable runtime is believed to show no performance change from its HIP predecessor either.

---

[5] It can not be compiled by trunk version either. The compilation error is because 557.pcsp defines a macro max which conflicts with the same function in the math header in Clang.

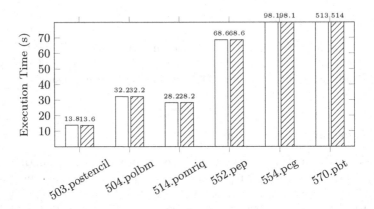

Fig. 2. Comparison between execution time of original device runtime (□) and that of our proposed new device runtime (▨) on Nvidia platform.

Table 1. Comparison of execution time of the two target regions in `miniqmc_sync_move` on Nvidia platform.

Target region	Version	Time (ms)	# Calls	Avg (μs)	Min (μs)	Max (μs)
`evaluate_vgh`	Original	1374.72	64512	21.309	19.744	32.384
	New	1376.59		21.338	19.776	33.760
`evaluateDetRatios`	Original	573.46	18202	31.505	25.247	44.480
	New	573.93		31.531	24.544	47.103

5   Conclusions and Future Work

OPENMP works well as a language to implementing GPU-only code libraries. The direct support for memory allocators and the precise dispatch through **declare variant** are clear advantages over C++. While minimal compiler modifications were required to match the CUDA and HIP semantics to the fullest, we expect those to be incorporated into the OPENMP standard over time.

Using OPENMP is especially suitable as the vehicle for implementing an OPENMP runtime library since the main prerequisite is an OPENMP compiler which needs to be implemented all targets in any case. Since the library ships with the LLVM repository, it can be built by any distribution which has built Clang. Vendor SDKs or compilers are no longer required.

Since the host and device runtime libraries can build as part of LLVM, we will coordinate with Linux distribution developers to ensure that people who install the distribution LLVM package onto a system that has a target device and driver available will be able to get this working "out of the box".

Acknowledgement. This research was supported by the Exascale Computing Project (17-SC-20-SC), a collaborative effort of two U.S. Department of Energy organizations (Office of Science and the National Nuclear Security Administration) responsible for the planning and preparation of a capable exascale ecosystem, including software, applications, hardware, advanced system engineering, and early testbed platforms, in support of the nation's exascale computing imperative.

References

1. Attributes in Clang. https://clang.llvm.org/docs/AttributeReference.html#loader-uninitialized
2. CUDA Toolkit Documentation v11.3.0. https://docs.nvidia.com/cuda/cuda-c-programming-guide/index.html#atomicinc
3. Intel® oneAPI DPC++/C++ Compiler. https://software.intel.com/content/www/us/en/develop/tools/oneapi/components/dpc-compiler.html
4. OpenMP Application Programming Interface Version 5.1. https://www.openmp.org/spec-html/5.1/openmp.html
5. OvO: OpenMP vs Offload. https://github.com/TApplencourt/OvO
6. QMCPACK/miniqmc. https://github.com/QMCPACK/miniqmc
7. Sollve/sollve_vv. https://github.com/SOLLVE/sollve_vv
8. Jacob, A.C., et al.: Efficient fork-join on GPUs through warp specialization. In: 2017 IEEE 24th International Conference on High Performance Computing (HiPC), pp. 358–367 (2017). https://doi.org/10.1109/HiPC.2017.00048

FOTV: A Generic Device Offloading Framework for OpenMP

Jose Luis Vazquez and Pablo Sanchez[✉]

University of Cantabria, TEISA Dpto, Santander, Spain
{vazquezjl,sanchez}@teisa.unican.es

Abstract. Since the introduction of the "target" directive in the 4.0 specification, the usage of OpenMP for heterogeneous computing programming has increased significantly. However, the compiler support limits its usage because the code for the accelerated region has to be generated in compile time. This restricts the usage of accelerator-specific design flows (e.g. FPGA hardware synthesis) and the support of new devices that typically requires extending and modifying the compiler itself.

This paper explores a solution to these limitations: a generic device that is supported by the OpenMP compiler but whose functionality is defined at runtime. The generic device framework has been integrated in an OpenMP compiler (LLVM/Clang). It acts as a device type for the compiler and interfaces with the physical devices to execute the accelerated code. The framework has an API that provides support for new devices and accelerated code without additional OpenMP compiler modifications. It also includes a code generator that extracts the source code of OpenMP target regions for external compilation chains.

In order to evaluate the approach, we present a new device implementation that allows executing OpenCL code as an OpenMP target region. We study the overhead that the framework produces and show that it is minimal and comparable to other OpenMP devices.

Keywords: OpenMP · Heterogeneous computing · Offloading · Generic devices

1 Introduction

Over the course of the past few years, more and more projects are looking to harness the efficiency and computing power of specific accelerator devices through heterogeneous computing techniques. These programs typically offload defined sections of highly data parallel computation to GPU devices [3, 5] or FPGA-based accelerators. In order to support heterogeneous computing programing, OpenMP 4.0 [4] introduced the "target" family of directives that the latest specifications have extended and improved. The "target" directives instruct the compiler to allocate and move data to and from a target device and to execute code on that device. Nowadays, compiler support for these directives extends to multiple CPU and GPU architectures [7–9].

However, the current approach has certain limitations. For example, the code for the target region is generated and compiled in parallel with rest of the program [5, 6], and

© The Author(s) 2021
S. McIntosh-Smith et al. (Eds.): IWOMP 2021, LNCS 12870, pp. 170–182, 2021.
https://doi.org/10.1007/978-3-030-85262-7_12

therefore the OpenMP compiler has to generate the target code, produce the target binary with a specific compilation chain and integrate all target binaries in a fat binary. Therefore, the integration of a new device typically requires specific compiler modifications that require OpenMP-compiler internal knowledge. Additionally, the OpenMP compiler generates the target binaries, which limits device-specific optimizations, performance analysis and target compilation chain. For FPGA-based accelerators, this limitation could have an important impact on performance. OpenMP 5.1 introduces the interop capability [4], allowing OpenMP to interface with other heterogeneous computing runtimes (e.g. OpenCL). While this is a step forward, it does not directly facilitate new device support.

The complex integration of new devices could limit the usage of OpenMP for heterogeneous computing. Other approaches, for example OpenCL [2], do not require modifying the host compiler, only some functions have to be implemented in a shared library. Additionally, OpenCL and OpenMP require a device specific compilation toolchain but, in OpenCL, the toolchain is not defined in the host compiler and the users can provide the kernel code or the kernel binary. This work explores a similar approach for OpenMP in order to facilitate new device integration.

We have integrated a generic device, FOTV (Future Offload Target Virtualization) in an open-source compiler (LLVM/Clang, version 13). The generic device is a container that supports new devices and target-region implementations in an OpenMP compiler. All the functionality that FOTV requires from a new device is encapsulated in a device-management component. Additionally, a target-region component defines all the functions that FOTV requires to execute an offloaded code in a particular device. These components define the set of functions (API) that the FOTV device requires to support in OpenMP a new device and/or device-specific target-region implementations. The implementations of these components are included in dynamic libraries that are loaded during the execution of the OpenMP program.

Additionally, a code generator extracts the target region code during OpenMP compilation. With this code, a device-specific toolchain could optimize, analyze and produce specific binary code after OpenMP compilation. These specific binaries will be loaded at runtime. The approach has been evaluated with a device that uses OpenCL code to implement the target region code.

The main contributions of the paper are the identification of an API for target device and implementation definition, the integration of a generic device (FOTV) in an OpenMP compiler and the definition of a methodology for dynamic loading of device-specific behaviors.

The rest of the paper is structured as follows. In Sect. 2, we describe the standard OpenMP offloading strategy and analyze its limitations to motivate this work. Section 3 presents the framework architecture and details two main components: the runtime library and the code extraction tool. The API for adding new devices and implementations is introduced in Sect. 4. Section 5 presents an example of a new device that uses OpenCL code. Section 6 evaluates the new device with several examples. Section 7 analyzes the related works and finally, Sect. 8 presents the conclusions and future work.

2 Background: OpenMP Offloading Infrastructure

This section briefly describes the OpenMP offloading strategy of Clang and analyzes the limitations that are faced in this work. A detailed definition of the offloading strategy is described in [5, 6]. Other compilers use a similar approach and therefore the conclusions of this work can be extended to them.

2.1 Offloading Strategy

The OpenMP offloading infrastructure integrates a runtime manager ("libomptarget"), some device specific libraries (device plugins), a target code-generation infrastructure and a binary bundler. The "libomptarget" module implements the interface between the host and the target devices. It defines a set of functions that the target devices have to implement in a specific device plugin, which provides device management functionalities such as device startup, data allocation and movement, target region launch and binary load.

The target-code generation infrastructure extracts target-region code in a compiler intermediate representation. This code is then compiled through a device-specific compilation toolchain that is compatible with the host compiler representation. The output binaries of all toolchains are embedded in a "fat binary": a single executable binary with the host and target binaries of all target regions. The bundler is used to make sure that the device binaries have the correct format when they are embedded into the host binary.

At runtime, the device plugins load the target specific binaries from the "fat binary" and launch target-region executions when it is required.

2.2 Advantages and Limitations

The previously commented strategy has several advantages such as a generic API for device management and device plugins for the specific implementations. However, it has several limitations:

- The runtime library ("libomptarget") is focused on device management but it has not control of the target regions that are loaded by the device plugins.
- Every time that a new device plugin has to be defined, the source code of the host compiler has to be modified.
- All the device tool chains have to be able to interact with the host compiler. Therefore, the integration of a new tool chain is not trivial.
- The host and device binaries have to be generated during the host compilation process and the OpenMP compiler has to support all required target devices.
- The target-code generation infrastructure produces a compiler-related code that cannot be easily adapted or modified for a specific device. OpenMP has introduced a new feature, the variant directive, that partially face this problem but the specific variant devices have to be supported by the host compiler.

Our proposal tackles these concerns by implementing a single OpenMP device plugin, an external runtime device/target-region manager and a source code extraction tool to interface with external device toolchains. This approach has several advantages:

- The extracted source code has the original syntax, which makes it easy to modify or adapt to specific targets.
- The approach supports off-line compilation with tool chains that are independent of the host compiler.
- Decoupling the process from the host compiler also means that new device support does not need any host compiler modifications.
- The framework loads both device and target region implementations at runtime. Consequently, there is no need to generate all implementations for all target regions during compilation.

For device manager, the proposed approach uses an API that is compatible with "libomptarget" in order to be easily integrated in an OpenMP compiler.

3   Architecture of the FOTV Generic Device Framework

The main elements of FOTV architecture are presented on Fig. 1. An open-source compiler (Clang) analyzes the OpenMP code. We have extended the last development version (v13) of Clang to support the FOTV device. The runtime library ("FOTVManager") manages FOTV-based devices and device-specific implementations at runtime. The compiler extension also includes a code generator that extracts, during OpenMP code compilation, the target-region code and some additional metadata such as file name, statement line, pragma directive and "for-loop" boundaries. All this information is stored in a "json" file.

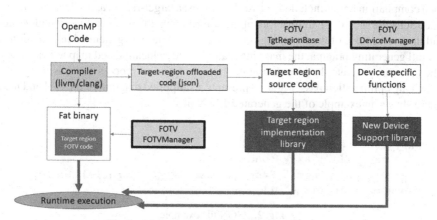

Fig. 1. Main elements of the FOTV architecture

3.1   The Runtime Library Components

The FOTV framework defines two components ("DeviceManager" and "TgtRegion-Base") that encapsulate all device and target-region specific functionality. For a particular device, the "DeviceManager" methods have to be implemented with device-specific code.

The "DeviceManager" component integrates most of the operations of a device, centered around data movement and target region association and execution. The "TgtRegionBase" component represents a device-specific implementation of a target region. The "DeviceManager" and "TgtRegionBase" objects are integrated in dynamic libraries. When these libraries are loaded, all declared objects are registered in specific lists that are used to manage the FOTV components at runtime.

At runtime, the "FOTVManager" component controls all devices that have been defined with the generic device framework at runtime. During execution startup, the manager looks for dynamic libraries that include information about new devices and implementations. It loads the device/target-code libraries, checks their integrity and associates the implementations to devices. When a target-region is executed in the FOTV device, the manager checks if an implementation is available. If there is no device-specific implementation, the host target-region code will be executed.

3.2 The Code Extraction Tool

The proposed approach can use compilation tool chains that are independent of the host compiler. These toolchains require target-region source code to produce device specific binaries. The code extractor identifies, during host compilation, the target-region source code and some additional metadata that can be used for automatic code generation. It also generates the infrastructure that is needed to load the target-region code at runtime. This infrastructure can be used to integrate device specific implementations that are not related to the OpenMP target region code. All the information that the extraction tool produces for a compilation unit is included in two JSON files: a target-region and a data region file. The JSON file includes parameter mapping information, the outlined function identifier and the source code of the target region. Among the meta-data generated information is the full generating pragma, the mapping clauses, source location and mapped variables. The tool will generate the files during the host compilation process and it is integrated in a Clang optimization pass. Figure 3 presents a simplified diagram of the tool and next figure shows an example of the generated JSON file.

```
'axpy_concurrent_region_111":{
  "source_file":"axpy_concurrent.c",
  "generating_pragma":"#pragma omp target parallel loop",
  "pragma_start_line":11,
```

Fig. 2. JSON file example.

4   Device Management API Description

This section introduces the basic elements of the approach. The DeviceManagement component functions are similar to those of "libomptarget", but they are modified to accommodate for the functionality of our runtime. The methods in the "TgtRegionBase" component are used to manage the target region implementations.

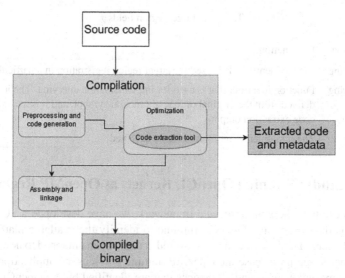

Fig. 3. Simplified compilation process and location of the extraction tool

4.1 DeviceManagement Component

A DeviceManagement implementation requires a minimum block of information that is used for identification and future compatibility with the OpenMP interop feature. This information includes an identifier string that is necessary for target region registration, a parameter block, an event queue and an internal host-to-device pointer mapping. The component contains 3 types of functions: basic runtime functions, memory management functions and synchronous and asynchronous data movement.

Basic Runtime Functions. These functions handle device operation. These include the implementation registration function for each device, functions to query the information block of a device, device synchronization routine, implementation registration, resource initialization and pause routines, and pointer map querying functions.

Synchronous and Asynchronous Data Movement Functions. These functions manage synchronous and asynchronous data movement in all directions: to the device, from the device and between devices.

Memory Management Functions. These functions are used to handle device memory and how it maps to the device. Includes the basic "alloc" and "free" operations as well as explicit pointer association and disassociation functions.

4.2 TgtRegionBase Component

The TgtRegionBase component is a simple wrapper with three fields. In certain cases, the user might need to extend the component with device-specific information. The core component fields are presented on Table 1.

Table 1. Target region fields

Name	Type	Explanation
dev_id	string	Device identifier. It is used for target region registration in a particular device
fn_id	string	Function identifier that is used for implementation querying. The identifier is derived from the original offloaded function symbol, and it is available in the code extraction output
fn	void *	The implementation function to be executed

5   Case Study: Running OpenCL Kernels as OpenMP Regions

In order to evaluate the generic-device framework, we have developed a FOTV-based device. This device uses the OpenCL runtime to identify the available platforms and hardware devices. These devices are discovered at runtime and mapped to new OpenMP devices. Therefore, in this case the OpenMP runtime provides the application with the compiler supported devices and all devices that are identified by the OpenCL runtime. The proposed approach also requires that the OpenMP target-regions be transformed into OpenCL kernels. Next sections describe the structure of the FOTV-based device.

5.1   The OpenCL Device Requirements

When a generic device infrastructure uses the OpenCL runtime, some problems have to be fixed. On the one hand, the runtime typically identifies more than one device at runtime and the "DeviceManager" component is designed to support only one specific device or device family. On the other hand, OpenCL requires some scaffolding code to be operated and it depends of the device and kernel. The generic device infrastructure assumes that the device functions are independent from the target-region functions and the OpenMP runtime uses these device functions to provide all the infrastructure that the target-region needs. This approach is not directly aligned with the OpenCL runtime.

These specific requirements make the OpenCL device a good use case to demonstrate the flexibility and efficiency of the proposed generic device. To comply with these requirements, the OpenCL device includes three elements that are presented on Fig. 4:

- A device-specific target region module (TgtRegionOpenCL). This new module includes the OpenCL kernel code. This code could be pre-compiled or an OpenCL C source built at runtime.
- A shared infrastructure (FOTVOCLEnvironment) between the device and the implementation. This object contains pointers to the OpenCL scaffolding as well as various ordered data mapping interfaces to be used by the target region module.
- An OpenCL specific device manager extension (OpenCLDeviceManagement). This extension consists of three major blocks: The first one is an OpenCL-specific implementation register. We also add initializer code that initializes OpenCL scaffolding. Finally, every extension requires device-specific implementations for the API introduced in the previous section, which in this case means OpenCL-specific implementations.

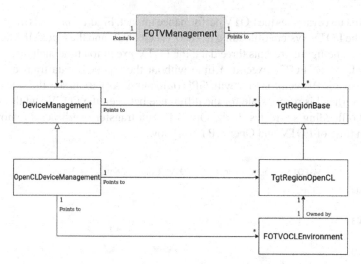

Fig. 4. Extended component diagram for OpenCL operation

6 Results

For benchmarking, we used an edge detection algorithm (Canny filter) in an image processing pipeline. The video pipeline includes four modules: a video capture, an image converter, an image filter and an image display module. The filter has a "target teams distribute parallel for collapse(2)" pragma in its top loop.

The tests were produced with code compiled using a FOTV version integrated in a development build of LLVM/Clang 13, using a standard workstation with the specs included in Table 2. The platform includes a CPU with 16 cores and a NVIDIA GPU with 768 cores. The FOTV device integrates the OpenCL backend that was presented in the previous section.

Table 2. Execution platform specs

Component	Type	Capabilities
CPU	Intel Xeon E5-2687W	16c/32t @ 3.1GHz
GPU	NVidia GTX1050Ti	6 CUs, 768 CUDA cores, 1392 MHz
Main memory	64 GB DDR3	
Operating system	Ubuntu Linux 18.04	OpenCL 2.0, LLVM/Clang 13

The OpenCL kernel code for the filter was manually generated from the JSON files, although it could be automatically created.

The main goal of the test is to evaluate the impact of the FOTV infrastructure and the flexibility that it provides to OpenMP. Two tests are proposed to evaluate these features.

The first test evaluates the FOTV performance impact. Figure 5 presents a comparison between the FOTV system offloading to GPU via OpenCL and the OpenMP native GPU offloading. The figure presents three data: the FOTV execution time including OpenCL data transfers, the FOTV execution time without the OpenCL data transfers and the standard OpenMP execution time with GPU offloading. As we can see, the OpenCL data transfer overhead is responsible for the difference between the FOTV and the standard OpenMP offloading strategies. If the OpenCL data transfer overhead is removed, the execution time of FOTV and OpenMP is very low.

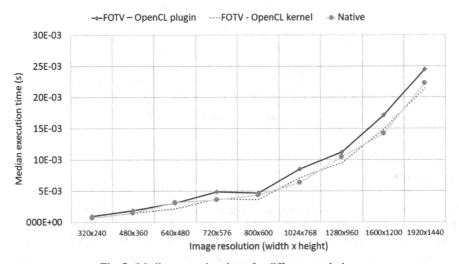

Fig. 5. Median execution times for different resolutions

The second test is oriented to evaluate the flexibility of FOTV. As we previously mentioned, FOTV can handle multiple devices with multiple interfaces. In Fig. 6, we are running the same test with a live device offloading reconfiguration of device swapping. In this case, the system has 2 offloading devices handled by FOTV: a local OpenCL-based GPU plugin and a remote POCL-r [15] based plugin. The remote POCL server provides access to a NVidia Quadro RTX4000 GPU. During the test, the remote access causes the large increase in execution time.

We observe a spike in the plot, just through a few images after device switching. This is produced largely by the implementation switch, while the extra execution time is caused by the remote communications and server load. This spike represents device switchover and the manager caching the new implementation function as well as device warmup, and averages out over the course of the run.

7 Related Works

The usage of dynamic libraries to define new devices and implementations was presented in Álvarez et al. [1]. However, it is a proof of concept that is not integrated in an OpenMP

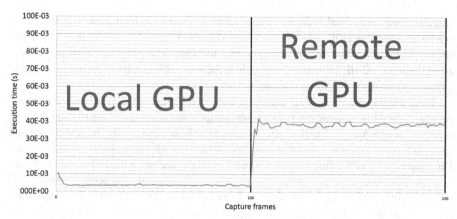

Fig. 6. Response time with a live device swapping for a local to a remote GPU

compiler and forces to use custom device implementations. The proposed FOTV generic device works seamlessly as an OpenMP device without any special requirements other than adding it as an offload target in compile time.

The addition of an external library for device management was inspired by the Aurora VE offload system [9]. The Aurora paper describes how to introduce the VE as an OpenMP offload target by introducing a custom toolchain that executes a source-to-source compiler and proprietary tools to generate the fat binary. After this process, they use the standard VE management library tools within a target device plugin to manage the device. This design allows higher flexibility than other device integrations such as the NVidia GPU [5, 6] support module that requires embedding architecture-specific runtime calls into the fat binary for operation. Unlike [9], this paper uses a compiler toolchain independent approach and defines a set of functions that facilitate the integration of new devices. Additionally, the proposed approach also dynamically loads the device-specific target-region implementations instead of including them in the fat binary. This provides a higher flexibility, as new devices don't require a tool-chain and/or backend to be integrated in the library, as well as giving the option of providing only relevant target implementations instead of having all target regions built for all devices.

Multiple works exist that extend the device pool of OpenMP with new features. The works range from adding an existing device into a different frontend [11], to adding entire cloud infrastructures as offloading devices [10]. In most cases, the new target still requires compile time code generation, making the approach device-specific and hard to extend. One of these implementations is the FPGA offloading device from Sommer et al. [12] that requires a High-Level Synthesis (HLS) compiler for the target device. This typically leads to very high compile times and very low FPGA occupation and performance, since CPU- and GPU-optimized code is notably inefficient in the FPGA architectures. Further work by Knaust [13] and Huthmann [14] attack this problem in different ways. The first one opts to prototype the FPGA device with OpenCL and compiler-specific interfaces, requiring IR (Intermediate Representation) backporting to make use of the HLS system and OpenCL interfaces. The second one creates a more efficient compilation toolchain, obtaining OpenMP-optimized HDL code to synthesize it in a faster and more efficient way. These approaches are still device-specific, which was our main concern when creating the generic interface. The proposed approach allows using the standard HLS process that provides the most efficient implementations. These implementations use dynamic loading at runtime.

More flexible than [13, 14] is the aforementioned Yviquel et al. [10] work. It does not generate target binary code but rather a Scala implementation (as a Java runtime binary) to be ran on any Apache Spark cluster. It uses a configuration file for authentication and configuration of a cloud cluster that is started on the RTL plugin device initialization call. The nature of this offloading infrastructure allows for more target flexibility than standard extensions, as the target is a cloud cluster middleware instead of specific hardware, but it's still limited to that specific runtime and would require rebuilding the code generation in case of an API extension. This work outperforms these approaches with the integration of a generic device in the OpenMP compiler and the definition or an API that simplifies the definition of new devices and the integration of specific implementations.

8   Conclusions and Future Works

In this paper we introduce FOTV, an offloading target for OpenMP that allows for extended device support through a runtime management library. We prove that it can handle otherwise unsupported devices by running OpenCL code through it, and show that it has minimal overhead over traditional OpenMP offloading. We also present a way the end user can optimize both device and implementations, allowing for better performance than other OpenMP device implementations.

This first version presents the base form of FOTV as a device bridge. A future goal would be to introduce an extended runtime library that manages resource loads for optimal performance and efficiency across multiple heterogeneous devices, exposing the entire platform as a single device to OpenMP. We also hope to create an automatic implementation generator, using information from the code extractor to create a rudimentary implementation function code that end users can then adapt to their particular devices.

Acknowledgement. This work was done as part of the FitOptiVis project, funded by the ECSEL Joint Undertaking, grant H2020-ECSEL-2017–2-783162, and the Spanish MICINN, grant PCI2018–093057. It was partially funded by the Platino project, funded by the MICINN, grant TEC2017–86722-C4–3-R.

References

1. Álvarez, Á., Ugarte, Í., Fernández, V., Sánchez, P.: OpenMP dynamic device offloading in heterogeneous platforms. In: Fan, X., de Supinski, B.R., Sinnen, O., Giacaman, N. (eds.) IWOMP 2019. LNCS, vol. 11718, pp. 109–122. Springer, Cham (2019). https://doi.org/10.1007/978-3-030-28596-8_8

2. Khronos Group, "OpenCL: The open standard for parallel programming of heterogeneous systems" (2010). https://www.khronos.org/opencl/

3. NVIDIA, CUDA – Compute Unified Device Architecture. https://developer.nvidia.com/cuda-zone

4. Open MP API Specification. Version 5.0 (November 2018). https://www.openmp.org/specif ications/

5. Bertolli, C., et al.: Integrating GPU support for OpenMP offloading directives into Clang. In: LLVM-HPC2015, Austin, Texas, USA, 15–20 November 2015

6. Antao, S.F., et al.: Offloading support for OpenMP in Clang and LLVM. In: LLVM-HPC2016, Salt Lake City, Utah, USA, 13–18 November 2016

7. Clang 13 documentation: OpenMP Support. https://clang.llvm.org/docs/OpenMPSupport. html

8. Offloading support in GCC. https://gcc.gnu.org/wiki/Offloading

9. Cramer, T., Römmer, M., Kosmynin, B., Focht, E., Müller, M.S.: OpenMP target device offloading for the SX-Aurora TSUBASA vector engine. Lecture Notes in Computer Science (including subseries Lecture Notes in Artificial Intelligence and Lecture Notes in Bioinformatics), 12043 LNCS, pp. 237–249 (2020)

10. Yviquel, H., Cruz, L., Araujo, G.: Cluster programming using the OpenMP accelerator model. ACM Trans. Archit. Code Optim. **15**(3), 1–23 (2018)

11. Özen, G., Atzeni, S., Wolfe, M., Southwell, A., Klimowicz, G.: OpenMP GPU offload in flang and LLVM. In: 2018 IEEE/ACM 5th Workshop on the LLVM Compiler Infrastructure in HPC (LLVM-HPC), 2018, pp. 1–9 (2018)

12. Sommer, L., Korinth, J., Koch, A.: OpenMP device offloading to FPGA accelerators. In: 2017 IEEE 28th International Conference on Application-specific Systems, Architectures and Processors (ASAP), 2017, pp. 201–205 (2017)

13. Knaust, M., Mayer, F., Steinke, T.: OpenMP to FPGA offloading prototype using OpenCL SDK. In: 2019 IEEE International Parallel and Distributed Processing Symposium Workshops (IPDPSW), 2019, pp. 387–390 (2019)

14. Huthmann, J., Sommer, L., Podobas, A., Koch, A., Sano, K.: OpenMP device offloading to FPGAs using the nymble infrastructure. In: Milfeld, K., de Supinski, B., Koesterke, L., Klinkenberg, J. (eds.) OpenMP: Portable Multi-Level Parallelism on Modern Systems. IWOMP 2020. Lecture Notes in Computer Science, vol. 12295. Springer, Cham (2020). https://doi.org/10.1007/978-3-030-58144-2_17

15. Solanti, J., Babej, M., Ikkala, J., Jääskeläinen, P.: POCL-R: distributed OpenCL runtime for low latency remote offloading. In: Proceedings of the International Workshop on OpenCL (IWOCL 2020). Association for Computing Machinery, New York, NY, USA, Article 19, pp. 1–2 (2020). https://doi.org/10.1145/3388333.3388642

Open Access This chapter is licensed under the terms of the Creative Commons Attribution 4.0 International License (http://creativecommons.org/licenses/by/4.0/), which permits use, sharing, adaptation, distribution and reproduction in any medium or format, as long as you give appropriate credit to the original author(s) and the source, provide a link to the Creative Commons license and indicate if changes were made.

The images or other third party material in this chapter are included in the chapter's Creative Commons license, unless indicated otherwise in a credit line to the material. If material is not included in the chapter's Creative Commons license and your intended use is not permitted by statutory regulation or exceeds the permitted use, you will need to obtain permission directly from the copyright holder.

Beyond Explicit Transfers: Shared and Managed Memory in OpenMP

Brandon Neth[1(✉)], Thomas R. W. Scogland[2(✉)], Alejandro Duran[3], and Bronis R. de Supinski[2]

[1] University of Arizona, Tucson, AZ 85721, USA
brandonneth@email.arizona.edu
[2] Lawrence Livermore National Lab, Livermore, CA 94550, USA
scogland1@llnl.gov
[3] Intel Corporation, Iberia, Spain

Abstract. OpenMP began supporting offloading in version 4.0, almost 10 years ago. It introduced the programming model for offload to GPUs or other accelerators that was common at the time, requiring users to explicitly transfer data between host and devices. But advances in heterogeneous computing and programming systems have created a new environment. No longer are programmers required to manage tracking and moving their data on their own. Now, for those who want it, inter-device address mapping and other runtime systems push these data management tasks behind a veil of abstraction. In the context of this progress, OpenMP offloading support shows signs of its age. However, because of its ubiquity as a standard for portable, parallel code, OpenMP is well positioned to provide a similar standard for heterogeneous programming. Towards this goal, we review the features available in other programming systems and argue that OpenMP expand its offloading support to better meet the expectations of modern programmers. The first step, detailed here, augments OpenMP's existing memory space abstraction with device awareness and a concept of shared and managed memory. Thus, users can allocate memory accessible to different combinations of devices that do not require explicit memory transfers. We show the potential performance impact of this feature and discuss the possible downsides.

1 Introduction

Heterogeneous systems are becoming the new norm in computing, from the smartphones in our hands to the largest computers in the world. GPUs, and the introduction of general purpose GPU (GPGPU) programming, have been the stars of this growth in popularity. Even so, leveraging the performance benefits of a heterogeneous system can be a time intensive process. One cause of this complexity is the variety of GPU programming systems available to programmers. Compounding this problem is the desire to write single-source code that will perform well across a variety of node architectures. While OpenMP*

© Springer Nature Switzerland AG 2021
S. McIntosh-Smith et al. (Eds.): IWOMP 2021, LNCS 12870, pp. 183–194, 2021.
https://doi.org/10.1007/978-3-030-85262-7_13

has supported heterogeneous programming to some extent since v4.0, managing memory among the execution units has been limited.

OpenMP's current support for memory allocation includes allocating host memory and allocating device memory. In contrast to this binary model, CUDA* supports a much wider variety of memory allocations, including device-accessible host memory, managed memory accessible by all execution units, and different levels of device-only memory, such as thread-private and thread-group-private memory. Similarly, OpenCL* 3.0 supports shared memory and different device memory allocations, while oneAPI Level Zero(Level Zero) supports a more relaxed model of memory ownership, where host memory allocations are device-accessible, and data movement does not need to be explicit.

If OpenMP is to stay competitive in this space, a more nuanced system of memory allocation is necessary. This paper presents such a system. The contributions of this work include:

- a survey of memory allocation and management features in existing heterogeneous programming systems,
- a proposed improvement to OpenMP's current allocation and management features, and
- an evaluation of the potential performance impact of such a change.

Section 2 summarizes OpenMP's current support for memory allocation. Section 3 surveys the approach to memory allocation and management in existing programming systems. Section 4 proposes new memory allocation features for OpenMP. Section 5 compares the performance of OpenMP's current capabilities with the capabilities of other programming systems. Section 6 concludes.

2   Current Support in OpenMP

2.1   Allocators

Because it was originally designed for shared-memory multi-core parallelism, OpenMP's memory model does not easily line up with those commonly used in offloading. One specific concept that is missing is accessibility of memories from more than one device. Instead, OpenMP supports two completely separate interfaces for memory on the host and memory on target devices.

2.2   Host Memory

The OpenMP allocator APIs support only memory that is accessible by the host. The allocator clauses can support device memory when executing a construct on that device, but only in certain circumstances. Rather than allocating for other devices, it allows a programmer to specify the properties they want for an allocation to allow allocation in lower latency, larger or higher bandwidth memories as appropriate:

- `omp_default_mem_space`: Default system storage
- `omp_large_cap_mem_space`: Storage with large capacity
- `omp_const_mem_space`: Storage optimized for reading rather than writing
- `omp_high_bw_mem_space`: Storage with high bandwidth
- `omp_low_lat_mem_space`: Storage with low latency.

Note that within these five predefined memory spaces, no clarification is made about the location of the memory in terms of device accessibility [5](2.13.1). Also they are all properties that change based on where code is running, so the context is important. The implicit context for all of these properties is that of the thread doing the allocation, not the one that creates the allocator.

Memory spaces are used by OpenMP memory allocators to request memory from the system [5](2.13.2). There are two ways to use an allocator within a target region. First, if the target region contains the `uses_allocators` clause, the target region can contain `allocate` directives that use the specified allocators. Second, default allocators and allocator routines can be used within a target region if the `requires(dynamic_allocators)`. clause is present [5](2.5.1).

2.3   Device Memory

OpenMP also supports directive-based data movement between the host and device for specific code regions. When a `target` region begins, the `map` clause indicates what data to move when, either host to device (`to`), from device back to host (`from`), or host to device and back (`tofrom`) [5](2.21.7.1). The particular nature of how this data is moved, copied, mapped, registered or even if anything is done at all, is implementation defined. So the programmer does not have control over how the memory becomes accessible to the device, only control over whether it needs to be made accessible.

Although it is not supported using directives, OpenMP has runtime functions for allocation and management of device memory. For allocation and freeing of device memory, programmers use `omp_target_alloc` and `omp_target_free`. Memory from the device is considered inaccessible from the host, and from other devices. Beyond that, the pointer returned by `omp_target_alloc()` isn't even considered a valid pointer (no pointer arithmetic allowed, can not be dereferenced, may not be unique) until it has been passed, and possibly fixed up, by passing it to the device it was allocated for with an `is_device_ptr()` clause. There is also support for queries about device memory: `omp_target_is_present` checks whether a pointer refers to memory that has been mapped with one of the mapping constructs, and `omp_target_is_accessible` checks whether memory can be accessed by a device. Copying is supported using `omp_target_memcpy` and `omp_target_memcpy_rect`, asynchronously by `omp_target_memcpy_async` and `omp_target_memcpy_rect_async`. Finally, `omp_target_associate_ptr` associates a device pointer to a host pointer so map clauses move the host pointer's data to the device pointer instead of potentially allocating new device memory [5](3.8). LLVM specific extensions also exist for allocating host-accessible, device-accessible, and migratable memory [1].

3   Survey

Multiple different programming systems are in use for heterogeneous computing. We survey those systems here, focusing on their approach to memory allocation and management.

3.1   OpenCL

Within an OpenCL program, the highest level scope is the *context*, which contains a host, some number of devices, command-queues, and memory. The memory model describes how the other elements of the context access and modify data values. It is broken into four parts: memory regions, memory objects, shared virtual memory, and consistency model [3](3.3).

Memory regions, named address spaces between which memory objects are moved, are divided into two top-level types. Host memory is the memory available to the host device. This is "normal" memory recognizable to homogeneous system programmers. Device memory is the memory available to the devices executing OpenCL kernels. Device memory is further divided into four address spaces. Global (device) memory is memory accessible to all parts of all devices. Constant (device) memory is similar to global memory, but it is initialized by the host and can not be changed by the devices. Local (device) memory is a memory region accessible by a single work-group. All work-items in the group can access local memory. Finally, private (device) memory is only accessible by individual work items.

Memory objects manage the transfer and manipulation of pieces of data. OpenCL contains three types of memory objects, all of which are part of global memory. The simplest memory object is the buffer. A buffer is a block of contiguous memory that can hold any data and is manipulable through pointers. Second is the image, which holds one, two, or three dimensional images. While as a data structure the image is more complex than the buffer, it is moved between host and device in the same manner as the buffer. The last memory object is the pipe, similar to the queue data structure. The pipe has two endpoints that kernels can connect to. One kernel connects to the write endpoint, where it produces values and writes them into the pipe. The second kernel connects to the read endpoint, where it consumes the values for its own computation [3](3.3.2).

Shared virtual memory (SVM), introduced in OpenCL 2.0, combines parts of the global and host memory regions to create a region accessible by all computing elements. OpenCL has three types of SVM. Coarse-grained buffer SVM works at the level of buffer memory objects. Explicit synchronization drives updates between the host and devices, so coarse-grained SVM mimics non-SVM in code design. However, because coarse-grained SVM does not move buffers between devices, pointer-based structures like trees can be used by devices. Fine-grained buffer SVM works at the level of individual accesses to the bytes within buffer objects, while fine-grained system SVM works at the level of individual accesses to the bytes of the entire host memory. For fine-grained SVM, consistency is guaranteed using explicit synchronization between devices [3](3.3.3).

The last piece of the OpenCL memory model is the consistency model, consisting of rules about the behavior of data manipulation. OpenCL's consistency model is based on that of ISO C11, using a relaxed memory consistency model. Depending on their needs, a programmer can specify what ordering they need for atomic operations, ranging from the less restrictive `memory_order_relaxed` to the more restrictive `memory_order_acq_rel`. Also, different memory scopes for the ordering constraints enable potential optimizations. For example, atomic operations at the work-item (thread) scope require much less synchronization than those at the global scope [3](3.3.5).

3.2 Level Zero

Unlike OpenCL, which has different named address spaces, Level Zero uses a unified memory design with a single address space. While it uses a single address space, memory can still be managed at a finer granularity. For devices, there is device-wide local memory (global memory in OpenCL terms) and two controllable cache levels (roughly local and private memory in OpenCL terms).

For allocations, three types are supported, based on the ownership of the memory. Host allocations are made out of system memory, but can still be accessed by devices. Because Level Zero uses a unified virtual address space, the same pointer is used on host and device. While host allocations can be accessed on device, they are not meant to be transferred from host memory to device memory, so all accesses must occur over interconnects. Device allocations are made and owned by a specific device. These allocations are not meant to be accessed by any device other than the one they are made on, but have high access speed. Device allocations can be explicitly copied to the host or another device if those devices need access. Last, shared allocations are intended to migrate between the host and devices. These allocations are comparable to CUDA's managed memory [2].

3.3 CUDA

The CUDA programming model, like OpenCL, has a different execution and memory model than OpenMP. Like OpenMP, individual execution units are called threads. Groups of threads are called blocks, and groups of blocks are called grids [4](2.2). This creates a 3 level hierarchy reflected in the memory model. Global memory is accessible by all threads, shared memory (local in OpenCL terms) by threads within a block (work group), and local memory (private) by individual threads [4](2.3). Furthermore, constant memory is a read-only section of global memory.

CUDA supports a variety of approaches to sharing data between host and device. The simplest is explicit transfers to and from the device. Before a kernel begins, the host allocates memory on the device using `cudaMalloc` and copies the host data to the device using `cudaMemcpy`. There are also functions to allocate and copy 2D and 3D arrays [4](3.2.2).

Another sharing technique uses pinned host memory to improve transfer speed and enable concurrent copying. The programmer can use `cudaHostAlloc` and `cudaFreeHost` to allocate and free pinned memory, and `cudaHostRegister` to pin pageable memory [4](3.2.5). Because pinned memory can be copied directly between devices using DMAs, it reduces the transfer cost. Furthermore, transfers can be overlapped with kernel execution. Finally, pinned memory can be mapped into the device address space. This technique is called mapped memory or zero-copy memory. While computation using mapped memory has lower bandwidth, it removes the need to explicitly allocate and transfer data to the device, and the computation and data transfer are automatically overlapped [4](3.2.5.3).

The final data sharing technique in CUDA is Unified Memory Programming. The fundamental component of Unified Memory is the managed memory space: a single memory space, visible and accessible by all devices, with a common address space. For this reason, it is used interchangeably with "managed memory". Like with mapped memory, managed memory removes the need for explicit allocations and transfers between devices. However, with mapped memory, the physical location of the memory is always with the host. With managed memory, data is moved towards where it is being used, so it may reside on any of the devices in the system [4](M.1). Programmers allocate managed memory using `cudaMallocManaged`, and on some systems, using system allocators [4](M.1.1).

By removing the explicit transfers between devices, Unified Memory also removes the synchronization inherent in the transfers. Thus, programmers need to use `cudaDeviceSynchronize` before the CPU uses results from a GPU kernel. This is another distinction between mapped memory and managed memory, because with mapped memory the CPU can access the memory while the GPU is active. Even so, some systems (those with the `concurrentManagedAccess` property), support simultaneous access of managed memory [4](M.2.2.2).

3.4   HIP

HIP is a runtime API and kernel language for creating single-source applications for both AMD and NVIDIA GPUs. Thus, much of HIP's memory and execution model is based on CUDA's, and its API is described as a "strong subset" of CUDA [7]. Of CUDA's memory sharing techniques described above, HIP supports explicit transfer and pinned/mapped host memory [6](3.3.1). HIP does not support managed memory [6](3.4.2.3).

4   Proposed OpenMP Extension

Detailed further in Fig. 1, across all of the models we've surveyed, we found support for:

- Device memory accessible only from that device, this OpenMP already supports.

	OpenCL	Level Zero	CUDA	HIP	OpenMP
Device-exclusive memory	Yes	Yes	Yes	Yes	Yes
Explicit transfers	Yes	Yes	Yes	Yes	Yes
Device-accessible host memory	Mapped buffers	Host allocations	Mapped memory	Mapped memory	No
Managed memory	Coarse-grained SVM	Shared allocations	Unified memory	In development	No
Shared memory	Fine-grained SVM	Shared allocations	Mapped memory, unified memory on some systems	Mapped memory	No
Unformatted allocations	Buffers	Memory	Linear memory	Linear memory	Arrays
Formatted allocations	Images, Pipes	Images	CUDA arrays	None	Rectangular subvolumes
Language-level variable qualifiers	__global__, __constant__, __local__, __private	None	__device__, __constant__, __shared__, __managed__	__constant__, __shared__	None

Fig. 1. Summary of feature support across programming systems. Table entries are the internal feature name.

- Host memory accessible from other devices: this memory usually also provides faster transfers due to being pinned to a specific physical memory resource.
- Managed memory, accessible from the host and at least one other device but may only be valid to access from one of them at any given time, requiring synchronization *even when concurrent access would not otherwise be a race condition.*
- Shared, shared virtual, or unified memory that can be accessed by all relevant devices simultaneously and provides some mechanism for finer grained coherence than managed memory.

There are several factors at play in this set of interfaces. If we leave off the memory that is only accessible to the device it was allocated for, which is already supported, then we are left with three forms of memory which are all accessible by the host and some set of other devices. Conventionally they map to three, or perhaps four, functions, but amount to three separate axes of memory properties: what devices can access the memory, what synchronization is required for accesses to be correct, and where is the memory allocated and initially resident.

To better support these features, we propose the following extensions to the OpenMP specification. First, we expand the memory space concept to include information about what devices need access to the memory space. Second, we introduce support for memory accessible from multiple devices in the form of shared and managed memory. Last, we'll discuss options for controlling where the memory is allocated, and possibly how it is allowed to migrate after allocation.

4.1 Memory Space Accessibility

In order to expand allocators to apply to multiple devices, we propose to add a way to request new memory spaces, in addition to those provided by default by OpenMP. The new `omp_get_target_memspace` function would accept an array of devices, and a default memory space, and return a new memory space that provides memory accessible from all the devices listed in the

array. This method includes the host, whose device number is accessible using
omp_get_initial_device() [5](3.7.7).

```
1  omp_memspace_handle_t * omp_get_target_memspace(
2    int count,
3    int *dev_nums,
4    omp_memspace_handle_t existing_memory_space);
```

Allocators created from the new memory space with omp_init_allocator
will allocate memory accessible from all relevant devices. This interface is currently slightly different from the other allocator interfaces in that it uses a *pointer*
to an omp_memspace_handle_t object. We decided to do that so that a NULL
return value could indicate that the requested memory space couldn't be con-
structed. The existing_memory_space argument serves to provide a hint to the
runtime about what should be prioritized for memory allocated from this space
as well.

4.2 Shared and Managed Memory

Ideally OpenMP should provide a way to request all the relevant allocation
types discussed above, but as always OpenMP also needs to remain portable
to a variety of hardware and foreign runtimes. The portability is a concern
because while the percentage of runtimes that support shared or unified memory
(henceforth shared memory) rather than just managed memory is growing, it is
still not universal. If we look at these properties across each type however, the
coherence and accessibility properties of host pinned memory and shared memory
are reasonably equivalent. Further, since managed memory requires more and
more stringent synchronization, using either in place of managed memory results
in a correct program. It is their performance characteristics that differ.

Since that is the case, any platform that can provide at least host pinned
memory could in principle provide semantically correct execution for programs
requesting managed or even shared memory, if at a low quality of implementation. That opens the way to use allocator traits to request the appropriate
synchronization model, where managed memory could be allocated as managed,
shared, or if necessary host pinned and shared could fall back to host pinned
as well. Thus, we propose to add a new allocator trait memory_access with values of managed or coherent. For coherent mode, the memory acts like common
shared memory, allowing (with other extensions) atomics and other fine-grained
synchronization. In managed mode, we would further require that all work on
the device had been synced to the host before the host is allowed to access the
memory. That roughly matches the requirement used by HIP and CUDA, but
currently lacks a method of tying a specific managed allocation to a stream. It
would require the"no mapping" mode of OpenCL SVM either to be available or
to be emulated by calls from the OpenMP runtime to perform the appropriate
mappings. Since OpenMP lacks an equivalent concept, we will need to consider
alternate mechanisms. An interface using a depend object may be an option,
but there's no clean mapping for that functionality.

One main downside to relying on this fallback behavior for portability is that it could pose a significant performance problem for code that relies on memory migrating automatically. While we could make it unspecified behavior to use these modes on systems where a fallback is necessary, or add a `requires` clause for it, it would reduce the portability of such code substantially and further subdivide implementations. We discuss some options for detecting and mitigating that in Sect. 4.3.

4.3 Memory Location Control

Much like selecting between `managed` and `coherent`, selecting the location of an allocation is better done at a finer granularity than the memory space. OpenMP needs a way to specify the context to use when allocating memory from an allocator, in a way that it can be used for both device selection and locality with other places on the host.

We propose that OpenMP adds two new allocator property keys to the allocator traits. `preferred_location` will take a device ID and `preferred_place` a place ID, indicating the users preference for allocations on that device and near that place.

```
omp_alloctrait_t traits[] = {{.key = preferred_location, .value = 0},
    {.key = preferred_place, .value = 1}};
```

Specifying the preferred location this way expands the flexibility of existing traits to allow requesting things like lowest latency with respect to a place, but makes allocating with different preferences across an application cumbersome. Having a way to specify an allocator property as part of an actual allocation, as an extension to the existing allocator API, could help mitigate that but there are several routines and directives involved which would make it a wide-ranging change. Adding a function to produce an allocator from an existing allocator with one property adjusted or added could also help with the proliferation of allocator objects, but exploring that is left for future work.

To offer control over whether memory should be allowed to migrate or not, we propose to leverage the existing `pinned` allocator trait as well. While that makes it partly overloaded, using it in this way avoids adding another trait, and makes it clear that the memory should not migrate even within the device.

Allowing the location and the memory access characteristics to be traits, and effectively hints, allows the API to remain consistent but adds to the challenge for programmers to understand the behavior of their code. If these interfaces become part of OpenMP, it will be important to expand the allocator API with a way to query or guarantee what access behavior, location and other trait properties are actually provided by a given allocation, or guaranteed by an allocator.

5 Evaluation

To evaluate the potential benefit of our proposal, we compare an OpenMP microbenchmark implementation with two CUDA implementations. The system we used for our evaluation uses two 24-core IBM Power9* CPUs and 4 NVIDIA* V100 Volta GPUs, however our evaluation only uses one GPU. For the OpenMP variant we used IBM's XL compiler, version 16.1.1. For the CUDA variants we used NVIDIA's nvcc compiler, version 10.1.243. We evaluated using a single node.

In our microbenchmark, we execute the `daxpy` (double precision `a*x + y`) kernel a number of times. In the OpenMP variant, we utilize a naive data movement strategy. Each time the kernel is executed, `map()` clauses move the data back and forth between the host and device. The kernel is extracted into the function shown in Listing 1.1. This microbenchmark simulates the potential data reuse between consecutive kernels in a larger application that does not use shared memory. Using this naive approach to improve the code's modularity comes at the cost of repeated data movement.

```
1  void omp_daxpy(int n, double a, double * x, double * y, double * z) {
2      #pragma omp target map(to: x[0:n], y[0:n], n, a) map(tofrom: z[0:n])
3      #pragma omp teams distribute parallel for simd
4      for(int i = 0; i < n; i++) {
5          z[i] += a * x[i] + y[i];
6      }
7  }
```

Listing 1.1. OpenMP microbenchmark kernel implementation.

In contrast, the two CUDA variants use either mapped (zero-copy) or managed memory. With these implementations, the kernel implementation remains modularized, but the data movement is not always performed and when it is it can happen asynchronously. The CUDA variants show the potential for OpenMP codes to maintain modularity and reduce unnecessary data movement without requiring modifying outer scope code as with using **target data**. Performance results for 1, 10, and 100 kernel repetitions are shown in Fig. 2. We report the average of three runs.

Figure 2 shows the high costs of offloading data transfers in OpenMP compared to mapped or managed memory. For the managed memory variant, the increase in execution time is minimal, driven by the increase in the size of the computation. In fact, between 1 and 10 repetitions, execution time increases only 7%. In contrast, for the OpenMP variant, execution time increases by 250% from 1 rep to 10 reps and by almost 700% from 10 to 100 due to the transfers back and forth on every iteration. The mapped memory variant increases 12× between 1 rep and 10 reps and 10× between 10 and 100. However, the mapped memory variant still outperforms the OpenMP variant at all tested repetitions. These results demonstrate the necessity for OpenMP to support other types of data sharing among devices if it is to remain competitive not only for functionality but in some cases for performance as well.

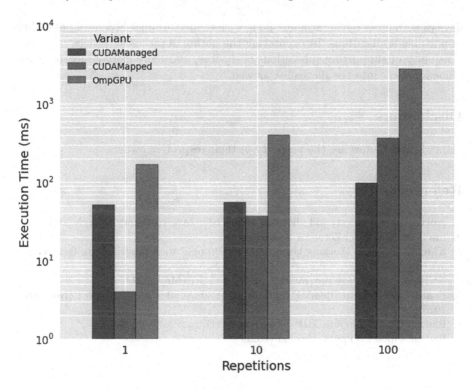

Fig. 2. Execution time for OpenMP offloading, CUDA mapped (zero-copy) memory, and CUDA managed memory variants (lower is better).

6   Conclusion

OpenMP endeavors to provide a comprehensive API for parallel programming, including of heterogeneous nodes since the release of OpenMP 4.0. While the flexibility and power of many of the interfaces for offload have been refined and extended since, support for memories accessible by multiple devices has largely stayed the same. The addition of `requires unified_shared_memory` helps for cases where true shared memory is available, but it's becoming ever more clear that enforcing an all-or-nothing switch on unified memory for an application is not sufficient to cover common uses across platforms anymore. Therefore, we present a survey of the state of memory accessibility and memory allocation interfaces across several APIs along with a proposal to extend OpenMP to cover a wider variety of commonly available memory types. Further we present a test case where the availability of a managed, or even pinned, allocation in an otherwise manually managed memory application allows for far greater efficiency and performance, 5× faster for this particular microbenchmark in the 100-run case.

Beyond what we have explicitly proposed here, bringing allocations supporting access from multiple devices into OpenMP opens the door to many more use-cases in the future. Fine-grained synchronization between host and target devices with cross-device atomics along with scoped atomics become a possibility in portable applications. Incorporating the notion of places in devices raises the possibility of supporting subsections of devices, and more closely incorporating offload devices into the places list as well.

Disclaimers

*Brands and names are the property of their respective owners.

References

1. grokos. [libomptarget] add allocator support for target memory (March 2021)
2. Intel. oneAPI Level Zero: 1.1.2 (2020)
3. Khronos OpenCL Working Group: OpenMP application program interface version 5.1 (April 2021)
4. NVIDIA. Cuda C++ programming guide v11.3.1 (May 2021)
5. Board, O.M.P.A.R.: OpenMP application program interface version 5.1 (November 2020)
6. Radeon Open Compute. HIP API (May 2021)
7. Radeon Open Compute. Hip-faq (2021)

Tasking Extensions II

Communication-Aware Task Scheduling Strategy in Hybrid MPI+OpenMP Applications

Romain Pereira[1,3(✉)], Adrien Roussel[1,2], Patrick Carribault[1,2],
and Thierry Gautier[3]

[1] CEA, DAM, DIF, 91297 Arpajon, France
{romain.pereira,adrien.roussel,patrick.carribault}@cea.fr
[2] Université Paris-Saclay, CEA, Laboratoire en Informatique Haute Performance
pour le Calcul et la simulation, 91680 Bruyères-le-Châtel, France
[3] Project Team AVALON INRIA, LIP, ENS-Lyon, Lyon, France
thierry.gautier@inrialpes.fr

Abstract. While task-based programming, such as OpenMP, is a promising solution to exploit large HPC compute nodes, it has to be mixed with data communications like MPI. However, performance or even more thread progression may depend on the underlying runtime implementations. In this paper, we focus on enhancing the application performance when an OpenMP task blocks inside MPI communications. This technique requires no additional effort on the application developers. It relies on an online task re-ordering strategy that aims at running first tasks that are sending data to other processes. We evaluate our approach on a Cholesky factorization and show that we gain around 19% of execution time on an Intel Skylake compute nodes machine - each node having two 24-core processors.

Keywords: MPI+OpenMP · Task · Scheduling · Asynchronism

1 Introduction

High Performance Computing (HPC) applications target distributed machines, which inevitably involve inter-node data exchanges that can be handled by MPI (Message Passing Interface). But, at compute-node level, the number of cores is increasing, and task programming models seem to be well-suited for efficient use of all computing resources and to satisfy the needs of asynchronism. Since 2008, OpenMP [1,14] defines a standard for task programming. This leads to codes that finely nest MPI communications within such OpenMP tasks. Furthermore, OpenMP 4.0 introduced data dependencies between tasks. Thus, within parallel regions exploiting tasks, applications can be seen as a single global data-flow graph which is distributed across MPI processes, where each process has its own OpenMP task scheduler with no view of the global graph. This may result in poor performance [12] and even deadlocks [19].

© Springer Nature Switzerland AG 2021
S. McIntosh-Smith et al. (Eds.): IWOMP 2021, LNCS 12870, pp. 197–210, 2021.
https://doi.org/10.1007/978-3-030-85262-7_14

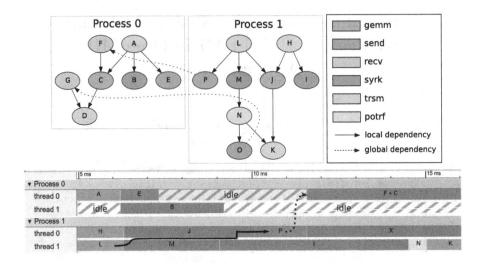

Fig. 1. Top: sub-graph of a distributed blocked Cholesky factorization mapped onto 2 MPI Ranks (matrix size: 2048 × 2048 with tile of size 512). Bottom: Gantt chart with 2 threads per MPI rank.

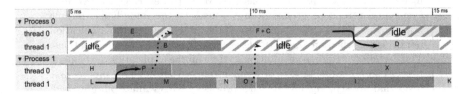

Fig. 2. Alternative scheduling for the graph in Fig. 1.

Deadlocks can be due to the loss of cores when threads execute blocking MPI calls within OpenMP tasks [11]. Several solutions address this issue [16,18,20] and enable working MPI+OpenMP(tasks) codes, but performance issues remain.

Task scheduling in this hybrid context can significantly improve the overall performance. As an example, Fig. 1 presents a subgraph of the task dependency graph (TDG) for a Cholesky factorization [19], and its scheduling trace on 2 processors of 2 threads each. Tasks are scheduled following a standard First In, First Out (FIFO) policy: once precedence constraints are resolved, the first tasks created are scheduled first. This policy leads to 61% idle time on Process 0, partially because it is waiting for data from Process 1. A similar result would be obtained with regular OpenMP runtimes (GNU-OpenMP [6], LLVM-OpenMP [8]) which uses a mix of FIFO and Last In, First Out (LIFO) policies. It is possible to reduce this idle time to 36% by adapting the scheduling policy to prioritize inter-process edges (see Fig. 2).

This paper proposes a communication-aware task re-ordering strategy for OpenMP that aims at reducing idle periods in hybrid MPI+OpenMP (tasks) applications by favoring tasks on a path to communications. This strategy relies on hybrid scheduling techniques and proposes an automatic TDG prioritization based on communication information. Our solution heavily leverages runtime interoperations but requires no OpenMP/MPI extensions and no further efforts on the user side on tasks prioritization. Section 2 presents related work. Then, Sect. 3 highlights our task scheduling strategy and Sect. 4 exposes its implementation and evaluation. Finally, Sect. 5 concludes and discusses future work.

2   Related Work

The Dominant Sequence Clustering (DSC) [22] was proposed as a heuristic for scheduling tasks on an unlimited number of distributed cores. This algorithm distributes a fully-discovered TDG onto cores - the clustering phase - and prioritizes tasks using global bottom and top levels. Our paper focuses on hybrid MPI+OpenMP(tasks) which are the widely used standards in the HPC community. With this programming model, the clustering is done by the user which distributes OpenMP tasks onto MPI processes. Each OpenMP tasks scheduler only has a view on its local subgraph (*i.e.* its cluster). The tasks *global* bottom and top levels (*blevel*, *tlevel*) are not known, which leads us to prioritize the TDG using purely local information.

MPI+OpenMP(tasks) model may lead to a loss of thread, when a thread executes blocking MPI code within an OpenMP task [11,12]. Many works addressed this issue [4,9,11,16,18,19]. Some approaches [4,11] consist of marking communication tasks from user codes and dedicating threads to communication or computation. This guarantees that both communications and computations progress and fix deadlock issues due to the loss of threads. However, it requires user-code adaptations and creates load balancing issues between communication and computation threads. In 2015, MPI+ULT (User Level Thread, Argobots) [9] proposed to run MPI code within a user-level thread, and make it yield whenever an MPI communication blocks. In OpenMP, yielding can be achieved using the `taskyield` directive. Schuchart *et al.* [19] explored various implementations of it, and having implementations that effectively suspend, enables the expression of fine MPI data movement within OpenMP tasks. This resulted in a more efficient implementation of the blocked Cholesky factorization with fewer synchronizations and led to new approaches on MPI+OpenMP(tasks) interoperability, such as TAMPI [18] and MPI_Detach [16]. TAMPI was proposed as a user library to enable blocking-tasks pause and resume mechanism. It transforms calls to MPI blocking operations to non-blocking ones through the `PMPI` interface and interoperates with the underlying tasking runtime - typically using the `taskyield` in OpenMP, or `nanos6_block_current_task` in Nanos6. The authors of [16] proposed another interoperability approach using the `detach` clause, which implies MPI specifications extensions to add asynchronous callbacks on communications completion, and also user code adaptations.

Among all these works, our solution on the loss of threads issue differs from [4, 11,16]: we aim at no user code modifications, and to progress both communications and computations by any thread opportunistically. Our approach is more likely a mix of [9,16,18] with automation through runtime interoperations. This part of our strategy is detailed in Sect. 3.1.

Other reasons can lead to threads idling. For instance, an unbalanced distribution of work between nodes leads to threads idling. CHAMELEON [7] is a reactive task load balancing for MPI+OpenMP tasks applications and enables OpenMP tasks migration between MPI processes. Another idling reason could be communication synchronization. A dynamic broadcast algorithm for task-based runtimes was proposed in [5] which aims at no synchronizations. Their algorithm consists of aggregating data-send operations to a single request, which holds all the recipients' information. Our work assumes that the task load is balanced across MPI processes and that applications only use asynchronous point to point communications. Thus, our scheduling strategy should be used alongside [5,7] to achieve the best performances in real-life applications.

Asynchronous communications progression in hybrid MPI+OpenMP tasks programming is discussed by David Buettner et al. in [2]. They proposed an OpenMP extension to mark tasks that contain MPI communications. This allows them to asynchronously progress MPI communication on every OpenMP scheduling point. We retrieved this technique in our paper, as part of our execution model. However, we propose it without the need to mark tasks on the user side, by adding runtime interoperability.

3 Task Scheduling Strategy

We target applications that nest MPI point-to-point communications within OpenMP dependent tasks. Our strategy aims at scheduling first tasks that send data to reduce idle time on the receiving side. For this purpose, let us denote respectively `recv-tasks` and `send-tasks` tasks that contain `MPI_Recv` and `MPI_Send` calls, or their non-blocking version - `MPI_Irecv` and `MPI_Isend` - paired with a `MPI_Wait`. We will discuss in Sect. 3.3 how to identify them. This section starts by the presentation of the assumed interoperation between OpenMP and MPI. Then it exposes, in a progressive way, different policies to adapt task scheduling in order to send data at the earliest: through manual (using OpenMP `priority` clause) or automatic computation of the required tasks annotation.

3.1 Interoperation Between MPI and OpenMP Runtimes

Each MPI process has its own OpenMP scheduler, which executes tasks according to their precedence constraints (expressed through the `depend` clause) and their priorities. To address the loss of cores issue introduced by a blocking MPI communication calls, and to keep asynchronous communication progression, we propose a mix of User Level Threads (ULT), TAMPI, and MPI_Detach [2,9,16,18]. On the MPI runtime side, whenever a thread is about to block, it injects a communication progression polling function inside OpenMP, to be called on every scheduling point - as it was proposed by D. Buettner and al. [2]. Moreover, the MPI runtime notifies the OpenMP runtime that the current task must be suspended. The MPI communication progresses on each OpenMP scheduling point, and whenever it completes, MPI notifies OpenMP runtime that the suspended task is eligible to run again. This solution enables the progression of both communication and computation asynchronously, by any threads opportunistically.

3.2 Manual Policies

This section presents a preliminary strategy to favor communication tasks based on source-code modification to evaluate the overall approach. To express the fact that a specific task contains an MPI communication or it is on a path to such operation, this strategy relies on the OpenMP `priority` clause. Thus, this section introduces 3 manual policies to annotate programs in order to fix the priorities of each task. We call this process *TDG prioritization*: Fig. 3 resumes the priorities setting by the policies.

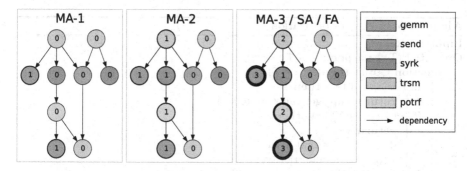

Fig. 3. Task priorities set by the various policies for the graph Fig. 1 - the value on the nodes corresponds to the task priority

MA-1. Relies on a binary priority 0 (the lowest) and 1 (the highest). Tasks with priority 1 are always scheduled - once dependencies are fulfilled - over the ones with priority 0. Here, the user has to manually sets priority 1 on `send-tasks`, and sets no priority on other tasks resulting in a 0 low priority internally. This way, whenever the scheduler has multiple tasks marked as ready (*i.e.*, with fulfilled dependencies), it may schedule `send-tasks` if there are any. This manual prioritization policy is presented in [17].

MA-2. In similar situations to the one depicted in Fig. 1, we would also like to prioritize all the tasks that precede a `send-task`, to fulfill its dependencies to the earliest. In this specific case, the user should prioritize the path (L, M, N)

to resolve 0 dependency constraint. MA-2 consists in setting to 1 the priority on send-tasks and on all their predecessors recursively.

MA-3. MA-2 does not allow to finely distinguish send-tasks and their path. However, this is important since sent data may be needed by a remote node earlier or later. The earlier the data is needed in a remote rank, the earlier it should be sent. MA-3 relies on discrete priorities to prioritize various send-tasks distinctly. One way is to use their depth in the local TDG: the shorter the path to the send-task in the local TDG, the higher the priorities on its paths. This prioritization follows Algorithm 1 and is illustrated in Fig. 3. Send-tasks are set with the maximum priority (line 3). If the task has no successor (lines 4–5) or if no path from it leads to a send-task (lines 8–10), then we set no priority for it. Otherwise, there is a path from the current task to a send-task and we set its priority by decrementing the value of the highest priority among its successors (line 12).

In practice, the MA-3 strategy requires the user to annotate every task on a path that contains a send-task.

Algorithm 1. Task prioritization

Input: Task T
Output: P(T) - the priority of T
1: **function** COMPUTEPRIORITY(T)
2: | **if** T is a send-task **then**
3: | | **return** omp_get_max_priority()
4: | **if** $Successors(T) = \emptyset$ **then**
5: | | **return** 0
6: | **for all** $S \in Successors(T)$ **do**
7: | | P(S) = ComputePriority(S)
8: | M = max($\{P(S) \mid S \in Successors(T)\}$)
9: | **if** $M = 0$ **then**
10: | | **return** 0
11: | **else**
12: | | **return** M - 1

3.3   (Semi-)Automatic Policies

While MA-3 reduces the idling periods by sending data to the earliest, manually prioritizing the TDG is tedious to implement at user level. Users will have to manually compute the depth of each tasks in the local TDG, and setting the priority clause accordingly. From the runtime point of view, this information could be tracked. So, we propose two runtime automations on the TDG prioritization to reduce user programming efforts to identify predecessors of a task as well as to identify communication tasks.

SA. In the Semi-Automatic (SA) approach, the user simply marks `send-tasks` with an arbitrary priority. Once a task construct is encountered, the runtime is guaranteed that all of its predecessors were already created too. So, the runtime internally sets its priority to the highest value, and automatically propagates it through the TDG following Algorithm 1.

FA. SA enables a more straightforward MA-3 implementation but it still requires the user to mark `send-tasks`. The Fully-Automatic (FA) approach enables a TDG prioritization similar to MA-3, but with absolutely no hints given by the users to the runtime, by adding fine collaboration between MPI and OpenMP runtimes. At execution time, whenever MPI is about to perform a send operation, it notifies the OpenMP runtime. If the current thread was executing an explicit task, it registers its profile with information such as its:

- size (`shared` variables)
- properties (tiedness, final-clause, undeferability, mergeability, if-clause)
- parent task identifier (the task that spawns current task)
- number of predecessors (fully-known at run-time)
- number of successors (may be incomplete)

Then, future tasks may be matched with registered profiles to detect `send-tasks`. This approach uses full-matching on the size, the properties, the parent task identifier, and the number of predecessors. It mainly targets iteration-based applications, where `send-tasks` profiles are likely to be identical between iterations.

The `send-tasks` cannot be detected until a task with a similar profile was scheduled, performed an MPI send operation, and registered its profiles in the OpenMP runtime. So unlike the SA policy, the prioritization cannot be done on task constructs with FA. We propose to perform it asynchronously during idle periods. This way, the runtime is more-likely to have detected `send-tasks` when performing the matching, and idle periods are overlapped by the prioritization without slowing down ready computations. Algorithm 2 is a single-threaded asynchronous TDG prioritization proposal. The parameter `ROOTS` corresponds to the task-nodes from which the prioritization should start, *i.e.* the blocking tasks. Line 9 to 17 consists of breadth-first-searching leaves, so we have them sorted by their depth in the TDG. Line 18 to 24 goes up from founded leaves to roots, matching tasks with registered profiles and propagating the priority to predecessors.

Table 1. Summary of approaches

Policies	MA-1	MA-2	MA-3	SA	FA
send-tasks	u	u	u	u	r
send-tasks path	N/A	u	u	r	r

u - user/manual

r - runtime/automatic

Algorithm 2. Priority propagation (single-thread, during idle periods)

```
 1: Variables
 2:    List D, U                                          ▷ D, U stands for DOWN, UP
 3:    Task T, S, P
 4:
 5: procedure PRIORITIZE(ROOTS)          ▷ Prioritize the TDG from given root nodes
 6:    D = [], U = []                                                   ▷ Empty lists
 7:    for T in ROOTS do
 8:       | Append T to D                                    ▷ Add T to the tail of D
 9:    while D is not empty do
10:       T = D.pop()                                        ▷ Pop T from D's head
11:       if T has successors then
12:          for S in Successors(T) do
13:             if S is not VISITED then
14:                Mark S as VISITED
15:                Append S to D
16:       else
17:          | Append T to U
18:       while U is not empty do
19:          if T is not queued then
20:             Set T.priority              ▷ match with registered task profiles
21:             for P in Predecessors(T) do
22:                if P.priority < T.priority - 1 then
23:                   P.priority = T.priority - 1
24:                   Prepend T to U
```

3.4 Summary

Table 1 summarizes the different approaches of computing priorities on tasks that perform MPI communications and tasks that contribute to execute communications (through OpenMP task dependencies). Almost all policies require user modifications of the application source code (through `priority` OpenMP clause) to mark tasks that perform send operations except the **FA** strategy that automatically detects such tasks by comparing profiles with previously-executed tasks. Furthermore, marking the whole path from the source task to the ones that perform MPI operations can be done manually (approaches **MA2** or **MA3**) or automatically (approaches **SA** or **FA**).

4   Implementation and Evaluation

4.1 Implementation

The scheduling strategy and the different policies presented in Sect. 3 were implemented into MPC [15]: a unified runtime for MPI and OpenMP [1]. It is based on hierarchical work-stealing, similar to [13,21], where red-black tree

---

[1] Available at: http://mpc.hpcframework.com/.

priority queues are placed at the different topological levels built from the hardware topology [10]. Each thread is assigned to multiple queues, and steal tasks from other queues when it falls idle. The task with the highest priority is popped from the selected queue.

To implement the interoperability approach presented Sect. 3.1, we made two modifications to MPC framework. First of all, we added an MPC-specific OpenMP entry-point to suspend the current task until an associated `event` is fulfilled - `mpc_omp_task_block(omp_event_t event)`. When a thread is about to block on an MPI call, it suspends its current task through this routine. The communication progresses, and on completion, `omp_fulfill_event(omp_event_t event)` is called so that the associated task is eligible to resume.

Furthermore, to avoid deadlocks, we added contexts to OpenMP tasks in MPC based on a modified version of the `<ucontext>` C library to handle MPC-specific TLS [3]. This add some extra instructions on tasks management measured using `Callgrind`. For each task, contexts added ~ 200 *instructions* on launch, ~ 2000 *instructions* on the first suspension, and ~ 200 *instructions* each time a task suspends.

Based on these modifications, we implemented the `MA-1`, `MA-2`, `SA` and `FA` approaches presented in the previous section. However, `MA-3` was not implemented since it is too tedious on the user-side.

Task prioritization is done synchronously on task construct in the `SA` policy. In the `FA` policy it is done asynchronously: whenever a thread falls idle, it runs Algorithm 2 with `ROOTS` being the list of tasks suspended through `mpc_omp_task_block`.

4.2   Evaluation Environment

We present the result of multiple experiments on the fine-grained blocked Cholesky factorization benchmark. We denote n the size of the matrix to factorize, and b the size of the blocks. The time complexity of the factorization is $O(n^3)$, and the memory used is about $8n^2$ bytes.

All experiments run onto Intel Skylake nodes (two 24-core Intel(R) Xeon(R) Platinum 8168 CPU @ 2.70 GHz, with 96 GB of DDR). Interconnection network is a Mellanox ConnectX-4 (EDR 100Gb/s InfiniBand) system. MPC (commit 702ce5c2) was configured with optimizations enabled, and compiled with GCC 7.3.0. We forked J. Schuchart fine-grained blocked Cholesky factorization benchmark.[2] The benchmark is compiled with MPC patched GCC [3], linked with Intel Math Kernel Library (MKL 17.0.6.256), MPC-MPI, and MPC-OpenMP. Each run uses SLURM `exclusive` parameter, which ensures that no other jobs may run concurrently on the same node. Each time corresponds to medians taken on 20 measurements.

To evaluate our strategy and different policies of Sect. 3 we compare measured performance against the FIFO reference policy, previously explained in Sect. 1.

---

[2] Sources are available at: https://gitlab.inria.fr/ropereir/iwomp2021.

This policy does nothing except that the MPC MPI and OpenMP runtimes interoperate to avoid deadlocks.

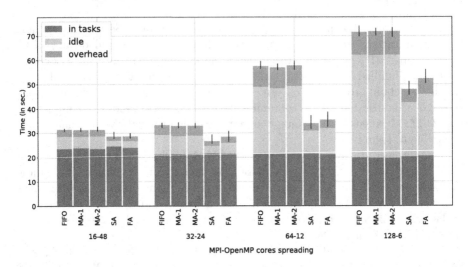

Fig. 4. Cholesky factorisation time based on the prioritization policy, and the MPI/OMP cores spreading on 16 Skylakes nodes (*e.g.*, 16–48 stands for 16 MPI ranks of 48 threads each) - with a matrix of size n = 131072, and blocks of size 512.

4.3   Experimental Results

Figure 4 shows the impact of cores spreading between MPI and OpenMP on the performance of each prioritization policy described in Sect. 3. The time was measured using a tool that traces every MPC-OpenMP tasks events and replay the schedule post-mortem to extract in-tasks (time spent in tasks body - MKL computation, non-blocking MPI communications initialization), idle (time spent outside tasks with no ready-tasks - idling, communications progression, prioritizations in FA), and overhead categories (time spent outside tasks with ready-tasks - tasks management, communications progression). The matrix size is $n = 131072$, and 16 fully-allocated Skylake nodes. The benchmark ran with different spreading configurations. On the left-most bars, there are 16 MPI ranks of 48 OpenMP threads each (1 MPI rank per node). On the right-most bars, there are 128 MPI ranks of 6 threads each (8 MPI ranks per node). In configurations with multiple MPI ranks on the same node, OpenMP threads of the same MPI rank always are on the same NUMA node. Note that the amount of computation between each configuration remains constant, there are precisely 2.829.056 OpenMP computation tasks in each run distributed across MPI ranks. The number of communication tasks increases with the number of MPI ranks and is depicted in Table 2.

Table 2. Number of point-to-point communication tasks in Fig. 4 runs

Cores spreading (MPI-OpenMP)	16–48	32–24	64–12	128–6
P2P communication tasks (overall)	388.624	640.632	892.640	1.372.880

This result demonstrates that tasks prioritization in MPI+OpenMP tasks applications can have significant impact on performance (as predicted in Figs. 1 and 2). First of all, MA-1 and MA-2 policies are not sufficient and they do not improve performance over the baseline FIFO policy. By prioritizing send-tasks and their path, the policies SA and FA significantly reduce idle periods. For instance in the 32-24 spreading, the total execution time and the idle time respectively are 33.2s and 8.0s for the FIFO policy, 28.4s and 4.4s for FA policy. However, being fully automatic has some costs. The FA policy is never as good as the SA one, with up to a 8% overhead in the 128-6 spreading. For FA, the prioritization only occurs once some send-tasks execution, their profile is registered and eventually a thread becomes idle to set and propagate the task priority. It means there is no prioritization for the first executed tasks. Moreover, the profile registering and matching mecanisms induce some overhead.

The 32-24 scheme reaches the best performance thanks to NUMA domain data-locality. MPC-MPI also optimizes intra-node rank exchanges, processing them in shared memory.

Table 3. Execution times of runs in Fig. 5

Number of MPI ranks	1	2	4	8	16	32
FIFO	22.28 s	24.05 s	25.82 s	26.46 s	31.02 s	33.36 s.
SA	22.67 s	24.46 s	24.58 s	24.91 s	25.96 s	27.01 s.
FA	22.63 s	24.48 s	25.05 s	25.38 s	26.27 s	27.89 s

Figure 5 is a weak-scaling on MPI ranks. Each time corresponds to the time spent by MPI processes in the factorization, given by the benchmark itself. The efficiency is relative to the mono-rank execution per prioritization policy, this is why times are also given in Table 3. Each MPI process fills a Skylake processor, with 24 OpenMP threads. The scaling starts from a single processor on 1 node, with a matrix factorization of size $n = 41286$, which represents 13% of the node memory capacity. The scaling ends at 16 nodes, with 32 MPI ranks, and a matrix of size $n = 131072$. The exact number of tasks is given in Table 4, where the compute category corresponds to potrf, gemm, syrk and trsm tasks, and the communication category to send-tasks and recv-tasks.

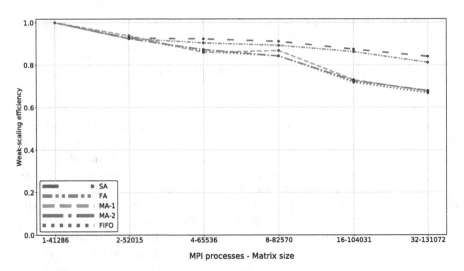

Fig. 5. Weak-scaling on MPI ranks, on the blocked Cholesky factorisation, with blocks of size 512, and MPI processes with 24 OMP threads per rank (Skylake socket)

Table 4. Figure 5 tasking details

Number of ranks	1	2	4	8	16	32
Matrix size (n)	41.286	52.015	65.536	82.570	104.031	131.072
Number of computation tasks	88.560	176.851	357.760	708.561	1.414.910	2.829.056
Number of communication tasks	0	10.100	32.512	102.082	243.616	640.632

In this application, the tasks graph is evenly distributed across MPI ranks. Data-dependencies are whether retrieved from local compute tasks or through `recv-tasks` completion. The weak-scaling result depicted in Fig. 5 scales the number of communications, while keeping constant computation work per MPI-rank. This experiment amplifies the inter-node data exchanges, and thus, the idling phenomenon we have introduced. We see that `MA-1` and `MA-2` prioritization does not improve the performance scaling compared to the reference `FIFO` prioritization. `SA` and `FA` prioritization enables better performance scaling, with up to 19% performance gain in the 32 ranks configuration.

5   Conclusion and Future Work

MPI+OpenMP task programming encounters some interoperability issues that lead to thread idling. Solutions were proposed to address the loss of cores, the load balancing, or the communication collectives, but scheduling issues remain. This paper proposes a task scheduling strategy for OpenMP schedulers to reduce idle periods induced by MPI communications, by favoring `send-tasks`. We propose and evaluate several policies from purely manual approaches which require user cooperation to fully automatic policy.

The best method significantly improves performance and scaling of the Cholesky factorization [19], with up to 19% performance gain in our largest run. Some overhead in the fully automatic strategy has been identified and we are planning to improve graph traversal to reduce the runtime cost.

For future work, we plan to validate our approach on a wider set of applications. Furthermore, in this paper, we only considered explicit data dependencies expressed through the depend clause: we consider adding support for control dependencies. Also, prioritization of send-tasks is purely based on local information (the dependency graph between OpenMP tasks) without taking into account task dependencies in other MPI ranks. We are thinking to improve our strategy by taking into account global information.

References

1. Ayguadé, E., et al.: A proposal for task parallelism in OpenMP. In: Chapman, B., Zheng, W., Gao, G.R., Sato, M., Ayguadé, E., Wang, D. (eds.) IWOMP 2007. LNCS, vol. 4935, pp. 1–12. Springer, Heidelberg (2008). https://doi.org/10.1007/978-3-540-69303-1_1
2. Buettner, D., Acquaviva, J.T., Weidendorfer, J.: Real asynchronous MPI communication in hybrid codes through OpenMP communication tasks, pp. 208–215 (December 2013). https://doi.org/10.1109/ICPADS.2013.39
3. Carribault, P., Pérache, M., Jourdren, H.: Thread-local storage extension to support thread-based MPI/OpenMP applications. In: Chapman, B.M., Gropp, W.D., Kumaran, K., Müller, M.S. (eds.) IWOMP 2011. LNCS, vol. 6665, pp. 80–93. Springer, Heidelberg (2011). https://doi.org/10.1007/978-3-642-21487-5_7
4. Chatterjee, S., et al.: Integrating asynchronous task parallelism with MPI. In: 2013 IEEE 27th International Symposium on Parallel and Distributed Processing, pp. 712–725 (2013). https://doi.org/10.1109/IPDPS.2013.78
5. Denis, A., Jeannot, E., Swartvagher, P., Thibault, S.: Using dynamic broadcasts to improve task-based runtime performances. In: Euro-Par - 26th International European Conference on Parallel and Distributed Computing. Euro-Par 2020, Rzadca and Malawski, Springer, Warsaw, Poland (August 2020). https://doi.org/10.1007/978-3-030-57675-2_28, https://hal.inria.fr/hal-02872765
6. GNU Project: GOMP - An OpenMP implementation for GCC. https://gcc.gnu.org/projects/gomp/
7. Klinkenberg, J., Samfass, P., Bader, M., Terboven, C., Müller, M.: CHAMELEON: reactive load balancing for hybrid MPI+OpenMP task-parallel applications. J. Parallel Distrib. Comput. 138, 55–64 (2019). https://doi.org/10.1016/j.jpdc.2019.12.005
8. LLVM Project: OpenMP®: Support for the OpenMP language. https://openmp.llvm.org/
9. Lu, H., Seo, S., Balaji, P.: MPI+ULT: overlapping communication and computation with user-level threads, pp. 444–454 (2015). https://doi.org/10.1109/HPCC-CSS-ICESS.2015.82
10. Maheo, A., Koliaï, S., Carribault, P., Pérache, M., Jalby, W.: Adaptive OpenMP for large NUMA nodes, pp. 254–257 (June 2012). https://doi.org/10.1007/978-3-642-30961-8_720

11. Marjanovic, V., Labarta, J., Ayguadé, E., Valero, M.: Effective communication and computation overlap with hybrid MPI/smpss, vol. 45, pp. 337–338 (2010). https://doi.org/10.1145/1693453.1693502

12. Meadows, L., Ishikawa, K.: OpenMP tasking and MPI in a lattice QCD benchmark. In: de Supinski, B.R., Olivier, S.L., Terboven, C., Chapman, B.M., Müller, M.S. (eds.) IWOMP 2017. LNCS, vol. 10468, pp. 77–91. Springer, Cham (2017). https://doi.org/10.1007/978-3-319-65578-9_6

13. Olivier, S.L., Porterfield, A.K., Wheeler, K.B., Spiegel, M., Prins, J.F.: OpenMP task scheduling strategies for multicore NUMA systems. Int. J. High Perform. Comput. Appl. **26**(2), 110–124 (2012). https://doi.org/10.1177/1094342011434065

14. OpenMP Architecture Review Board: OpenMP application program interface version 3.0 (May 2008). http://www.openmp.org/mp-documents/spec30.pdf

15. Pérache, M., Jourdren, H., Namyst, R.: MPC: a unified parallel runtime for clusters of NUMA machines. In: Luque, E., Margalef, T., Benítez, D. (eds.) Euro-Par 2008. LNCS, vol. 5168, pp. 78–88. Springer, Heidelberg (2008). https://doi.org/10.1007/978-3-540-85451-7_9

16. Protze, J., Hermanns, M.A., Demiralp, A., Müller, M.S., Kuhlen, T.: MPI detach - asynchronous local completion. In: 27th European MPI Users' Group Meeting, pp. 71–80. EuroMPI/USA 2020, Association for Computing Machinery, New York, NY, USA (2020). https://doi.org/10.1145/3416315.3416323

17. Richard, J., Latu, G., Bigot, J., Gautier, T.: Fine-grained MPI+OpenMP plasma simulations: communication overlap with dependent tasks. In: Yahyapour, R. (ed.) Euro-Par 2019. LNCS, vol. 11725, pp. 419–433. Springer, Cham (2019). https://doi.org/10.1007/978-3-030-29400-7_30, https://hal-cea.archivesouvertes.fr/cea-02404825

18. Sala, K., Teruel, X., Perez, J.M., Peña, A.J., Beltran, V., Labarta, J.: Integrating blocking and non-blocking MPI primitives with task-based programming models. Parallel Comput. **85**, 153–166 (2019). https://doi.org/10.1016/j.parco.2018.12.008

19. Schuchart, J., Tsugane, K., Gracia, J., Sato, M.: The impact of taskyield on the design of tasks communicating through MPI. In: de Supinski, B.R., Valero-Lara, P., Martorell, X., Mateo Bellido, S., Labarta, J. (eds.) IWOMP 2018. LNCS, vol. 11128, pp. 3–17. Springer, Cham (2018). https://doi.org/10.1007/978-3-319-98521-3_1

20. Seo, S., et al.: Argobots: A lightweight low-level threading and tasking framework. IEEE Trans. Parallel Distrib. Syst. **29**(3), 512–526 (2018). https://doi.org/10.1109/TPDS.2017.2766062

21. Virouleau, P., Broquedis, F., Gautier, T., Rastello, F.: Using data dependencies to improve task-based scheduling strategies on NUMA architectures. In: Euro-Par 2016. Euro-Par 2016, Grenoble, France (August 2016). https://hal.inria.fr/hal-01338761

22. Yang, T., Gerasoulis, A.: DSC: scheduling parallel tasks on an unbounded number of processors. Parallel Distrib. Syst. IEEE Trans. **5**, 951–967 (1994). https://doi.org/10.1109/71.308533

An OpenMP Free Agent Threads Implementation

Victor Lopez[✉][ID], Joel Criado[ID], Raúl Peñacoba[ID], Roger Ferrer[ID],
Xavier Teruel[ID], and Marta Garcia-Gasulla[ID]

Barcelona Supercomputing Center (BSC), Barcelona, Spain
{vlopez,jcriado,rpenacob,rferrer,xteruel,martag}@bsc.es

Abstract. In this paper, we introduce a design and implementation of the free agent threads for OpenMP. These threads increase the malleability of the OpenMP programming model, offering resource managers and runtime systems flexibility to manage threads and resources efficiently. We demonstrate how free agent threads can address load imbalances problems at the OpenMP level and at an MPI level or higher. We use two mini-apps extracted from two real HPC applications and representative of real-world codes to demonstrate this. We conclude that more malleability in thread management is necessary, and free agents can be regarded as a practical starting point to increase malleability in thread management.

Keywords: OpenMP · Tasks · Free agent · Malleability · Dynamic load balancing

1 Introduction

In the current race for exascale, the new HPC architectures are going in two main directions to achieve their goal. On the one hand, adding accelerators to the compute nodes, and on the other one, increasing the number of cores per socket. These trends challenge parallel programming models to provide support, transparency, and performance in these new architectures. When increasing the number of cores per socket, the challenge is using a high number of cores efficiently. To address this challenge, undoubtedly, all heads are turning to look at OpenMP as the most widely used shared memory programming model.

Noise, load imbalance, complex code, or lack of parallelism, among others, are some of the pitfalls that can jeopardize efficiency when using architectures with a high number of cores per socket. To address these issues is no longer enough to fight them; we need to adapt. Parallel programming models need to offer flexibility (i.e., the execution model is not predetermined, several external factors need to be considered, such as the current state of the system) and malleability (i.e., the ability to increase or decrease the hardware resources used at any time) to adjust the execution at runtime and make it transparent and

© Springer Nature Switzerland AG 2021
S. McIntosh-Smith et al. (Eds.): IWOMP 2021, LNCS 12870, pp. 211–225, 2021.
https://doi.org/10.1007/978-3-030-85262-7_15

straightforward for the user or developer of the code. Moreover, the different layers of the software stack, job schedulers, resource managers, distributed memory programming models, or shared-memory programming models must cooperate and coordinate.

This paper presents a design and implementation of the free agent threads in the LLVM OpenMP runtime. The free agent threads increase the malleability and flexibility of OpenMP, allowing extra threads to execute tasks in idle computational resources, and at the same time, offering a tool that will help coordinate the workload between different resource managers or runtime systems. Since tasks were introduced in OpenMP, there has been an interest in having free agent or task-only threads in the model [18]. Now it is one of their objectives in their roadmap for OpenMP 6.0 [5].

The remainder of this paper is organized as follows. In Sect. 2, we review the current state of the art of different task-based programming models and their malleability and other approaches that try to exploit malleability to improve efficiency. Later, in Sect. 3, we discuss the design decisions regarding the definition and context of the free agent threads within the OpenMP standard. In the following section, we explain some relevant implementation details of our proposal. In Sect. 5, we present the evaluation of the proposal. For this evaluation, we consider two use cases, in the first one a load imbalance problem at the OpenMP level among different parallel regions. The second use case considers a load imbalance between MPI processes that can be solved using a Dynamic Load Balancing Library and the free agent threads implementation. Finally, in Sect. 6, we will summarize the conclusions gathered from this work in the last section.

2   Related Work

Several programming models are implementing a pure task-based approach versus a thread-based one. A pure task-based programming model relies on creating work units that could be executed by any processing element available on the system and does not usually tie the resulting parallel decomposition to any hardware resource.

The OmpSs [4,8] programming model expresses the application parallelism through task-generating constructs. A task construct is a compiler directive or a source code comment that the compiler can interpret with well-defined semantics. Tasks are also annotated with clauses to specify certain behaviors (e.g., the data associated with the task; and if this data is read, written, or updated). In addition to these task-generating constructs, the programmer has another mechanism to handle the synchronization among tasks and guarantee correctness accessing shared memory.

The Intel Threading Building Blocks [12] component, currently known as oneTBB, is a C++ template library that allows parallelizing an application breaking it down into tasks. The programmer may use any of the TBB pre-packaged high-level interfaces (i.e., Generic Parallel Algorithms, Parallel STL, or Flow Graph interfaces) or directly using its low-level interface to create tasks. A TBB task is an entity that defines a small computation unit and its associated data. With that information, the runtime can create a task dependency graph and execute tasks in parallel.

Intel Cilk++ SDK [11] is a language compiler add-on and a runtime library included in the Intel compiler family. It allows expressing parallelism using only three keywords: `cilk_spawn` (to create a task), `cilk_for` (to parallelize loops), and `cilk_sync` to wait for completion. In addition to these three fundamental keywords, the Cilk++ SDK offers other services to handle most parallel programming challenges (locks, reducers, etc.). The current incarnation of the Cilk language families is the OpenCilk [13] project, maintained by the Massachusetts Institute of Technology. The project also includes an open-source implementation of the Cilk concurrency platform, compatible with the Cilk Plus language extension to C and C++.

The OpenMP [16] programming model, in its version 3.0 [14], also included a task-based approach. With the `task` construct, programmers were able to annotate tasks. Since its version 4.0 [15], they could also annotate them with the `depend` clause, enabling the runtime to compute the task dependency graph and properly synchronize the task execution order. The main problem of this tasking extension is that the execution model is still bound to the creation of parallel regions, perpetuating the rigid fork-join pattern of this model.

Task-based parallel approaches ease the malleability of parallel executions. And malleability allows adapting the use of underlying resources, and, in some instances, it also allows to adapt it dynamically. This is the case of the aforementioned OmpSs programming model. Its implementation includes a module, the Thread Manager, which determines the number of threads and their binding to the underlying CPUs. Furthermore, this module may agree with an external component (e.g., a resource manager) which may decide to extend or reduce the number of CPUs used at any given time. The resource manager may collect information from different processes running in the node, which improves the quality of this decision.

The Dynamic Load Balance library (DLB [9]) is one of these resource managers. This software implements several policies to decide the usage and/or the ownership (DROM [7]) of CPUs by a set of parallel processes linked to it. Then, the library can shrink (in the phases it has not declared enough parallelism) or expand (when the application reaches stages with a significant number of concurrent tasks) the number of threads for a given process. The ideal situation occurs when a process may yield its CPUs to another one that requires them.

DLB can easily interoperate with OmpSs due to the remarkable malleability of this programming model [10]. OmpSs can increase or reduce the number of threads participating in the execution of a given program almost at every single point. This is not the case with the OpenMP programming model. Once the application starts executing a parallel region with a certain number of threads, it is impossible to change the number of participants; it will break the semantics of work-sharing. But the execution of tasks does not require a constant number of worker threads, neither that just threads from the current parallel region are the only candidates to execute these tasks.

Some extensions of OpenMP attempt to include the idea of using additional threads, not participating in the current parallel region, to help in the execution of the instantiated tasks. Using the hidden helper threads implementation [19], the authors propose to leverage not currently active worker threads to participate in the offload of target regions to the device. This is a common use case: offloading kernels to a GPU while executing the sequential part of the OpenMP program and losing potential performance due to unused CPUs. The main difference of this extension compared to our proposal is that hidden helper threads do not allow dynamically changing the number of threads, where the OpenMP standard does not impose any restriction. In addition, our proposal aims to be more generic, and it allows executing any task rather than restricting these threads to execute target tasks. This is also the main reason we have not used this implementation as a comparison counterpart. We are not targeting devices other than host, and, in addition, we base our fundamental source of improvement on dynamically changing the number of threads (which is not possible with this implementation of hidden helper threads).

3   Proposal

We present our design of free agent threads as an addition to the OpenMP specification to increase the malleability of the programming model. Our proposal is driven towards making free agent threads as much flexible as possible. They should be treated as helper threads that can be enabled or disabled, and the OpenMP runtime will use them whenever possible.

The OpenMP specification distinguishes between *implicit task*, which is the task implicitly assigned to any thread participating in a parallel region, and *explicit task*, which is the task generated by a `task` construct. In our proposal, free agent threads are *OpenMP threads* that will not be considered when encountering a parallel region. Their only purpose is to execute *explicit tasks*.

Free agent threads will neither participate in any team synchronization point, such as `barrier` constructs or *implicit barriers*. They will, however, be part of the initial thread contention group and will participate in other synchronization constructs such as `critical` or `atomic`.

A task executed in a free agent thread may contain other parallelism-related constructs, although we have not explored all the possibilities, and further investigation would be needed. The `parallel` construct is one of them, and probably the one that presents more difficulties to compose with free agent threads concerning nesting level, CPU bindings, etc. We believe that this construct should be initially restricted for tasks executed in free agent threads. A free agent thread could also encounter a `taskgroup` or a `taskyield` construct, or any other construct that causes a task switching point. The only issue here is that the free agent thread is not guaranteed to exist when the task becomes ready again. Therefore, all tasks executed in a free agent thread should be considered *untied tasks*.

3.1   Considered Aspects in the Design

Free Agent Threads Are Not Organized in Teams. OpenMP threads are typically grouped in *teams*. An *OpenMP team* is a set of one or more threads created for a specific parallel region, whether the implicit parallel region or a region generated from a `parallel` construct. In the case of explicit parallel regions, the thread that encounters the `parallel` construct creates the *team*. All the threads in that team will participate in the execution of the parallel region.

During the initial design discussions, we explored the idea of free agent threads being part of the same team, as in the hidden helper thread implementation. It certainly has some benefits, like an already defined task scheduler model and implementation. But, it makes the model too strict for the use cases that have motivated us for this article. We want to propose a model where free agent threads are free to steal explicit tasks from any other team, not just the tasks bound to a specific team or a thread set. Furthermore, the term *team* is well defined in the OpenMP specification, and we believe that expanding its definition for including free agent threads would be confusing.

By not constituting an exclusive *team* or forming part of any other regular *team*, free agent threads will not participate in some team-wide synchronization constructs, such as *barriers*. But they acquire some advantages:

- The number of participating free agent threads may be dynamic. Unlike *teams*, the free agent threads group is an asynchronous structure. It will be created during the initialization, but the number of participating free agent threads might be modified at any time by using a runtime library routine.
- The execution of explicit tasks by free agent threads is not limited to tasks bound to their *team* since there is none. Explicit tasks are still bound to the thread set of the current team and optionally to the free agent threads set.

Free Agent Threads Might Be Dynamically Enabled or Disabled. There is a necessity for application developers, users, and third-party tools to have mechanisms to set the initial values or to dynamically change the number or the state of free agent threads. The runtime must provide tools in the same way that allows setting or modifying the number of threads.

These mechanisms are detailed in Sect. 3.3, but we distinguish some concepts. They may be explicitly set using an environment variable, a runtime library routine, an OMPT entry point, or decided by the implementation. First, the total number of *existing free agent threads* is self-explanatory but does not tell their situation, only that they are known. Then, the global *free agent threads policy* is a single value that affects all the existing threads and states whether they are enabled or disabled. And last, the *free agent thread state* is a per-thread value that manages whether a specific free agent thread may execute some explicit tasks, but only if the global policy allows it.

3.2   The free_agent Task Clause

Free agent threads are intended for executing explicit tasks in situations where the parallel region cannot exploit all the parallelism in the system. The task construct generates an explicit task from the code for the associated structured block, with an accordingly created data environment for the task that will be destroyed when the structured block is completed. Since the task becomes an independent entity of work, any free agent thread will execute it as long as the task has been deferred.

Although, until now, tasks were supposed to be executed by any team member, so developers may have written code relying on that. Listing 1.1 shows a task where some data is stored in a private buffer indexed by *thread number*. The operation is not protected with a mutual exclusion because the developer expected only one thread to modify this address. If omp_get_thread_num() returns 0 then the above assumption is invalidated; if it returns a unique number, the program will probably incur a memory access violation.

Listing 1.1. Task invoking a team related function.

```
#pragma omp parallel
{
    #pragma omp task
    buffer[omp_get_thread_num()] += f();
}
```

Another example is shown in Listing 1.2, where at the end of the parallel region, the participating threads perform a reduction of their respective *thread-private* variables. In this example, if a free agent thread would have executed any task, their accumulated value in counter will not be added to result.

Listing 1.2. Reduction assuming that tasks are executed by threads in the team.

```
int counter = 0;
#pragma omp threadprivate(counter)
...
#pragma omp parallel
{
    #pragma omp taskgroup
    #pragma omp task
    counter += f();

    #pragma omp for schedule(static)
    for(int i=0; i<omp_get_num_threads(); ++i)
        #pragma omp atomic
        result += counter;
}
```

There may be other programming patterns where developers did not foresee that threads might execute explicit tasks outside the team. For this reason, we propose the new clause free_agent(bool-expr) for the task and taskloop constructs.

Since adding a new clause to many constructs might be time-consuming for application developers, we also propose an environment variable to set the default behavior: OMP_FREE_AGENT_TASKS={true,false}.

- In a `task` or `taskloop` construct, if a `free_agent` clause is present and evaluates to *true*, or if the environment variable `OMP_FREE_AGENT_TASKS` is set to `true` and a clause `free_agent` does not evaluate to *false*, the generated task may be executed by any thread in the team or by any free agent thread.

3.3 Proposed Mechanisms to Manage Free Agent Threads

We propose the following OpenMP environment variables to configure the initial state of free agent threads in an OpenMP program. We also offer a set of runtime library routines for applications to modify the state at run time. And finally, we propose a set of entry points in the OMPT callback interface for OMPT tools to gather information of free agent threads and enable or disable specific ones.

Environment Variables

- `OMP_FREE_AGENT_NUM_THREADS`: sets the initial number of free agent threads to use.
- `OMP_FREE_AGENT_PROC_BIND`: sets the thread affinity policy to be used for free agent threads. The value of this environment variable might be `true`, `false`, `initial`, `close`, or `spread`. This variable is the equivalent of `OMP_PROC_BIND` for free agent threads, except that it is relative to the initial thread.
- `OMP_FREE_AGENT_PLACES`: sets the place partition for free agent threads. The allowed values are the same as in `OMP_PLACES`.
- `OMP_FREE_AGENT_WAIT_POLICY`: sets the desired behavior of free agent threads that are waiting. Possible values are `active` or `passive`.
- `OMP_FREE_AGENT_POLICY`: sets the initial policy for free agent threads. Possible values are `enabled` or `disabled`. If the value is `enabled`, free agent threads will be able to execute explicit tasks. If the value is `disabled`, free agents must be suspended or even yet not created, and they must not execute any explicit task.
- `OMP_FREE_AGENT_TASKS`: sets whether all tasks are considered to have the `free_agent` clause.

Runtime Library Routines

- `int omp_get_num_free_agent_threads(void)`: returns the number of existing free agent threads.
- `void omp_set_num_free_agent_threads(int num_threads)`: affects the number of free agent threads to be used by the runtime. If `num_threads` is greater than the current number of free agent threads, the runtime may create new ones. If `num_threads` is less than the current number of free agent threads, exceeding threads are destroyed or suspended, but they will not count as existing free agent threads.
- `void omp_set_free_agent_policy(omp_free_agent_policy_t policy)`: sets the global policy, same as the variable `OMP_FREE_AGENT_POLICY`.

Entry Points in the OMPT Callback Interface

- `int ompt_get_num_free_agent_threads(void)`: returns the number of existing free agent threads.
- `int ompt_get_free_agent_thread_id(void)`: returns the internal thread identifier of the free agent thread. The number must be in the range of $0..n-1$, where n is the number of existing free agent threads.
- `void ompt_set_free_agent_thread_state(int free_agent_id, int state)`: sets the individual state of the specified free agent thread. The `state` argument can be either `enabled` or `disabled`.

4   Implementation

We have implemented a subset of the free agent threads proposal in the LLVM OpenMP runtime [1]. Of the ∼80 kSLOC of the runtime (not counting the library for `target` support), our implementation required changing ∼800 SLOC. This suggests that a complete implementation of our proposal would have reasonable implementation complexity.

The runtime creates one operating system thread (a `pthread` in Linux) for each free agent thread. The number of free agents threads is defined by the environment variable `OMP_FREE_AGENT_NUM_THREADS`. Free agents can be enabled or disabled, and `OMP_FREE_AGENT_POLICY` characterizes their initial state. Creation of the free agent threads happens simultaneously the runtime initializes, typically upon encountering the first OpenMP construct or OpenMP API call.

The LLVM OpenMP runtime keeps two data structures related to the team of a parallel region. One corresponds to the proper *team of threads*, and another one is named the *task team*, which exists only if threads of the team create explicit tasks. There is one queue of explicit tasks ready to be executed for each thread of the team. When a task team is first created, all the free agent threads are *allowed* to execute tasks of that task team. During the finalization of the parallel region (when all the explicit tasks of that team have been completed), free agents are not allowed to execute tasks of the finishing task team anymore.

The lifecycle of an enabled free agent thread is a loop for each of the allowed task teams. Once the free agent thread *enters* a task team, it executes as many explicit tasks as possible. It does this by stealing tasks from other (regular) threads of the task team. While executing an explicit task, a free agent thread is logically inside the task team, but it does not belong to the team of threads. The semantics of team-requiring operations such as a call to `omp_get_thread_num` or usage of `threadprivate` variables are for now intentionally left undefined. Once no more tasks remain in the task team, the free agent thread *leaves* it. Once all the allowed teams have been processed, the free agent thread is suspended to avoid a busy loop.

When a thread of the team creates an explicit task, if there is a suspended free agent thread, then the runtime will resume it. Free agent threads are also resumed when they are enabled by the user code and periodically when threads of the team are executing tasks.

A free agent thread (with free agent thread number n) can create an explicit task while executing another explicit task. When this happens, the new task is added to the queue of the corresponding thread number n of the task team (modulo the number of threads of the team).

In general, the LLVM OpenMP runtime does not defer the execution of explicit tasks created in inactive parallel regions (regions executed by teams with only one thread). However, to support detached tasks, the LLVM OpenMP runtime can defer tasks also in inactive parallel regions. Our implementation leverages this feature to allow deferring tasks created in such regions when free agents are available. This enables a scenario where OMP_NUM_THREADS=1 and OMP_FREE_AGENT_NUM_THREADS ≥ 1.

5   Evaluation

The free agent threads implementation presented in this article has been tested with applications to evaluate its performance. We expose two different use cases to demonstrate the potential of free agent threads in different scenarios.

We analyze a pure OpenMP application in the first use case that presents a load imbalance between two nested parallel regions. Free agent threads execute explicit tasks encountered in the most loaded parallel regions, thus alleviating the load balance issue.

The second use case shows a task-based MPI+OpenMP application that presents a load imbalance among processes. A third-party tool, DLB, can exploit the free agent threads enable and disable mechanism to modify the number of productive threads assigned to a process to fix the load imbalance in hybrid applications.

All the results have been obtained on the MareNostrum 4 supercomputer. It is composed of compute nodes with two sockets Intel Xeon Platinum 8160 2.1GHz 24-core and 96 GB of main memory. Regarding the software, we used the Intel compiler (version 17.0.4), a modified LLVM OpenMP runtime (based on LLVM 11.0.0, OMP version 5.0.20140926), and DLB 3.0. Since we used the Intel compiler, we have not implemented the free_agent clause, and we assume that free agent threads can safely execute all tasks.

5.1   Use Case: Fixing Load Imbalance Between Parallel Regions

When an OpenMP thread reaches a task scheduling point, it may suspend the execution of the current task and switch to a different task bound to the same team. This task scheduling model allows, among other things, to use threads that may have already finished their work to execute other pending explicit tasks encountered in the same team. This model is crucial to avoid load balance issues when the task creation is not perfectly distributed. Also, it does not necessarily impact the performance in simpler algorithms such as a single thread creating all the explicit tasks since all the threads in the team will participate in their execution. However, threads may only switch to other tasks in the same team.

In cases where the application has nested parallel regions, idle threads in one parallel region cannot help and execute the tasks of a different parallel region.

The Density Matrix Renormalization Group (DMRG++) is a condensed matter physics application developed at ORNL used to study the superconductivity properties of materials. For our study, we used a mini-app [3,6] that captures the computation core of DMRG++. The code has been slightly modified from previous versions; the structure of the code used is shown in Listing 1.3.

Listing 1.3. DMRG++ code structure.

```
for (int it = 0; it < NIts; ++it) {
  #pragma omp parallel for num_threads(X)
  for (int ipatch = 0; ipatch < npatches; ipatch++) {
    // ...
    #pragma omp parallel for schedule(dynamic, 1) num_threads(Y)
    for (int jpatch = 0; jpatch < npatches; jpatch++) {
      // ...
      #pragma omp taskloop
      for (int k = 0; k < k_size; k++) {
        // Loop body
      }
    }
  }
}
```

Figure 1 shows two Paraver [2,17] traces of two different DMRG++ executions. The Paraver traces in the figure represent a timeline in which the X-axis is the elapsed time, the Y-axis the OpenMP threads, and explicit tasks are shown in blue for each thread that executes them. The first trace shows an iteration of a DMRG++ execution with two levels of nesting; 4, 4, distributed on 16 logical CPUs. The program has been executed with OMP_PLACES="{0,1,2,3},{4,5,6,7},{24,25,26,27},{28,29,30,31}" to bind each OpenMP thread to a specific core. It can be appreciated how the load imbalance of one of the innermost parallel regions causes the threads of the other team to wait.

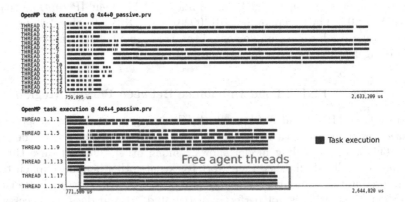

Fig. 1. DMRG++ trace execution with a 4,4 nesting running on 16 CPUs, and same execution running with free agent threads. Both traces are at the same duration time scale.

The second trace is the same configuration but enabling free agent threads at the end of the iteration. Those free agent threads are different *pthreads*, and Paraver draws them in another row, but they use the same logical CPUs as the threads that just finished their region. As done with the execution without free agents, the same `OMP_PLACES` is used, and the clause `OMP_FREE_AGENT_PLACES="`{0,1,2,3,4,5,6,7,24,25,26,27,28,29,30,31}`"` is used to determine where the free agents can be executed. This use case shows how free agent threads can be exploited on otherwise unproductive CPUs to increase the parallelism when needed.

The performance results of DMRG++ with free agent threads are shown in Fig. 2. Different nesting configurations have been evaluated with a variable range of free agent threads and wait policies *active* and *passive*. The nomenclature $N \times M$ in the legend represents the OpenMP threads per nesting level: N for level 1, M for level 2, executed in as many CPUs as needed to bind only one OpenMP thread to a logical CPU, without considering free agent threads, e.g., the configuration "2×4 passive" has been executed with `OMP_NUM_THREADS=2,4`, `OMP_WAIT_POLICY=passive`, and using only eight logical CPUs, regardless of the number of free agent threads used. The speedup values represent the relative performance of each case with zero free agent threads, so only the effect of free agent threads is shown. The number of free agent threads is limited to the number of threads in the second level. Since free agent threads are running on the CPUs of the faster parallel region, it would not be efficient to increase the number of free agent threads to higher values.

DMRG++ Speedup with free agent threads

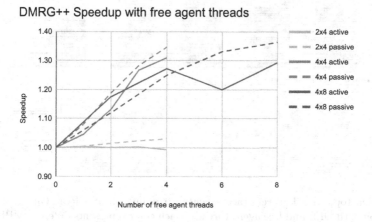

Fig. 2. Speedup of DMRG++ with free agent threads.

As it can be observed in the figure, the runtime can dynamically enable the free agent threads to increase the number of active threads executing tasks. Thus, load imbalance between parallel regions may be reduced and improve the overall performance execution. In this case, we obtain up to a 36% speedup when using free agent threads on a pure OpenMP application.

5.2 Use Case: Solving Load Imbalance in a Hybrid Application with DLB as an OMPT Tool

In the second use case, we analyze a more common situation: load imbalance among processes. However, to efficiently use the free agent threads to solve this load imbalance, we need a third-party tool responsible for enabling and disabling the free agent threads of each process.

For this use case, we analyze a kernel extracted from Alya [20], a computational fluid dynamics (CFD) code optimized for HPC environments developed at BSC. This kernel presents an iterative pattern of MPI communications followed by a region of task-based computation with a slight load imbalance, $LB = 0.74$. The task-based region also challenges resource balance techniques since the average task duration is only 200 μs. Figure 3 shows a Paraver trace of a hybrid MPI+OpenMP execution and a trace of the same configuration with DLB. In the second trace, DLB runs as an OMPT tool monitoring the OpenMP events of each MPI process and selectively enabling or disabling free agent threads to fix the load imbalance with temporary helper threads. The right-hand side of the figure shows a zoom of a few processes at the end of an iteration. It can be appreciated how some free agent threads are enabled, acting as helper threads only when a logical CPU becomes idle after another process reaches an MPI synchronization call.

Fig. 3. On top, Alya Paraver trace execution running on 48 CPUs. On the bottom, execution with DLB and free agent threads. Each color represents different MPI ranks. Both traces are at the same duration time scale.

Figure 4 shows the speedup comparison of the Alya kernel running with 48 MPI ranks, 1 OpenMP thread each, and a variable number of free agent threads. Due to the fine granularity of the tasks, using more threads than needed causes a slight performance drop, which may have been caused either by our implementation or by some scheduling decision in DLB. There is still some future

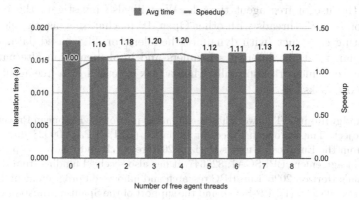

Fig. 4. Time and Speedup of Alya running 48 MPI processes, with DLB and a variable number of free agent threads.

work in how DLB manages free agent threads, but even with a proof of concept implementation, the execution was always 10–20% faster.

6   Conclusions and Future Work

In this paper, we have presented a proposal to extend the OpenMP programming model and execution model. Our proposal intends to relax the rigid fork-join approach by allowing the OpenMP threads to participate within the parallel region and outside of it. This approach enables leveraging the assigned processing elements when the OpenMP program has not fork threads yet. For nested parallelism, we can generalize this statement as free agent threads may participate in the execution of work units when the application has not reached the inner level of parallelism it was designed for.

The free agent threads are designed to execute tasks. We consider tasks are helpful to guarantee the required malleability of an application. A resource manager can further exploit this characteristic to balance assigned resources between processes. As the free agent threads are not directly bound to a parallel region, their number may increase or decrease during the program execution. Then, tasking models and dynamic free agent threads are a powerful combination to maximize the application performance.

In Sect. 5, we have presented the results of two different scenarios: intra- and inter-process levels. In both cases, we have proved performance benefits by using a small set of free agent threads. In the intra-process use case, we handle fixing the imbalance between OpenMP parallel regions, obtaining up to a 36% speedup. In the inter-process use case, we solve the load imbalance of a hybrid application using the DLB resource manager, and it obtains up to 20% speedup compared to the baseline.

As future work, we plan to further develop more use-cases that can potentially leverage the use of free agent threads. We will also investigate the potential interaction of such threads with other OpenMP mechanisms, as it could be the work-sharing construct (with dynamic schedulers) or TLS based data. Finally, we also plan to study different schedulers and implementation alternatives of our reference framework, especially when a task executed by a free agent thread creates more tasks.

Acknowledgements. This work has been done as part of the European Processor Initiative project. The European Processor Initiative (EPI) (FPA: 800928) has received funding from the European Union's Horizon 2020 research and innovation programme under grant agreement EPI-SGA1: 826647. It has also received funding from the European Union's Horizon 2020/EuroHPC research and innovation programme under grant agreement No 955606 (DEEP-SEA); and the support of the Spanish Ministry of Science and Innovation (Computacion de Altas Prestaciones VIII: PID2019-107255GB).

References

1. LLVM OpenMP Runtime. https://openmp.llvm.org. Accessed 18 May 2021
2. Paraver: a flexible performance analysis tool. https://tools.bsc.es/paraver. Accessed 21 May 2021
3. Alvarez, G.: The density matrix renormalization group for strongly correlated electron systems: a generic implementation. Comput. Phys. Commun. **180**(9), 1572–1578 (2009)
4. Barcelona Supercomputing Center: OmpSs Specification. https://pm.bsc.es/ompss. Accessed 04 Nov 2020
5. de Supinski, B.R.: Recent, Current and Future OpenMP Directions: OpenMP 5.1 and More!. https://www.openmp.org/wp-content/uploads/OpenMP_SC20-deSupinski.pdf. Accessed 01 July 2021
6. Criado, J., et al.: Optimization of condensed matter physics application with OpenMP tasking model. In: Fan, X., de Supinski, B.R., Sinnen, O., Giacaman, N. (eds.) IWOMP 2019. LNCS, vol. 11718, pp. 291–305. Springer, Cham (2019). https://doi.org/10.1007/978-3-030-28596-8_20
7. D'Amico, M., Garcia-Gasulla, M., López, V., Jokanovic, A., Sirvent, R., Corbalan, J.: DROM: Enabling Efficient and Effortless Malleability for Resource Managers, p. 41 (2018)
8. Duran, A., et al.: OmpSs: a proposal for programming heterogeneous multi-core architectures. Parallel Process. Lett. **21**, 173–193 (2011)
9. Garcia, M., Labarta, J., Corbalan, J.: Hints to improve automatic load balancing with LeWI for hybrid applications. J. Parallel Distrib. Comput. **74**(9), 2781–2794 (2014)
10. Garcia-Gasulla, M., et al.: MPI+ X: task-based parallelisation and dynamic load balance of finite element assembly. Int. J. Comput. Fluid Dyn. **33**(3), 115–136 (2019)
11. Intel Corporation: Intel Cilk++ SDK Programmer's Guide (2009). https://www.clear.rice.edu/comp422/resources/Intel_Cilk++_Programmers_Guide.pdf
12. Intel Corporation: Intel Threading Building Blocks (2011). https://www.inf.ed.ac.uk/teaching/courses/ppls/TBBtutorial.pdf

13. Massachusetts Institute of Technology: OpenCilk Language Extension Specification Version 1.0 (2021). https://cilk.mit.edu/docs/OpenCilkLanguageExtensionSpecification.htm
14. OpenMP Architecture Review Board: OpenMP Application Programming Interface, Version 3.0 (2008). http://www.openmp.org/
15. OpenMP Architecture Review Board: OpenMP Application Programming Interface, Version 4.0 (2013). http://www.openmp.org/
16. OpenMP Architecture Review Board: OpenMP Application Programming Interface, Version 5.1 (2020). https://www.openmp.org/wp-content/uploads/OpenMP-API-Specification-5-1.pdf. Accessed 22 March 2021
17. Pillet, V., Labarta, J., Cortes, T., Girona, S.: Paraver: A tool to visualize and analyze parallel code. In: Proceedings of WoTUG-18: Transputer and Occam Developments, vol. 44, pp. 17–31 (1995)
18. Sunderland, D., Olivier, S.L., Hollman, D.S., Evans, N., de Supinski, B.R.: Making OpenMP Ready for C++ Executors (2019). https://www.osti.gov/biblio/1559921
19. Tian, S., Doerfert, J., Chapman, B.: Concurrent Execution of Deferred OpenMP Target Tasks with Hidden Helper Threads. Springer (2020)
20. Vázquez, M., Houzeaux, G., Koric, S., et al.: Alya: multiphysics engineering simulation toward exascale. J. Comput. Sci. **14**, 15–27 (2016)

Author Index

Printed in the United States
by Baker & Taylor Publisher Services

Printed in the United States
by Baker & Taylor Publisher Services